D0453740

PRAISE FOR
THE ZOOKEEPERS' WAR

"As riveting as any Cold War spy novel. *The Zookeepers' War* is an immaculately researched, moving tale of two zoo directors whose careers became a microcosm of the struggle between two antagonistic ways of life. A captivating read."

—Elena Gorokhova, author of *Russian Tattoo*

"J.W. Mohnhaupt's engrossing tale features a mix of just about everything: outsized ambitions, clashing personalities, Cold War drama, and animals galore. It also encapsulates Germany's history from the end of World War II until reunification. Quite a feat—and a must-read."

—Andrew Nagorski, bestselling author of
1941: The Year Germany Lost the War

"With the Stasi chipping in for a pair of bears, Ho Chi Minh sending an elephant, and the Kennedys gifting a decrepit bald eagle, J.W. Mohnhaupt's portrait of two dueling Berlin zoos gives us a new understanding of the term 'political animal.' This quirky and delightful account of captive critters and soft (and occasionally scaly) diplomacy is colorful, provocative, and ultimately about the very human notions of power, pleasure, and the nature of freedom."

—Abby Tucker, bestselling author of
The Lion in the Living Room

"A highly entertaining true story that is sure to delight history buffs and general audiences alike."

—*America* magazine

"The book is subtitled 'An Incredible True Story from the Cold War,' and for once that's no exaggeration."

—*Daily Mail*

"A charming account of a decades-long rivalry between Heinrich Dathe, the dour, scholarly, former Nazi zoologist and educator who founded and directed East Berlin's zoo, called the Tierpark, and Heinz-Georg Klös, the opportunistic, insecure veterinarian turned administrator . . . of the West Berlin zoo. . . . As frenemies for nearly half a century, they encapsulate the larger saga of the great city, the era, and a world in conflict."

—*Air Mail*

"The liveliness of [Mohnhaupt's] storytelling and the wonderful eccentricity of his subject matter make this book well worth a read."

—*Star Tribune* (Minneapolis)

"Cold War Berlin bursts to life in this riveting, lively German bestseller chronicling the fierce rivalry between zoos on either side of the Iron Curtain. . . . Mohnhaupt is a keen guide to the difficulties of a divided Berlin and to the enchantment of a career devoted to wild animals."

—*Publishers Weekly*

"An offbeat tale from the Cold War . . . with plenty of near-comical turns."

—*Kirkus Reviews*

THE
ZOOKEEPERS' WAR

AN INCREDIBLE TRUE STORY
FROM THE COLD WAR

J.W. MOHNHAUPT

TRANSLATED BY SHELLEY FRISCH

SIMON & SCHUSTER PAPERBACKS

NEW YORK   LONDON   TORONTO   SYDNEY   NEW DELHI

Simon & Schuster Paperbacks
An Imprint of Simon & Schuster, Inc.
1230 Avenue of the Americas
New York, NY 10020

Copyright © 2017 by Carl Hanser Verlag München
Originally published in 2017 in Germany as *Der Zoo der Anderen* by Carl Hanser Verlag

All rights reserved, including the right to reproduce this book or portions thereof in any form whatsoever. For information, address Simon & Schuster Subsidiary Rights Department, 1230 Avenue of the Americas, New York, NY 10020.

First Simon & Schuster trade paperback edition November 2020

SIMON & SCHUSTER and colophon are registered trademarks of Simon & Schuster, Inc.

For information about special discounts for bulk purchases, please contact Simon & Schuster Special Sales at 1-866-506-1949 or business@simonandschuster.com.

The Simon & Schuster Speakers Bureau can bring authors to your live event. For more information or to book an event, contact the Simon & Schuster Speakers Bureau at 1-866-248-3049 or visit our website at www.simonspeakers.com.

Interior design by Carly Loman

Manufactured in the United States of America

10 9 8 7 6 5 4 3 2 1

Library of Congress Cataloging-in-Publication Data is available.

ISBN 978-1-5011-8849-7
ISBN 978-1-5011-8850-3 (pbk)
ISBN 978-1-5011-8851-0 (ebook)

The translation of this work was funded by Geisteswissenschaften International—Translation Funding for Work in the Humanities and Social Sciences from Germany, a joint initiative of the Fritz Thyssen Foundation, the German Federal Foreign Office, the collecting society VG WORT, and the Börsenverein des Deutschen Buchhandels (German Publishers & Booksellers Association).

For Juliane

CONTENTS

THE
ZOOKEEPERS' WAR

PROLOGUE

ANIMAL PEOPLE

*City dwellers in general, and Berliners in particular,
love animals more than their fellow men.*

—Wolfgang Gewalt, former director of the Duisburg
Zoo, in an interview with *Die Zeit*, 1966

The following anecdote stems from the late 1980s, with the world on
the brink of crisis, when it seemed that the Berlin Wall would stand
for at least another hundred years, and West Berlin's Zoo and East
Berlin's Tierpark were not only their respective countries' most popular recreational facilities, but also symbols of their systems of government. The city of Berlin had been divided for nearly thirty years,
and the only sign of unity was the two zoo directors' dedication to
cultivating their mutual aversion. It is hard to know who started the
feud; as so often in life, though, it all came down to who had the biggest of whatever was being compared—in this case, elephants.

The setting was the West Berlin Zoological Garden, where Heinz-
Georg Klös, the director, had recently enlarged his elephant enclosure
and bought a few new animals, which he was now showcasing. Klös
was an avid animal collector, and his zoo had the largest number of

species in the world. He attached great importance to having more elephants than his counterpart in the East, because, in the world of zoos, elephants are prize possessions. Having more elephants meant winning a battle. Back in the 1960s, Willy Brandt, West Berlin's mayor at the time, was said to have gone over the head of his own Department of Finance to secure the money needed to purchase additional elephants, with the sole aim of flaunting this acquisition in front of the East Berlin Tierpark and its director. At least, that's how Klös remembered it.

Courtesy now dictated that Heinrich Dathe, the director of the Tierpark ("animal park"), be invited to the unveiling of West Berlin's new elephant enclosure. Dathe's presence could be to Klös's advantage: the director of the Zoo would be able to make sure his rival saw just how badly he had been bested—after all, Dathe had been struggling for more than ten years to get funding for a new pachyderm pavilion despite East Germany's floundering economy.

Dathe did not think much of Klös, professionally or personally. And Dathe, who was sixteen years older, made his junior counterpart fully aware of his disdain—he once made a show of serving dumplings at a gathering, pointing out the resemblance between the German word for dumplings (*Klösschen*) and his guest's last name.

And so, when Dathe criticized the new elephants in the Zoological Garden for looking "a little puny," Klös had reached the limit of his patience. One word led to another, and eventually a shoving match ensued between the two aging men—neither much taller than five foot five—right there among the elephants.

Top Dogs Behind Tall Walls

In retrospect, we have to wonder which was more responsible for driving these two men apart: their similarities or their differences.

Both came to divided Berlin in the 1950s: Heinrich Dathe in 1954 from the city of Leipzig, several hours to the south, in order to create the world's largest and most modern zoo in the capital of the newly formed communist German Democratic Republic (GDR); Klös three years later from Osnabrück, a smaller city way off in the country's west, to restore the oldest zoo in the Federal Republic of Germany to its former glory. The Tierpark and the Zoo became their missions in life, and before long an intense rivalry developed. Jürgen Lange, the longtime director of West Berlin's aquarium, described the relationship between the two: "If one of them buys a miniature donkey, the other buys a mammoth donkey."

Dathe was an educator by nature. A short, stocky, prematurely balding man with a round head and horn-rimmed glasses, he tried to hide his receding hairline by combing his remaining strands of hair over the bald spot above his forehead. But he made no attempt to conceal his singsong, backwoods Saxon accent, pronouncing cockatoos "gagadoos" and camels "gamels." Dathe was sought after not just locally, but throughout the world, owing both to his expertise and to his control of the central quarantine station for the transport of animals from the Eastern Bloc to Western Europe. He also published the influential trade journal *Der Zoologische Garten*. Everyone reached out to Dathe, and everyone wanted something from him.

On the other side of the Berlin Wall, Klös ran the richest and most important zoo in West Germany, but he lacked Dathe's self-assured personality. Everything seemed to come easily to Dathe; Klös always came across as eager, yet oddly insecure. He was forever trying to wriggle his way into any new plans. If some organization was starting up, he would find a way to get involved.

Klös had the disadvantage of being "only" a veterinarian—someone who traditionally had a harder time of it in the world of zoo directors than a zoologist did. Today, a background in veterinary medicine isn't unusual for a zoo director, but then it was regarded as a shortcoming. Klös, however, was a superb organizer and manager, with a knack for badgering politicians and business tycoons until they handed over money. "Don't eat dinner next to Klös, otherwise you'll lose your purse" went a rhyming quip in West Berlin. Some people claimed Klös was so good at rustling up money out of nowhere that he must also be able to pull rabbits out of hats.

Klös could be dogged, certainly, but he was determined to maintain his institution's relevance to a country from which West Berlin had been physically blocked off. With the West German capital four hundred miles away, the far-off Bonn, he made every effort to ensure that each West German president visited his zoo at least once—and he got them all, even Gustav Heinemann, a confirmed hater of animals.

For Dathe in the East, it was important to gain a foothold for himself and his animal park not only within the GDR, but also beyond the confines of its borders. Cozying up to the men in the Politburo paid off handsomely, particularly if they were also animal lovers, such as Friedrich Ebert Jr. and Günter Schabowski, high-ranking members of East Germany's Socialist Unity Party. "Dathe would not have worked out in the West any better than Klös would have in the East," says Lothar Dittrich, the director of the Hanover Zoo and a close friend of Heinrich Dathe. "They were two top dogs—each in the place that best suited him." In the other's Germany, they would have failed miserably.

But while Dathe and Klös were masters of their respective games, both could be naive. Through to the end of the GDR, Dathe clung to the belief that the East German secret police had never kept tabs on him, while Klös proved still more obtuse when he recommended that his predecessor, Lutz Heck, an old Nazi and close friend of Hermann Göring, be named an honorary member of the Association of German Zoos. Politics sparked their interest only where their animals were concerned.

For both men, their zoos came first, well before anything else—even their own families. Their zoos *were* their families, wives and children often little more than hangers-on. In Berlin, in the Cold War, being a zoo director was more than a nine-to-five job; it was a calling. Klös and Dathe were "animal people," a description used by zookeepers and circus performers to describe those who get along better with beasts than with their fellow men.

Politics by Other Means

The political and social influence the two zoo directors had in their halves of the divided city was possible only in the context of the Cold War—but it was also an outgrowth of the special bond between Berliners and their animals. Berliners are not just animal lovers; they are animal-obsessed. No other city has made so many of its nonhuman residents VIPs, from Bobby the gorilla, the first of his species to join the Berlin Zoo in the late 1920s, to Knautschke the hippo, one of the only animals to survive World War II, to Knut the polar bear, who in death received almost as many flowers, condolence cards, and stuffed animals as Princess Diana.

The Wall was the bulwark between the administrators' separate turfs, where they reigned without competition, the existence of the zoo on each side providing the justification for the other to flourish. Both became symbols of their half of the city and embodied its political system: the Zoo was the treasure of the island that was West Berlin, a cornucopia of species packed within the constricted space of a city hemmed in by the Wall. On the other side of the Iron Curtain, the Tierpark was spacious and expansive, planned on a drawing board, but not designed of a piece and never fully completed: the socialist utopia as a work in progress.

In divided Berlin, in the words of historian Mieke Roscher, whose research at the University of Kassel focuses on human-animal relationships, "the feeling of being enclosed within a border was palpable everywhere. In a sense, West and East Berlin were themselves two zoos." Amidst the tensions of the Cold War, animal parks were havens in which visitors might get a glimpse of an unspoiled world. Yet within the gates of these purported paradises, rigid hierarchies ruled. And those in the know claimed the two zoos were run as strictly as any city hall, court of law, or international military alliance set up to guard against the outbreak of World War III.

CHAPTER 1

WAR AND CROCODILE TAIL SOUP

There would surely be no more bombs that day. In the early evening, fog had settled in, and now thick clouds veiled the sky over Berlin. How could enemy pilots possibly locate their targets in this weather? The Zoological Garden was dark and quiet, the visitors were long gone, and the gates were shut.

It was November 22, 1943. Over the past few months, Royal Air Force raids on Berlin had been stepped up, but apart from six hits two years earlier, the zoo had thus far emerged largely unscathed. Even so, Lutz Heck was prepared. The director held repeated drills to teach his staff what to do if firebombs hit. He also readied for the possibility of animals escaping by buying two elephant guns, 11-millimeter caliber. In some other zoos, predators had been shot dead as a precaution; these guns allowed Heck to avoid such drastic preemptive measures, at least for now.

Heck, who had been a supporting member of the SS since 1933 and a member of the Nazi party since 1937, was a close friend of Hermann Göring, Germany's Reich Master of the Hunt. Göring, second in command in the Third Reich, always kept a pet lion cub (brought to him by Heck) at his country residence, Carinhall, in the Schorf-heide forest outside Berlin. When the cub grew too large and dangerous to live in a private home, Heck arranged for it to be picked up, and promptly supplied Göring with a replacement.

Among zoologists, Heck was a controversial figure. Together with his brother, Heinz, the director of Hellabrunn Zoo in Munich, he bred back aurochs, an extinct species of European cattle, by crossbreeding various domestic cows until the young animals bore a resemblance to the wild form. Many colleagues criticized this back-breeding effort as unscientific, but Lutz Heck knew he could quickly silence his adversaries by threatening them with the Reich Master of the Hunt. Göring was keen on promoting breeding projects in hopes of creating new, extraordinary hunting trophies. In 1938, he appointed Lutz Heck head of nature conservation in the Reich Forestry Office, and on April 20 of the same year—the Führer's birthday—he granted him the title of honorary professor. Several years earlier, Göring had even rewarded Heck with a substantial expansion of the premises north of the Berlin Zoo, where a special "German Zoo" was established: from black grouses to beavers to brown bears, only animals from within the Reich were on display. Oak trees bordered the enclosures, and the animal identification signs were emblazoned with little swastikas.

Heck had been the director of the Berlin Zoo since 1931. Founded in 1844, it was Germany's oldest, and with more than 4,000 animals from 1,400 species, the most biodiverse in the world. The zoo was owned by an association of shareholders, with 4,000 shares broadly distributed across the residents of Berlin. In lieu of receiving monetary payments, shareholders and their families were granted free entrance. So the zoo belonged to its visitors—at least to those who could afford to buy stock or were lucky enough to inherit it.

Lutz Heck took over his post from his father. Privy councilor Ludwig Heck, who had made the zoo famous, liked to brag that he had been a National Socialist before the term even existed. His son ran the zoo in complete accord with Nazi guidelines. In July of 1938, Jewish shareholders were required to sell their shares back to the zoo, generally far below their fair value, and the zoo then resold them at higher prices. By the end of the year, Jews were no longer allowed to visit.

Heck had attempted to get himself put in charge of all German zoos. The Nazis felt this would exceed the reasonable number of posts for him to hold, however, so permission was denied. Even so, the Heck family's close ties to the party proved advantageous for the country's other zoos, especially after the outbreak of World War II. In times of war, there were often problems with animals' feed supplies, which Lutz Heck was generally able to rectify quickly—unlike in World War I, when many zoo animals had starved to death. But it was his own Berlin Zoo that would reap the most direct profits from the war: Heck used forced laborers, and the Russian campaign enabled him to bring animals over from Eastern European zoos.

But by November 1943 the days of expansion were done. The war had long since come home. Heck saw one question written all over the faces of his zookeepers as they tended to their animals: "Will we get out of here alive?" He had taken the precaution of evacuating part of the zoo's collection—750 animals from 250 species—to other cities: a Tasmanian devil went to Frankfurt, a giraffe to Vienna, garpikes from the aquarium to Leipzig, and wild donkeys and lions to Breslau. To protect those that remained, Heck had steel boxes with slits built into the ground and covered with earth; they looked like oversized molehills. The caretakers were told to stay in these shelters until danger passed. An underground air raid shelter was also built at the entrance to nearby Budapester Strasse.

A flak tower, nicknamed Gustav, had begun to give him a queasy feeling. The reinforced concrete colossus sat enthroned on the northwest border of the zoo, like a medieval fortress. The tower was intended to provide refuge to soldiers and civilians during air raids, but Heck feared it was far too easy a target for British and American bombers. "Will we get out of here alive?" was a question Heck was now pondering as well.

It seemed that at least this mid-war Monday would end without any major incident. In a staff apartment at the edge of the zoo, several caretakers were celebrating the birthday of a colleague with a few bottles of beer. Beyond the zoo's walls, people were, as usual, seeking distraction from the everyday wartime routine. Many headed to the opera on Kantstrasse, paying no attention to the instructions on the program for what to do in case of an air raid. Others went to one of the nearby movie theaters to see *Münchhausen*—one of those new color films, with the ever-popular Hans Albers flying through the air on a cannonball—or *Melody of a Great City*, which people would later say was the last film to show an as yet undestroyed Berlin in all its glory. But on this foggy November evening in 1943, no one could have anticipated that.

At 7:25 p.m., the telephone in the zoo's gatehouse rang. The message was from air raid warning headquarters: "Strong combat units approaching from Hanover, heading east. Several waves to follow." The gatekeeper rushed to pass along the news. Within a few minutes, all sections of the zoo had been informed. The caretakers sent their wives and children to the air raid shelter, which could hold about twenty thousand people on five levels, and then moved into their molehills. "Nothing much will happen tonight," they assured one another. "In this foggy weather? Impossible!"

Half an hour later the first airplanes reached the city. Over the next twenty minutes, 753 British bombers dropped 2,500 tons of explosives. Twenty-one major fires raged in the zoo that night. The roof of the elephant pagoda caved in, killing a white rhinoceros and seven elephants; one was buried under a roof beam, his entrails hanging out of his belly, thick as rolled-up mattresses. Siam, the male elephant, was the only survivor. Of the two thousand animals that had remained in the zoo, seven hundred were dead.

The next day, the worn-out caretakers, their faces blackened with soot, joined up with a group of prisoners of war and went about cleaning up. They put out fires and cleared away debris, under which they kept finding dead animals.

The following night brought renewed attacks, which devastated the neighborhoods of Charlottenburg and nearby Hansaviertel. Once the raids were over, the zookeepers rushed out of their hide-outs to put out more flames. The bombs had destroyed many of the city's water pipes, making it necessary to transport water in vats and buckets. Everyone pitched in. Katharina Heinroth, the wife of aquarium director Oskar Heinroth, stood in front of the red-brick hippopotamus house with a relatively intact hose and tried to quench the flames on the burning roof. Next to her, the hippos circled nervously in their outdoor tank with terrified, wide-eyed stares. One-year-old Knautschke would not budge from his surrogate mother's side.

Heinroth did not know how long it took her to put out the fire, but sometime in the early morning she finally managed to do so. From the charred roof beams, the water dripped down onto the hippos.

Rubble Woman with a PhD

Katharina Heinroth, born in Breslau, near the Polish border, in 1897 as Katharina Berger, was the second wife of the aquarium director.

Both she and Oskar Heinroth were already divorced when she began working as his secretary in 1932, helping him type up the manuscript of his book, *The Birds of Central Europe*. Even though Oskar had had a key role in building the Berlin Aquarium and leading it to world renown, he was first and foremost an ornithologist. Their work soon brought them closer, and they married the following year. On the rooftop terrace of their apartment above the aquarium they kept carrier pigeons and together studied their sense of direction.

Katharina Heinroth had remarkable credentials herself. At the age of twenty-two, she had enrolled in PhD courses in zoology, botany, paleontology, geology, and geography at the University of Breslau, despite the dismal job prospects for a young woman looking to go into those fields. She collected four marriage proposals before graduation, almost as many as she did areas of academic interest, and her dissertation adviser often worried that with all the time she spent "going through men," as he called it, she would not have enough time to devote to her studies. But after four years, she became the first woman to receive a doctorate at the university's Zoological Institute—summa cum laude, no less. In the two decades since graduation, she'd spent her nights conducting research on bees and springtails (invertebrates less than a quarter of an inch long); during the day, she earned a living as a secretary, librarian, or administrative assistant. That was as far as a woman could go at the time.

◆

While Katharina Heinroth put out the fire in the hippopotamus house, rumors circulated through Berlin that animals had escaped from the zoo. Elephants were said to be making their way across the Kurfürstendamm, Berlin's main thoroughfare, and lions were roaming about the ruins of the Kaiser Wilhelm Memorial Church.

A tiger reportedly made it all the way to bustling Potsdamer Platz, ate a piece of traditional honey-glazed "bee-sting cake" in the bomb-gutted Café Josty, and promptly died for reasons unknown. But the animals who survived the inferno were too scared to flee: they cowered in the ruins. Even the vultures and eagles did not fly away, but remained on the branches of their shattered cages. A tapir—a tropical relative of the rhinoceros, but piglike in appearance—pressed up against the bars of its enclosure to draw warmth from some smoldering carbon piled in front of it. A crocodile was found lying at the entrance to the aquarium on Budapester Strasse. The force of the explosions had hurled it out of the tropical hall, and the night frost had been the death of it. Since the meat was kept fresh by the cold, the following days brought crocodile tail soup for the famished zoo staff, who were grateful for the added bit of meat.

Meanwhile, the air raids kept escalating. During the day, the Americans bombed Berlin; at night, the British took over. And every day, the Red Army moved closer and closer to the capital from the east.

So it went for eighteen months, until just before Easter of 1945, when Oskar Heinroth was slowly recovering from a bout of pneumonia. All the time spent in the cold air raid shelter had taken a terrible toll on the seventy-four-year-old aquarium director. He was getting an injection to help him back on his feet when the nurse accidentally hit a nerve and paralyzed his right leg. Katharina, who for so many years had supported her husband in his research, now added nurse to her responsibilities. When he developed a nutritional edema, she asked Lutz Heck for a daily ration of goat milk. But food was scarce, and the zoo director had never liked Heinroth's pigeon research, much less his contacts with Jewish and dissident scientists.

The conversation quickly turned ugly, dredging up old resentments. "Herr Heinroth would have been better off sticking to his own job at the aquarium," Heck said sharply. "In the future I'll be sure that everyone's research agenda is prearranged."

"In that case, you can forget about any discoveries," Katharina snapped back, restraint having never been one of her strong points. "No work of genius has ever come out of civil service!"

They argued back and forth for quite some time, until Heck gave in and authorized the goat milk for her husband. "I've never fought with anyone for so long," he said, impressed. He wasn't used to being contradicted, let alone by a woman.

Trenches in the Zoo

By late April, it was evident that the "future" Lutz Heck alluded to was not to be. Some obstinate souls who still believed in the possibility of a German victory attempted to keep the advancing Red Army at bay with antiaircraft guns. The huge flak tower in which these guns were housed was an obvious target, and many of the shots fired in its direction exploded in the adjoining zoo.

Heck arranged for his wife and sons to be evacuated and sent west. Katharina Heinroth was also trying to figure out how to get herself and her husband to safety. But Oskar could no longer walk. And even if he could have fled, it would not have occurred to him to leave the zoo, especially his aquarium, which he had run for more than thirty years. "Let's stay here," he said to her quietly. "I'd rather go down with everything."

In the final days of April, the eastern front ran right through the zoo. Several Soviet tanks had already battled their way to its walls. The remaining zookeepers were conscripted into the German national militia, known as the Volkssturm, and had to dig trenches on the zoo grounds. During lulls in combat, they tended to the few animals that remained.

By the evening of April 30, it was clearly just a matter of time until the Red Army attacked the zoo. Lutz Heck bolted before they could. He sensed what lay ahead for him: the Russians had been told he'd seized animals from Eastern European zoos, and abducted a team of wild horses from Ukraine. With barely any working vehicles left in Berlin, he fled on a bicycle and succeeded in making his way to Leipzig, more than a hundred miles, where he rode to the home of zoo director Karl Max Schneider.

Schneider was surprised to open his door and see who was standing in front of his home. "As a fellow zookeeper, I'm asking you to put me up for the night," Heck said, without further explanation.

Fifty-eight-year-old Schneider had lost his left lower leg while serving as a lieutenant in World War I. An old Social Democrat, he'd refused to join the Nazi party until 1938, when he succumbed to pressure from on high. He cast a skeptical eye on Heck before reaching into his pants pocket to pull out a keyring. "Here's the key to my apartment," he said, "but I will not spend the night under a roof with you. When I return tomorrow morning at six o'clock, you'll be gone." Schneider left, and spent the night with friends. When he returned the next day, Heck had vanished. He'd stay hidden for quite some time.

◆

Smoke lay over Berlin. When the dull thuds of the explosions had at last gone silent, the grounds of the zoo had been reduced to rubble. Two stone elephants sat at the Budapester Strasse entrance like silent sentinels, the gateway they'd watched over destroyed, apart from a narrow crumbling arc somehow still balanced between two shattered pillars. The antelope house, originally built in the Moorish style, was now just a pile of debris with two minarets and a chimney sticking out. A young horse poked around for a trace of grass between heaped-up bricks, while an emaciated wolf gazed over from his enclosure, hungry but too weak to chase after it.

Once director Heck had fled, Katharina Heinroth took charge, tending to injured Berliners in the zoo's air raid shelter—her dying husband among them. She had attached a white cloth with a red cross to the door of the bunker in the hope the Russians would spare them from combat operations. From his sickbed, Oskar instructed her how to treat gunshot wounds and apply dressings. A few hours later the first Red Army soldiers entered the zoo.

Oskar asked his wife for one last favor. "The poison pills," he whispered, "get them for me." But the pills were in a drawer in Oskar's study in their demolished apartment. How was she supposed to get there? The place was swarming with soldiers, and besides, she had no intention of leaving her husband alone, so she tried to reassure him, telling him gently, "We'll get through this somehow." He sighed in disappointment.

The next morning, the soldiers herded everyone out of the air raid shelter. Katharina was able to carry her husband to a dry, quiet corner in the basement of the aquarium, but they were unable to stay hidden for long. As the days dragged on, different sets of soldiers made their way past the smashed walls, on the search for something to eat or drink, or just an opportunity to show the Germans who was now in charge. Men who did not obey, or tried to protect their wives, were shot, and their wives raped. Several times Heinroth and her husband moved from one level of the ruin to another, but they were found again and again. *"Raboti, raboti!"* the soldiers shouted when they saw Katharina. The men held her down and raped her.

Finally, she was able to get her husband out of the aquarium. He was too ill to stand on his own, so she sat him in a wheelbarrow and went looking for a new hideout. But most of the cellars in the area were overcrowded. They had to keep moving on every few days.

Once the Soviet troops had left the zoo, Katharina Heinroth went back to her old apartment and put a room in some semblance of order. Then, with the help of two zookeepers, she brought her husband back home.

Oskar Heinroth died on May 31. Katharina was now alone. She asked the zoo's carpenter to make a coffin out of doors from bombed-out buildings and had her husband cremated. Several weeks went by before she could bury him on the zoo grounds.

Now she had to go on, and Katharina Heinroth recalled the motto of her dissertation adviser in Breslau: "Doing something will make you feel better." She had always abided by the saying, and it had helped her to cope with dark times in her life. So she and the remaining zoo staff set about making order out of the chaos. As they cleaned things up, they found the corpses of eighty-two people amidst the rubble. Like the dead animals before them, the bodies were buried in mass graves.

Only ninety-one animals had survived the war. These included a reindeer, a rare Oriental stork from Japan, a shoebill—a bird about the size of a crane, with gray feathers and a clog-shaped beak, whose natural habitat is the swamps of the Nile—the male elephant, Siam, and Knautschke, the young hippo. In the final days of the war, bombs had destroyed the hippo house and wounded Knautschke's mother so severely that she died. The zookeepers poured water over Knautschke several times a day to keep his skin from drying out. Several other animals disappeared soon after, slaughtered by hungry Berliners. The rest of the animals were

placed in temporary enclosures, the shoebill in one of the few un-
damaged bathrooms.

After Heck's disappearance, the zoo lacked a director. The former managing director, Hans Ammon, had tried to take over, but
once a former zoo chauffeur revealed that Ammon had been a Nazi
party member, he was forced to leave—while the chauffeur was installed as head of the zoo's cleanup efforts by the Soviets. He brought
together two hundred *Trümmerfrauen* ("rubble women"), and by July
1, 1945, some semblance of a restored zoo could be opened. A few
weeks later, yet another man turned up—a former part-time waiter
in the zoo's restaurant—who claimed to have been put in charge
of running the zoo. Since neither the telephone nor mail systems
were operational, no one could confirm or deny this. The bickering
between the two "directors" resounded through the zoo for weeks.
Still, they agreed on one thing: they sent Katharina Heinroth to work
with the rubble women, where the most she was allowed to do was
make a couple of signs for the animal enclosures.

While this rebuilding was underway, the governments of the
United States, the Soviet Union, Great Britain, and France formally
assumed joint control of Germany, dividing the country into four
semi-autonomous occupation zones. Berlin, located deep inside the
Soviet zone, was also split into four, with one sector given to each
Allied Power to administer. The Berlin Zoo suddenly found itself
under nominal British control.

When the occupying forces got wind of the leadership chaos at
the zoo, they charged the newly established Magistrate of Greater
Berlin—the city's highest administrative authority, tasked with overseeing all four sectors—with clearing up the matter once and for
all. Shortly thereafter, Katharina Heinroth received a written request

from the magistrate to appear at the Old City Hall on August 3. The request did not specify why.

Werner Schröder had also received a letter from the magistrate, and on the morning of August 3, he started out on the five-mile walk from his apartment in the district of Wilmersdorf to the city center. He was to report to the Public Education Department. He, too, was left in the dark as to why.

Werner Schröder had come in contact with Oskar Heinroth while he was studying zoology at Berlin's Friedrich Wilhelm University in the 1930s, but he did not know Katharina. They met for the first time that day, when Josef Naas, head of the magistrate's cultural bureau, informed them that Heinroth would serve as the interim head of the zoo and Werner Schröder as the managing director and her deputy.

Heinroth was well aware that she had been given this opportunity only because of the unusual circumstances of this moment in history: there were not enough politically untainted men to fill the country's vacant positions. She'd later joke to friends, "They surely thought I was Oskar when they asked me to come to city hall."

And so Heinroth and Schröder, who was also politically above reproach, set about rebuilding the zoo. Because the boundary walls had been smashed, street traffic ran right through the grounds. During the night, gangs came to plunder what they could. The zookeepers attempted to drive them away with whistles, but a silver fox, a wild boar, and a deer fell victim nevertheless.

In late September Heinroth was appointed the zoo's permanent director, and a good month later the Allied Powers officially recognized the institution's cultural value, guaranteeing public financing, which kept the zoo afloat—albeit barely. During that first year following the war, there was hardly any reconstruction. The sewer system and electricity supply had to be put into operation again, and there was little food for the animals. Vegetables were planted on the fallow lands, as was tobacco; cigarettes were an indispensable currency. Heinroth had signs made up to guide visitors through the muddle of half-destroyed cages and enclosures to find the ones in which animals were still alive. One day she caught a thief trying to make off with the wooden planks from a wrecked stable. When she confronted him, he snapped, "As a zoo shareholder, I have every right to do this!"

In January 1946 the Associated Press would write, "Only about 200 animals still live in the dreary ruins of this once so colorful and beloved institution." Even so, things were much less dire than they had been the previous year. There was no money to purchase new animals, but several hundred Berliners had brought their pets to the zoo, especially their parrots, thinking they they could get better care there than at home. A giraffe named Rieke who'd been evacuated to Vienna was returned to Berlin, and the staff chipped in a month's salary to acquire at least a few new species. Heinroth used the money to buy penguins. She also offered a consultation hour for worried pet owners hoping to find out why their parrot was plucking out its feathers or why their dog disobeyed them.

Cabbage for Knautschke

In late August 1947 the zoo was again rocked by explosions; British troops were trying to blast apart the nearby air raid shelter. All 649 animals had to be lured into wooden crates, one after the after, and brought out of the zoo. But the bunker was too massive, despite the twenty tons of explosives detonated. The attempt would have to be repeated the following year. By then, explosions were a minor concern compared to the new problems facing the zoo.

The blockade of West Berlin, which lasted almost a full year, posed entirely new problems for the zoo. The occupying forces had been arguing for years about creating a unified German currency, and now in June 1948 the three Western Powers announced that they would be introducing the new deutsche mark in their sectors of Berlin. The Soviets, who had not been consulted on this move, reacted promptly. On the night of June 23, 1948, the lights went out in the western part of the city, the electricity supply was switched off, and all streets and waterways were closed by the Red Army. The island of West Berlin, which depended on supplies from the outside world, was cut off from that world except by air. The Allies used an airlift to supply food to the two million residents.

The zoo was expected to do its part to save the city from starvation. The new British commander informed Katharina Heinroth what had to be done: fell all the trees, plant spinach on the open spaces, get rid of all the animals, and set up chicken coops instead.

Heinroth was shocked as she pictured the grand oaks falling, some of them four hundred years old. The zoo would have to close down, and she knew that once a zoo had been closed, it was almost impossible to reopen it. She was painfully aware of what had happened in Düsseldorf, where the Zoological Garden, founded in 1876, was closed on what was supposed to be a temporary basis during World War II, and hadn't opened its gates again. She wanted to spare her zoo—Oskar's zoo—from that fate.

Heinroth resisted the order. She tried to stall, filing complaints at the headquarters of the British forces and at the Berlin bureau for open space planning. The commander relented, and again visited Heinroth at the zoo. This time he brought a map with trees sketched in. He asked her to mark the trees that absolutely had to be preserved. A major portion had been damaged in the war, with many treetops lopped off. But Katharina Heinroth marked every tree, without exception. The commander threatened her with legal action, but Heinroth stood her ground; she had argued with a whole host of characters over the years. Sometime later, she received a visit from another British officer from headquarters. "Forget about that business with the trees," was all he said. In the end, not a single tree was felled.

◆

In May 1949, the American, British, and French occupation zones coalesced into a sovereign state, the Federal Republic of Germany. West Berlin became a *de facto* part of this new country—although the Soviet Union would continue to dispute the city's status for decades. Five months later, in October 1949, the former Soviet zone was rechristened the German Democratic Republic. East Berlin became the capital of the new socialist state.

The Berlin Zoo kept its gates open throughout this upheaval. During the blockade, Berliners had fed Knautschke the hippo, their favorite animal, heads of cabbage, which they had scrimped and saved for. Now the new resident of West Germany would be getting a lady visitor from the East.

After the war, hippos were rare in European zoos. Katharina Heinroth had Knautschke, and Leipzig's zoo director, Karl Max Schneider, had two females, Grete and Olga. Schneider and Heinroth had been trading animals back and forth for quite some time, undeterred by the fact that their zoos were in two different and increasingly hostile countries. They were not about to be stopped by political borders. After all, far more was at stake: the survival of a species. And so they sent the animals on their honeymoons.

The females, Grete and Olga, took several trips on a freight train to West Berlin, where they were briefly housed in a hippo house that had been patched together. The British soldiers called the building a "pis-soir," but it did the job. The ownership of the hippos' offspring followed a time-honored farmer tradition: the female goes to visit the male, and the first male issue becomes the property of the female's owner.

Meanwhile, managing director Werner Schröder was trying to come to grips with the Berlin Zoo's dire financial situation. The zoo was barely bringing in enough money to pay the keepers and cover the costs of feeding the animals. Somehow or other he would have to entice more people to visit.

Schröder had always been a big fan of boxing; as a student he had even twice been German champion. He decided to organize boxing and wrestling matches in a small arena on zoo premises. He also set up animal fairs, and was able to sign on two circuses, Astra and Busch-Aeros, to give performances on an open area near the antelope house. He thought of arranging an Oktoberfest too. Katharina Heinroth was underwhelmed by that idea.

"What about all the animals?" she asked. "They definitely won't be able to cope with the noise and commotion."

Schröder worried about that as well, but he knew the zoo's losses, and they were alarming.

"We're up to our necks in trouble," he said. The dark circles under his eyes accentuated his anxious look. "We have to try this."

Berliners were a bit perplexed when they saw the zoo's new promotional posters, which featured two grinning hippos toasting each other with beer steins. Each sported a gingerbread heart around its neck, one saying Gretchen and the other Knautschke. Above them cursive script announced: "Oktoberfest in the Zoo." There would be shooting galleries and carousels in with the reindeer, parrots, and bears? As it turned out, any misgivings were unfounded; the festival was a roaring success. More than half a million visitors came in the four weeks, providing the zoo substantial revenue that assured its survival. Contrary to Heinroth's fears, the animals barely noticed all the commotion.

Even the two advertising icons were unimpressed, but they had other reasons to be excited. In May 1950 a male hippo named Schwabbel was born; he went to Leipzig, as stipulated. Two years later came a female, Bulette, who could eventually become a new partner for Knautschke. The incestuous nature of this union was beside the point. Hippos were rare and drew large crowds; it made no sense to be too picky.

◆

Young hippos were not the only new attractions during this time. By 1951, there had been no elephants for four years, ever since the old male, Siam, the only elephant to survive the wartime bombings, had died in 1947. Heinroth was convinced that a zoo without elephants could not be a real zoo, but she lacked the funding to buy a new one. At some point she read in the newspaper that India's head of state, Pandit Nehru, had made a gift of a young elephant to a foreign zoo. She lost no time in establishing contact with the Broadcasting Service in the American sector, which ran a program for local schools; she hoped her request would have a greater chance of success if it came from the children of Berlin. Heinroth's plan worked, and soon a young female elephant, Dathri, was located. Dathri, who was three years old and five foot three inches tall, was soon renamed Shanti.

There was no longer an elephant house, so at first Shanti lived in the so-called equid house, a thatched half-timbered building, next to the horses and zebras. But something was wrong. When she was let out onto the enclosure every morning, she was so exhausted that she threw herself down in the sand and slept for hours. This was not how Heinroth had pictured her; after all, people don't come to the zoo to see an elephant lie around all day. Shanti's keeper stayed on for night shift after night shift to find out what was keeping the young elephant awake all night—a mouse, perhaps, or one of the other animals next to her in the stable. But he found nothing.

At some point Heinroth recalled a photo she had received from Mumbai. Wasn't Shanti chained up in that picture? Heinroth was relieved to find that yes, two of the elephant's feet had indeed been chained to a tree. No sooner was Shanti chained up in the equid house than she slept through the night and romped about during the day.

◆

Now that the zoo's finances were relatively stable, Werner Schröder was finally able to devote himself to a project he'd cared about for years: rebuilding the demolished aquarium. Schröder's great passion was for everything that crept and swam. As a little boy, he'd caught frogs, newts, bugs, and fish in the Wilmersdorf fen and kept them in preserving jars at home. His mother patiently observed her son's interests, but his father attempted to get this "obsession with critters," as he called his son's hobby, out of his system, and dragged him to imperial military parades. His efforts were unsuccessful.

As a student, Schröder had visited the aquarium frequently, bringing reptiles from his travels in Greece and North Africa. After the war he often spent time when the workday was through standing in the dilapidated structure, in which trees were now growing, and gazing into the evening sky.

In September 1952, after two years of construction, the Berlin Aquarium reopened as the home to one thousand animals, purchases made possible in part by the annual Oktoberfests, which continued to enjoy great success. Over the next twenty-five years it would be Schröder's mission in life to bring new glory to the aquarium, making it one of the most important institutions of its kind in Europe.

While Schröder was rebuilding the aquarium, a new elephant house—the zoo's first new building since the war's end—was approved for construction. Heinroth had until then worked primarily on repairs, such as to the historic antelope house, and on simple stopgap solutions. Sensing that her critics were waiting for her to slip up on this first major undertaking, she showed the plans for the elephant house to Karl Max Schneider, her friend and colleague in Leipzig, who found no problems with them.

The elephant house opened in 1954, after two years of construction. In addition to Shanti and two newer elephants, the long building with a high glass facade and green-tiled interior welcomed the zoo's first rhinoceros in eleven years, along with a tapir and a sloth.

A Woman in a Man's World

During the years of reconstruction it became evident that Katharina Heinroth and Werner Schröder made a good team. Heinroth always pitched in when a tree needed to be planted, and bawled out zookeepers to keep them in line, while Schröder remained in the background. "Let her handle it," he would think, with a chuckle. He was the one to keep things calm. When a zookeeper had problems, he was more likely to confide in the unruffled Herr Schröder than in the effusive Frau Heinroth, who had had to learn to assert herself in a man's world. Schröder, by contrast, lived by the motto, "Step on those above you if you need to, but never step on those below you." Still, in spite of their differences in temperament, Heinroth and

Schröder liked and relied on each other. Some people even claimed that Katharina Heinroth had a bit of a crush on her scrawny, stern-faced colleague with dark circles under his eyes.

Even though Heinroth had successfully guided the zoo through the formative years of the Federal Republic of Germany, she continued to face hostility at every turn. Back in 1945, shortly after the end of the war, the zoo's supervisory board had handed her a letter at one of its first sessions in which Hans Ammon, the former managing director who'd failed in his bid for the top job when he was outed as a Nazi, called for her dismissal. He claimed that although it could "not be held against her that she has no overall grasp of the situation, this is quite simply a job for a man."

Four years later, while Heinroth was recovering from an illness in the hospital, several members of the board went to see Werner Schröder. After much hemming and hawing and talk of how running the zoo was evidently too strenuous for a woman, Schröder knew what they were looking for from him. Before they could ask him directly whether he wanted his boss's job, he ended the conversation by saying, "We're a good team, and our personalities complement each other for the good of the zoo. Besides, I want to build the aquarium."

Despite the lingering mistrust of the zoo's board, Heinroth enjoyed a very good reputation in professional circles. When the first four German zoo directors were reaccepted into the International Union of Directors of Zoological Gardens in 1950, Heinroth was among the favored few.

And in spite of all the hardships, Heinroth enjoyed the postwar years. Cultural life in the damaged city was gradually coming back, and the restored zoo restaurant and banquet hall were once more hosting conferences and balls. Expectations had risen. Even if Berlin was no longer the capital of all of Germany, it could regain at least some of its old sparkle. The new era of the "economic miracle" had come to West Berlin, and the burgeoning City West downtown shopping and commercial center was especially well placed, right near the zoo. There were plans to build a nearly two-hundred-foot-high, sixteen-story office building directly at the corner of Hardenbergplatz and Budapester Strasse, although Heinroth was skeptical about the project. Because of the way the building was laid out, large parts of the zoo would be in shadow.

Heinroth arranged a meeting with the architect and a new member of the zoo's board named Walter Rieck. As Heinroth tried to persuade the architect to build the high-rise with a north–south rather than an east–west orientation, so as not to rob the zoo of too much sunlight, Rieck cut her off, saying, "As you know, dear lady, the interests of the city come first. In this instance, the zoo has to take second place." Heinroth turned to him and replied gruffly, "In that case, you'd seem to be the wrong man for the zoo." The building was eventually constructed in accordance with Heinroth's wishes, but her attitude had made her unpopular with the board once again.

Meanwhile, men who had vanished after the war were back, and had no intention of holding their tongues. Lutz Heck, the former zoo director, was now living in the western half of the country, in the city of Wiesbaden, and making statements about the goings-on at the zoo to the West Berlin daily newspaper *Der Tagesspiegel*. He bemoaned the difficulties in saving the zoo from going under after the war. When Heinroth read that comment, she was furious, and wrote a letter to the editor setting the record straight about how Heck had fled the city before the war had even ended. The letter was published in late May 1954 alongside readers' views on refugees and foreign words in the German language.

But the events of the past would have sadly little impact on the future. The women who had rebuilt the city—as rubble women or zoo director or even as mayor—had fulfilled their roles. Louise Schroeder, the mayor of Berlin from 1948 to 1951 and a close confidante of Heinroth, had bowed out of the zoo's supervisory board, and Heinroth was continuously undermined on zoo grounds. Just weeks after her indignant letter to the editor, the weekly magazine *Der Spiegel* wrote, "Before the month is out, a decision will be made as to whether Frau Dr. Käthe Heinroth—the only female zoo director in Germany—can remain the head and director of the Berlin Zoological Garden."

This article was prompted by a call by Otto Radke, a Berlin businessman and the spokesman for the zoo shareholders (as well as, coincidentally, an old friend of Lutz Heck). For the upcoming shareholders meeting he had drawn up a plan that included holding new board elections and mounting a scathing attack on the director. Management of the zoo, he declared, "belongs in the hands of a man with an international reputation." Even though she held a doctoral degree in zoology, Katharina Heinroth was still regarded by the old boys' club as nothing more than a top-notch secretary and "trained beekeeper," in Radke's words. She was an interim solution—that was all.

When Heinroth read Radke's plan, she shook with anger. She wanted to go to court to fight his accusations, but one of the board members, a jurist, dissuaded her with assurances that the board stood behind her. But just one week later, *Der Tagesspiegel* published a report on shareholders who blamed Heinroth for "the Berlin Zoo's continuing to make a parochial impression nine years after the end of the war." Some visitors from across Germany who came to Berlin with memories of the venerable zoo were disappointed to find such a small number of exotic animals. Aside from the newly constructed elephant house and Knautschke the hippo, there were few star attractions—not worth the trip to Berlin, they concluded. "Of course we need to bear in mind," *Der Tagesspiegel* went on to write, perhaps a tad hyperbolically, "that no other zoo has lacked visitors with disposable income from surrounding areas as Berlin has since 1945."

But Heinroth's adversaries did not care about these fine points, and they did not drop their opposition. Heinroth, along with Schröder, had saved the zoo from closing down and slowly steered it back to profitability, but demands to entrust Germany's formerly most important zoo to a man only increased.

CHAPTER 2

THE ZOO ON THE OTHER SIDE

The train slowly made its way into the Treptower Park station, stopping at the paved platform as usual. "Treptow," as the locals called it, was the final station before the border between the occupied zones, and the beginning of the American sector of West Berlin.

Since 1949, Germany had been divided into two states, but there were still four powers in Berlin. The borders between the sectors existed only on paper, but the East German regime frowned on its Berliners traveling to the capitalist West.

Several people got in or out, and the train started up again, but those who figured they were in the clear were sadly mistaken. After just a few yards, the train stopped again at a long wooden walkway. No one got out here. Werner Philipp looked through the train window and saw several *trapos* waiting outside, along with a group of men in long dark brown leather coats. They boarded the train and walked slowly along the rows of seats, with the "coats" remaining in the background.

The transport police, known as *trapos*, monitored the Berlin railway network. Philipp was well acquainted with their little game. If you answered their question of where you were going by saying you were headed to the West to go to a bakery or the movies, the *trapo* would come back with a patronizing reply, like "The capital of the GDR has movie theaters and cakes too." But Philipp knew how to outsmart them. He had recently bought a new Western printing machine for his father, who was working as a tax accountant in the East, and had been determined not to let the *trapos* catch him with it. That could have gotten dangerous, particularly because his father's profession was considered suspiciously capitalist. So before boarding the train Philipp had bought the latest edition of the party newspaper, *Neues Deutschland*, pushed the shipping crate under the table in his compartment, and made a show of opening the paper to the page with Socialist Unity Party leader Walter Ulbricht's latest speech. The *trapos* didn't bother him.

Now one of the *trapos* was standing right in front of him. "And where are you headed?" the man asked.

"Well, I want to go to the zoo," Philipp replied.

The policeman turned up his nose, unable to come up with a retort. If there was anything that did not exist in the capital of the GDR, it was a zoo.

Werner Philipp had been going to the zoo since his early childhood; he had worn through several pairs of shoes there. As a child he was often sick and feverish, but whenever his father had free time during the week and suggested, "Tomorrow we can go to the zoo," his fever seemed to melt away. In the late 1930s, the zoo was still one of Berlin's major cultural attractions. Families came for a weekend getaway and wore their Sunday best. People sometimes joked that "the zoo never needs sweeping, because the ladies' long dresses wipe up the dust from the paths." Werner Philipp's parents dressed him for these outings in a sailor suit, and made him wear scratchy knee socks. But he put up with all that, as long as they were going to the zoo. Long before the train stopped at the Zoological Garden station, Philipp could see the elephant pagoda in the distance—a massive building that resembled an Indian temple. Every time he looked at the towers with their reddish gold adornments, anticipation welled up within him, and he felt terrible whenever his parents did not get out there, but simply passed by on their way to other stations. He'd keep looking back at the towers until they had disappeared behind the rows of houses. By the next day, he was typically back to feeling sickly.

Even then, Werner Philipp knew he wanted to become a zoo director. But he was nineteen years old now, and his parents could not afford to finance his university education. Besides, there were more important things going on in the spring of 1953.

Just three and a half years old, the GDR was already experiencing its first economic crisis. The young state, which wanted to expedite the "advancement of socialism" as quickly as possible, prioritized heavy industry (iron and steelwork) over all other areas of development. This resulted in a shortage of food and consumer goods. The so-called workers' and farmers' state reacted by forcing farmers to collectivize and by raising minimum work quotas on construction sites by 10 percent. But the true "enemies" the state targeted were members of the middle class. Entrepreneurs, retailers, and wholesalers lost their businesses as state priorities shifted away from their services, and taxes were increased.

Werner Philipp's father was one victim of these policies. Not long before his son made what was to be his last journey through Treptow to visit the zoo, the tax office carried out one of its notorious audits of his company and determined that he had to pay one million marks in back taxes for the previous year, even though his annual revenue was only about 90,000 marks; after paying his three bookkeepers, only 25,000 marks remained for himself and his family. The "back taxes" left him bankrupt. On top of that, the tax office accused him of vague "economic crimes" and threatened him with three years in prison. The family would soon drop everything and flee to the West, taking along only the bare minimum and traveling separately. But even with so much else on his mind, Werner Philipp would not give up his passion for the zoo.

The Competition Begins

By the spring of 1953, more and more people were leaving the GDR every day; 300,000 had already slipped past the guards and across the border since the previous year. Moscow saw that the GDR was overextending itself with its ambitious construction plans, overlooking the well-being of the people, and so the Soviet Union called on the Socialist Unity Party leadership to change course. In early June, these leaders conceded that they had made "a few mistakes," and agreed to reverse the expropriations, return property, review arrests and sentences pertaining to so-called economic crimes, and improve the food supply. But they continued to insist on their new work quotas, and so on June 17 construction workers went on strike, marching down the most prestigious construction site in the country: Stalinallee, the new central boulevard of the capital. The police looked on helplessly, while the government fled to the headquarters of the Soviet occupation force, which eventually quelled the rebellions with tanks and soldiers.

The Politburo in East Berlin was starting to realize that things could not go on like this. You couldn't just keep raising production targets; people needed to feel as though they'd been given something in return.

That October, Karl Max Schneider, the director of the Leipzig Zoo, was awarded the National Prize of the GDR for "outstanding creative work in scholarly fields." During the festivities, Prime Minister Otto Grotewohl and Soviet ambassador Mikhail Pervukhin took him aside and told him of their plans to build a prestigious zoo in the eastern part of Berlin.

The Magistrate of Greater Berlin (as the city government of the socialist sector continued to call itself) did not want East Berliners traveling to the British sector to visit the zoo there, as they would be maintaining contact with the West and throwing their money at capitalism. Besides, GDR state officials had to seek approval from the Ministry of the Interior just to go see a few animals. Having a zoo of their own in the East would solve these problems, the two men explained.

Back in Leipzig, Schneider told his assistant, Heinrich Dathe, what he had learned. Neither Schneider nor Dathe thought much of the idea of establishing another zoo. Both felt that there was already plenty that needed to be done to repair the country's three existing zoos. While the zoo in Halle had come through the war relatively unscathed, many buildings in the Leipzig Zoo had still only been patched together. The zoo in Dresden, which was, at one hundred years, the oldest in the new country, had suffered damage on an entirely different scale: in February 1945, a firestorm had raged through the city after a British bombing, damaging the zoo so badly that it took more than a year after the end of the war for it to reopen. But if the gentlemen in Berlin were serious about their plan, the two zookeepers knew what that meant. There was really only one individual qualified to be the director of this new Berlin zoo: Schneider's right-hand man, Heinrich Dathe.

Forty-three-year-old Dathe was a passionate zoologist. Even as a child he went birdwatching, binoculars in hand, as often as he could in his rural hometown in Saxony. If he were to become rich, he wrote in an essay for school when he was twelve, he would build a big hall where "snakes, lizards, hummingbirds, insects, sloths, apes, and flying dogs" could live. Back then, he regarded the traditional zoo as nothing but "a prison where animals are locked up."

When he was thirteen years old, his parents relocated to Leipzig, where his father took a job as an office manager. Dathe completed his college entrance exams and in the early 1930s began to study zoology, botany, and geology at the University of Leipzig. He frequently visited the city's zoo to sketch the animals and began working there as an assistant while still a student. He quickly rose in rank over the next decade to become director Schneider's deputy. His career seemed mapped out for him, until it came to a sudden halt. The past—both Germany's and his own—had caught up with him.

From Ornithologist to Nazi

In 1932, at the age of twenty-one, Heinrich Dathe had become a member of the Nazi party. At Leipzig University, National Socialism had enjoyed widespread support; many professors were in the party. And Dathe was a child of the 1920s. He had experienced the consequences of the Treaty of Versailles—which he, like so many others, believed Germany had been bullied into accepting—as well as the subsequent period of inflation and the ensuing global economic crisis. He was determined to contribute what he could to help Germany regain its former standing in the world. However, his eagerness to complete his expensive studies as quickly as possible and begin earning money clashed with his political commitment. And so, until the mid-1930s, Dathe held the lowest rank in the Nazi party hierarchy, putting him in charge of collecting membership dues. His neighbors would later testify that he was an affable sort of Nazi.

Two days after the start of the war he was drafted and sent to the western front, where his right arm was severely wounded in 1940 in northern France. In the sick bay he met his future wife, Elisabeth, a nurse, from Saxony like himself. He was attracted to the beautiful way she rolled her "r"s. After an extended convalescence at home, during which their daughter, Almut, was born, he returned to the front in 1945, this time to Italy, where he wound up in American captivity. He spent much of the remainder of the war giving zoological lectures to his fellow prisoners and keeping up with his birdwatching.

Shortly after the war's end he received offers of employment from several West German zoos, but his wife, their three-year-old daughter, and their two-year-old son, Holger, who was born during his time as a prisoner of war, were waiting for him in Leipzig. He was flattered by the offers, but Dathe wanted only to get back to Leipzig and his zoo. Once he had returned, however, he saw that life had gone on without him. At first, his children wished that the stranger who wanted to be their "Papi" would go away. And Dathe soon learned he had been fired in absentia from the zoo because of his membership in the Nazi party. When he applied for a teaching position at the Kürschner-Schule, a continuing education institute, he was rejected for the same reason. In order to feed his family, he took temporary jobs as an editor, and earned money mimicking bird sounds on the radio. He had always found it unpleasant to ask for a favor, or even to ask for directions, but now found himself struggling in an era in which bribing was called "trading" and stealing "hoarding." Even his old boss, Karl Max Schneider, could not help him, as he had been fired from the zoo as well. Dathe's career seemed to have ended before it had begun.

Hope sprang anew when Schneider returned to the zoo after two of his successors proved inept. The once and future zoo director wanted to round up his old team again—Schneider needed every available man, and his former deputy most of all. The state recognized that it would be impossible to manage in the long run without pardoning at least some of the men who had been in the Nazi party, so Dathe was asked to undergo an assessment to establish whether he was a confirmed Nazi. A publisher and one of his wartime companions attested to his humane and scientific qualities, and eventually Heinz Keil, the administrative director of the zoo and a concentration camp survivor, spoke in his favor. After several conversations, he had concluded that Dathe had not internalized Nazi ideology and issued a clearance for him, which meant that Dathe was now free to return to the zoo. In July 1950 he started there again as a research assistant.

In light of these experiences, Dathe arrived at a decision: never again would he belong to any political party. Doing so had practically cost him his career, and he valued his career above all else.

◆

It took a good three quarters of a year for the fantasy of a new zoo in the East German capital to crop up again. At a special parliamentary session in early June 1954, the Magistrate of Greater Berlin proposed a program referred to as "our Berlin moving along even faster on the new track." In addition to building additional housing, a new clinic in Treptow, and sightseeing tours for West German visitors, the program would set up animal enclosures in all districts and "construct a zoo in the democratic sector," as East German politicians sometimes referred to East Berlin. The zoo in the Western sector was said not to measure up to the "standards of the capital, which was growing larger and more beautiful." That the zoo might simply be in the wrong part of Berlin went unmentioned.

Shortly afterward, Karl Max Schneider received an invitation from the deputy mayor of East Berlin, Herbert Fechner, to attend a meeting at which the issue of a new zoo would be discussed. On the appointed date, however, Schneider would be at a conference of zoo directors in Copenhagen, so his deputy had to fill in for him, reluctantly. No one needed a second zoo in Berlin, least of all Dathe.

Early in the muggy Monday morning of June 21, 1954, Heinrich Dathe made his way to the Leipzig train station. His carriage was packed with people who all looked as though it was their first time in a train.

The day's plan was to tour the three sites in East Berlin they had to choose from: Plänterwald, a marshy woodland whose southeast side adjoined Treptower Park; Wuhlheide, a public park in the district of Köpenick; and Schlosspark Friedrichsfelde, an overgrown park in Lichtenberg. The last of these, Friedrichsfelde, would be the first destination.

The car Fechner provided headed east along Stalinallee. Looking through the side windows, Dathe saw the new "workers' palaces" (large apartment buildings with porcelain tiles) going by, with a sixteen-foot-high bronze statue of Stalin smiling placidly into the distance from its pedestal. One year earlier, there had been riots here, with Soviet tanks rolling up, rocks flying, and numerous casualties. Now the construction workers on the scaffolding looked like ants, having long since returned to work. It was as though the East Berlin workers' uprising of June 17, 1953, had never occurred.

As they drove along, the area grew less formal, with cottages rather than stately older buildings lining the street. In 1821, Peter Joseph Lenné, a Prussian garden architect, had created a palace garden in Friedrichsfelde on the estate of the noble Treskow family. The palace suffered only minor damage in World War II, but afterward it was nationalized and left untended, as was the park. Dathe was still skeptical when they entered the estate, but as the car drove to the overgrown park grounds, his disinclination gradually gave way. He later wrote in his diary, "It felt almost ceremonial for us to be riding along the plane-tree-lined avenue to the little old palace." The group spent an hour walking the grounds, Dathe listening to the calls of different birds in the trees and in the undergrowth. The farther he walked, the more he shed his initial reluctance, until he felt something he had never experienced before, something like euphoria, and an awareness of a new era dawning. "Something could be made of this," he thought to himself. He was already picturing enclosures being built between the trees. All of a sudden he sensed quite clearly that here he would be able to design a zoo according to his own specifications. "This is the opportunity of a lifetime," he told himself. "You get this only once!"

After months of insisting that Berlin had no need for a second zoo, he was now determined to build that zoo right here. But Heinrich Dathe would not have been Dathe if he'd made this known to the others on the spot. His decision had been made, but when Deputy Mayor Fechner asked him what he thought about Friedrichsfelde, he asked for time to mull it over.

Still, the rest of the group had noticed the way he scrutinized the spacious grounds. They didn't even visit the other two sites that day, and those later turned out to be poor options anyway: the Plänterwald was too swampy and would have had to undergo a thorough draining, and Wuhlheide was too far out of town.

Heinrich Dathe did not care in the slightest; the only thing on his mind was the overgrown park. When he got home at one in the morning, the first thing he did was wake up his wife to tell her about his change of heart. Still half-asleep, she heard him out. What else could she do? There was no way of changing his mind. He raved to her about Friedrichsfelde until four o'clock. Later, after just a few hours' sleep, he sent a telegram to Copenhagen to update his boss: "Meeting in Berlin took place after all. Outcome as predicted. Regards, Dathe." He did not yet tell people about his decision, as he had misgivings about leaving the Leipzig Zoo and his benefactor if he went to Berlin. But when Schneider came back and Dathe informed him of his plans, Schneider's reaction was not what Dathe had feared. His only concern was for the future of the trade journal *Der Zoologische Garten*, which Dathe helped him edit. And because Dathe had trouble saying no, he agreed to continue doing his editorial work for the magazine from Berlin. Dathe was raring to throw himself into his new job.

The Old Plan for the Second Zoo

Another meeting in Berlin with Fechner soon followed, during which Schneider imposed a condition: "Before the press finds out about the construction, I would like to inform Dr. Heinroth of this development." The new zoo could in no way compete with the venerable one in the western part of the city, and a rivalry would not be beneficial to a project that was still on shaky ground. Fechner agreed.

That afternoon, Schneider and Dathe visited Katharina Heinroth in her study. Hanging on the wall behind her desk was a weekly calendar decorated with giant colorful butterflies and studded with appointment reminders. Next to it hung a portrait mask of a gorilla named Bobby, who in the late 1920s had been something of a celebrity. Beside the desk was a big birdcage in which a black hill myna hopped around, calling out "Come in." Heinroth was sitting off to one side of her chair, as she usually did, her left elbow propped up on the desk. There was organized chaos everywhere: piles of opened letters and partially read manuscripts next to mountains of reference books.

Schneider began by discussing several routine business matters. Finally, he said, "One more thing you should hear from us: East Berlin will be getting a zoo."

After almost ten years as director of the Berlin Zoo, Heinroth was not easily thrown. So she tilted her head and pressed her chin into her hand. "Oh," she said, slowly raising her eyebrows. "That's been proposed so many times."

There certainly had been numerous plans for a second zoo in Berlin. As far back as 1909, Hamburg animal dealer Carl Hagenbeck envisioned setting up a "people's animal park" in the northern part of Charlottenburg. Two years earlier he had caused quite a stir in Stellingen, just outside Hamburg, with his fenceless zoo featuring outdoor enclosures and ostentatious craggy backdrops. There had never been a zoo like it. He was planning something of this sort for Berlin, and had even gained the Kaiser's support, but before the plans could take concrete form, Hagenbeck died. The next year, World War I broke out, and the plans were scrapped. Then in the late 1920s, Theodor Knottnerus-Meyer, a zoo director who'd fled Rome to escape the Fascists, took up the idea of a people's animal park. Lutz Heck was wary, fearing that his Berlin Zoo would meet the same fate as the old Hamburg Zoo. Soon after the opening of Hagenbeck's animal park, the number of visitors to the old zoo dropped off sharply, and it was forced to close. Heck also had plans of his own to collaborate with his good friend Hermann Göring to establish a spacious branch of the Berlin Zoo on the outskirts of the city.

Heinroth had been pitched the idea of adding a second zoo herself. Shortly after the end of the war, two Russian veterinarians suggested she build a zoo in Treptower Park. But she turned them down, saying "I already have more than enough on my hands with one zoo."

Karl Max Schneider may not have been a keen observer of human nature, but he had known his colleague long enough to deduce her wariness about the likelihood of a second zoo ever being built, so he assured her, with an impish grin, "This time it's for real."

"Well," Heinroth replied, trying to avoid sounding overly snide, "if they're banking on our destruction, we're fifty years ahead." It would take at least half a century, she thought, for the new zoo to become a real threat to hers.

Rather than engage with this barb, Schneider simply informed her that Dathe would be the director.

Now Heinroth was truly surprised, and straightened up in her chair. "Well, what do you know," she said. "He could have come to me. I would've been happy to have him work as an assistant."

But Dathe had had quite enough of playing a subordinate role.

◆

Hermann Henselmann, the GDR's head architect, recommended that a young colleague of his named Heinz Graffunder oversee the building of the animal park, and on August 27, once Dathe had selected his preferred site, the Berlin Magistrate officially approved construction. But the future director seems to have been kept in the dark about this development. In a letter to Graffunder dated September 4, Dathe wrote, "I have to admit to you frankly that I'm disappointed by the course of events." The planning was going far too sluggishly for his liking. He had yet to hear anything from the government about whether building could proceed. All he knew was that a board of trustees had been set up. He found it vexing "that speed is of the essence only when spurring into action a crowd of people who don't know a thing about the matter at hand yet are perfectly willing to meddle, while the obvious steps are not taken."

Even with construction approved, it was not yet certain how— and with what—the animal park would be built. All projects for the coming year were already accounted for. There were neither funds nor materials nor workers available for this one. Dathe knew that without additional resources and support from the people of Berlin, all his planning could come to naught. All this "ambling about," as he called it, unsettled him. He was still grappling with his decision to leave his hometown and "relocate to the sea of houses that made up the giant city of Berlin." At times he even thought of chucking it in and staying in Leipzig.

One short week later Deputy Mayor Fechner visited to let him know that the go-ahead had been given. Heinz Graffunder had been awarded a contract to design the new zoo on the grounds of the Friedrichsfelde park. The animal park, to be named Tierpark Berlin, would comprise four hundred acres, making it more than five times larger than the old zoo in the West.

The following week, Dathe traveled south to the city of Cottbus to look at a park in which a small zoo for domestic animals was being set up. Quite in vogue at the time, these were mostly simple enclosures featuring native wildlife species, often begun by local forest rangers, vocational school groups, or animal lovers acting on their own. Then Dathe continued on to Berlin.

There, an entirely different task lay ahead for him, arguably his most difficult one yet: he had to convince the people of Berlin that they wanted an animal park. Berliners were curious about everything new and unfamiliar, but quite obstinate when it came to parting with cherished traditions. The Western sector already had a zoo—and one that was cheap to visit, with one East German mark worth four Western ones. They had no need for a second zoo, let alone one with a Saxon as its director.

About two hundred people showed up at the school building on Rüdersdorfer Strasse that September evening. When Dathe entered the room, no one recognized him. The visitors sat in small groups: a few elderly women up front who were determined to kill the project that very evening, farther back several garden plot holders poised to fight for the bungalows they'd built illegally at the edge of the overgrown castle grounds. Somehow, Dathe thought to himself as he took his place at a long table at the front of the room, he had to get all these people on his side.

Dathe began by showing a short film about the Leipzig Zoo in order to set the visitors' minds at ease. (Animals always did the trick.) Grumbling gradually yielded to a murmur of approval. Now it was time to introduce his plans.

Animals Onstage

In the two decades that he had been in the field, Dathe had come up with his own philosophy of zoos. Zoos were there, he insisted, for visitors, not for experts. It did not matter to him whether visitors noticed *why* a zoo was beautiful, so long as they noticed *that it was*. Its crucial functions were to educate and entertain. He wanted to move away from the classic zoo, and he sought to whet Berliners' appetites for a new zoo, to show visitors what the cramped urban zoo in the

West could not provide: an expansive park with spacious enclosures for large groups of animals. But if he announced that here, to Berliners still enamored with the only zoo they knew, he might as well pack up his bags and leave. So he tried to involve the public, asking people for their suggestions for what the new park should be like. Dathe emphasized that he intended the animal park to complement the zoo in the West in its design and choice of animals. He aimed to present the animals as though they were on a theater stage. No pens, no fences, little decoration on the enclosures—nothing to divert visitors' attention. That was nothing new. Back at the beginning of the twentieth century, Carl Hagenbeck had enticed people to his animal park in much the same way. The zoos in Leipzig and even Berlin had been using this principle for quite some time. But no zoo director had ever had as much space to work with as Dathe would.

"But don't expect us to perform magic!" he warned his audience. "It will take years."

Also on the evening's program were East Berlin's deputy mayor, Herbert Fechner, Heinz Graffunder, the animal park's architect, and Leipzig Zoo director Karl Max Schneider. Dathe had Graffunder present the first sketches of the enclosures so that people could visualize them and look forward to seeing more. Finally it was Schneider's turn. He started by heaping praise on Dathe and declaring that he was bidding Dathe goodbye with a heavy heart. Dathe, hearing his boss express this sort of sentiment for the very first time, was quite taken aback.

Schneider announced that he would make a gift to the new zoo. Since the 1920s, the Leipzig Zoo had been famous for its lion breeding, earning it the nickname the "lion factory." Several thousand cubs had been born in the ensuing decades for export all the way to South Africa. "The only way to escape receiving a lion as a gift from Leipzig is by suicide," Schneider quipped that evening in his closing remarks. A lion was not the kind of animal he had in mind, however. With a big smile, Schneider continued, "But a bear would be more suitable as the heraldic animal of Berlin, so we're breaking with tradition. Berlin will have to bear with its first bear." His punning pronouncement was greeted with approving applause.

Schneider sat back down with a grin. Only he and Dathe were aware that his generous gift of a bear suggested not only originality, but also frugality. A bear is much cheaper to acquire than a lion.

One of the garden plot holders in the back row stood up and made his way to the front of the room. "Here we go," Fechner murmured to Dathe, who until then had been relieved by how smoothly everything had been going. But there was no cause for concern. "Everything you've presented us here, gentlemen, sounds really good," the man said. "So I promise you on behalf of the District Association of Small Livestock Breeders, Garden Plot Holders, and Homesteaders that we'll support the animal park. And just so you can see I mean that seriously, I'll donate the first hundred marks for spades." Another man went on to pledge ten hours of construction, as did a student at the Academy for Planned Economy. These gestures proved decisive in turning public opinion around. The press soon chimed in, mustering support from the rest of Berlin.

◆

In late October of 1954 the planning began. Graffunder's architects and draftsmen in white smocks moved into the Friedrichsfelde palace. "Design Agency Building Construction II, Greater Berlin, Tierpark Group" the white sign next to the doorway read. Because the fire department had shut off the furnace for safety reasons, they were soon freezing in the drafty mansion.

One of the architects was Heinz Tellbach, a twenty-three-year-old Graffunder knew from their student days at the Building Academy in Neukölln, and whom he'd now recruited for his collective. It was a promising time for young architects—most of the older ones had died in the war or fled to the West, and the young GDR wanted a fresh workforce with fresh ideas. But while Graffunder was able to travel and gather inspiration from zoos around Europe, his aides had to settle for those in nearby Leipzig and Halle. For them, and for so many others involved in the project, all this was terra incognita. And a first inspection of the grounds left them with some odd impressions of what they'd have to work around: in addition to the illicit bungalow colony that had sprung up on the outskirts of the park, there was also a Red Army training site, which was still in active use.

Dathe likewise had no practical experience in designing and building animal enclosures. The only construction he'd overseen in Leipzig entailed a few reroofings and some fence replacements. Now he had to design an entire zoo—and a zoo of the future, no less.

The plan was to start by building enclosures for hardy hoofed animals—deer, camels, and buffalo—as these did not require elaborate heating. Since the architects did not know how tall the individual animals would grow to be, Dathe took them to the sites where the various stables and fences should be placed. Dathe would often come to an abrupt stop somewhere and bend his arms in front of his chest, as though wanting to gauge something with his bare hands. "How much is one yard?" he'd ask the group, and one of the architects would show him on a measuring tape. "No, that's too little," Dathe would then usually say. He'd stretch out his arms even more and say, "Add this much to it." The architects would hasten to measure the distance between his hands. And thus the first site plan came into being.

Dathe liked young Tellbach. He called him by his nickname,

Teddy, as though he'd known him forever. He also liked Tellbach's wife, and enjoyed flirting with her when she came to pick up her husband from work. He made a habit of winking at her—and sometimes at her husband as well, but only at meetings when the head architect, Heinz Graffunder, launched into one of his long discourses about politics. When Tellbach's first daughter was born, Dathe sent the couple a telegram that read, "Congratulations on the animal park's first breeding success." Once he had come up with a good joke, there was no stopping him from telling it.

His own family, who remained in Leipzig, rarely saw him during those months. In Berlin, Dathe lived in sublets or shabby rooming houses. Every morning he cursed the city anew. When his driver picked him up at seven o'clock, they would have to search for a restaurant that served breakfast. Hardly any were open at this hour, so most of the time they wound up at some smoke-filled, gloomy train station dining room that served leftovers from the previous evening.

He had only two or at most three days at a stretch in Berlin to get everything set up for the construction of the Tierpark before he had to go back to Leipzig. Schneider was not about to let Dathe neglect his duties there, which included training his successor.

Lothar Dittrich had just recently arrived at the zoo as a research aide—an unpaid position, as was then customary. Instead of earning money, the twenty-two-year-old could gain experience, and at the start of the new year he would be promoted to a paid assistant. Dittrich had already known Dathe from the university, where Dathe had lectured on the taxonomy of vertebrates, a terribly dry subject. But Dathe had such a vivid narrative flair that Dittrich found some of his descriptions unforgettable, such as his account of eels, whose slimy exterior enables them to move across land to get to their spawning grounds in the sea. "Anyone who has held an eel in his hands knows what slippery means," Dathe told his students. And he described the typical zigzag flight patterns of small wading birds called snipes by saying, "If the hunter takes aim during the 'zig,' it's already up to the 'zag.'" This casual approach appealed to his students.

Over time, a friendship would form between the two men, but for now Dathe was Dittrich's superior. He took Dittrich along on his morning rounds and showed him how to write reports about the animals' latest developments, filling him in on the individual quirks of each animal—which tiger was nervous, which seal irritable.

As if that were not enough, Dathe spent his spare time—not that he had any—writing his postdoctoral thesis.

◆

Somewhere around this time, Heinrich Dathe stood on the balcony of the dilapidated Friedrichsfelde palace and spoke into a recording device that Karin Rohn held in front of him. Rohn, a young radio reporter, was interviewing him for a new program in which Dathe would report on the developments in the Tierpark. Working with journalists was a tricky matter; Dathe couldn't stand the idea of reporters covering the zoo without speaking with him personally. He liked Karin Rohn right away, perhaps because the way she rolled her "r"s reminded him of his wife. He told her about his vision for a spacious nature park with moats rather than fences and bars. Then he took a piece of paper out of his jacket pocket, unfolded it, and pointed to the path that led southeast from the palace. "You see," he said, "this will be a promenade with rhododendron bushes, and over there, large colorful parrots will be sitting on swings. And camels will graze on the Linné meadows."

Rohn did not know what to trust less—her ears or her eyes. She was looking at bare trees and an overgrown pathway. Behind her the palace's stucco crumbled, giving the impression of an abandoned robber baron's castle. She couldn't stop thinking of the meat ration tickets in her pocket. "Berlin is still broken," she thought, "and he's talking about a nature park?"

While the architects were completing their sketches in the palace, construction began on the first of the animal enclosures and walkways in early April 1955. This piecemeal start was necessitated in part by a particularly harsh and long winter, even by Berlin standards. Time was now short; the opening ceremonies were to be held on July 2.

It seemed almost impossible to construct a zoo in three months and so the public was asked to pitch in. Volunteer work had enabled the construction of Stalinallee, the main thoroughfare through the eastern part of the city, two years before. Now, in Friedrichsfelde, people shoveled sand, leveled paths, and cleared out undergrowth. Volunteers were rewarded with stickers for their service cards, and anyone who collected enough stickers got a badge. But that was not the point. The point was to contribute to the development of socialism—at least that was the official line.

The idea caught on. Numerous construction companies and volunteers helped after work and on Sundays to build the Tierpark, putting in roughly 100,000 hours. Schoolchildren with tin cans went through streetcars to collect money, or searched Wuhlheide Public Park for beechnuts and acorns to use as food for the boars and deer in the Tierpark. Anyone who came across a brick brought it to Friedrichsfelde, because everything was needed there. Working in the Tierpark became one of the state's most popular unpaid projects. Heinrich Dathe sensed the outbreak of a veritable zoo fever.

The West German media saw the matter differently. A writer at the weekly newspaper *Die Zeit* made no attempt to hide his malicious glee on a visit to Friedrichsfelde in May 1955, a few months before the Tierpark opened. "Retirees, schoolchildren, Free German Youth members, and a handful of workers are now digging in Friedrichsfelde to make the first enclosures ready for occupancy," he wrote. "There is not a hint of enthusiasm for this construction. The only sign of initiative so far has emanated from the single animal inhabitant of the 'world's greatest animal park': Dr. Dathe's guard dog, who never stops barking."

Spectacled Bears from the Stasi

The first animals were brought to the Tierpark from the nearby Lichtenberg freight depot, with hundreds of gawking spectators lining the streets. They'd never before seen a camel led through the streets of Berlin on a leash. The first animals were gifts from other Eastern European zoos and GDR businesses. The Halle Zoo contributed a Bactrian camel and a black stork. The city of Strausberg donated ostriches and a bed manufacturer more storks. The children's magazine *Bummi* collected money from readers for two giraffes, the ministry for heavy industry and the newspaper *Neues Deutschland* each provided an elephant, and the State-Owned Refrigeration Company and the Köpenick Consumers' Cooperative gave polar bears. Johannes Dieckmann, president of the People's Chamber, the GDR's unicameral legislature, donated a nilgai antelope from India, and the State-Owned Painting and Glazing Company five guanacos, creatures closely related to llamas. The Stasi, East Germany's secret police, contributed two spectacled bears. "Our comrades felt that one spectacled bear would be bored, and the response was so robust that the call for funding brought in triple the planned sum of money," the official communication stated.

On the morning of July 2, 1955, Dathe, GDR president Wilhelm Pieck, and Berlin deputy mayor Friedrich Ebert walked a few steps ahead of a swarm of people headed in the direction of the Friedrichs-felde palace. Katharina Heinroth and Werner Schröder were in the crowd. Dathe considered it essential for them to be present at the opening ceremony, to show that Berlin's two zoos were not working at cross-purposes. When he was warned not to invite his Western counterparts, he threatened, "Then you will have to do without me."

The throng of people stood still in front of red tape stretched across their path. Actually, when seventy-nine-year-old Pieck finally cut the tape with a tiny pair of scissors to celebrate the park's official opening, construction crews and volunteers were still laboring away in other corners of the extensive grounds. They would remain hard at work in the coming months—and indeed years. But unlike so many other projects made possible by volunteer work, East Berlin-ers identified with this one. This was not some grand boulevard that would never be completed, a project to be appreciated primarily by people like the city's head architect, who would gaze down upon it from his penthouse apartment in the neighborhood's choicest build-ing. This was the people's animal park, which they themselves had helped build.

◆

For the state government, the new zoo in the capital was an impor-tant showcase project. And its director was a person of particular interest, especially when he was as fond of travel and socializing as Heinrich Dathe. Shortly after the Tierpark opened and Dathe was on one of his visits to Leipzig, a member of the Stasi called up his secretary, Irene Engelmann. "We would appreciate your keeping us informed about the Tierpark. It's all quite exciting," the man said in a friendly tone. "And Herr Doktor surely gets quite a few visitors from colleagues from the West."

Engelmann didn't know how to respond. When Dathe came back, she wasted no time in telling him about the ominous call. Dathe knew just what it meant, and it was the last thing he needed. He jotted down the telephone number, picked up the receiver, and dialed. Without waiting to find out if he had the right person on the line, he shouted, "I refuse to let anyone put tabs on me in this manner," and slammed down the receiver. His overzealous entry into the Nazi party in 1932 had come close to ruining his career; he was not about to let that happen again.

It was not the Stasi's first attempt to keep tabs on Dathe. When he was still working at the Leipzig Zoo, he had gone through something similar. Shortly before he was to leave for a conference, Schneider had called him into his office. There was a man sitting at the director's desk, someone Dathe had never seen before, but who showed great interest in his trip.

"Is it correct that you'll be going to West Germany shortly?" the stranger asked.

"That's correct," Dathe answered warily.

"Then surely some other colleagues will be going there from the GDR, won't they?"

"Of course," said Dathe, still unsure where this unknown man's questions were heading.

"Ah," said the man, "I would just be interested in learning what sorts of things will be said."

Dathe, taken aback, glanced over at Schneider, who kept looking straight ahead with a blank expression, as though this had nothing to do with him. Now Dathe realized what was going on. "Oh, you mean I ought to work as an informer?" he hollered. "You know what? I'll stay here."

Now it was the stranger who grew nervous. "Oh no. No, please take your trip," he said.

Dathe never heard from the man again.

◆

Less than four months had passed since the Tierpark's opening when on October 26, Karl Max Schneider died at the age of sixty-eight. He was buried with military-style honors, a tribute that had never before been bestowed upon a zoo director. Now Heinrich Dathe had to run the Leipzig Zoo in addition to the Berlin Tierpark. He had spent years working toward running the zoo in his hometown, and now that the time had come, it was but one more task among many. His interim deputy director in Leipzig, Lothar Dittrich, was just twenty-three years old.

For the Leipzig Zoo, the loss of such a formative individual would take a long time to recover from. Very soon, the new Berlin Tierpark would surpass it as the most important zoological institution in the GDR.

Meanwhile, in Berlin, Dathe was trying to retain the impression of a peaceful coexistence with West Berlin's Zoological Garden. Two days before the Tierpark opened, he announced in the GDR newspaper *Neues Deutschland*: "The Berlin Zoo and our new Berlin Tierpark differ so fundamentally in their structure that any 'competition,' which no one wishes to have, is impossible."

The decision for whether the two zoos would become rivals, however, would soon be taken out of his hands.

CHAPTER 3

THE FOURTH MAN

On a rainy morning in October 1955, Katharina Heinroth traveled
to Leipzig to bid farewell to an old companion. She was on her way
to the funeral of Karl Max Schneider, where she would be giving the
eulogy. She had often exchanged animals with Schneider, building
a successful hippopotamus breeding operation that crossed political
borders. And Schneider had stood up for her every time she was
attacked by the Berlin Zoological Garden's shareholders or board.

"I'm down by yet another friend," Heinroth thought as she
strode behind Schneider's coffin, which was borne through the city
to the South Cemetery. Afterward, the mayor of Leipzig, Hans Erich
Uhlich, approached her to say that he was still looking for Schneider's successor. He offered her the position.

A year earlier, Heinroth had received a similar offer from the
Wuppertal Zoo, in the West. She was flattered by these efforts to
entice her away from Berlin. Her work was being recognized after
all, even if it was disregarded by those closer to home. Just recently
there had been problems in the predator section: a tiger and two
young leopards had stopped eating, and were vomiting and produc-

ing bloody diarrhea. No one could identify the cause. "The last thing we need is to have a death just before the annual board meeting," Heinrich wrote to her mother, to whom she regularly reported zoo news and in whom she would continue to confide for many years to come. "The bellyaching will let loose all over again."

Katharina Heinroth was now fifty-eight years old. Her second in command, Werner Schröder, had his hands full with the aquarium, and she could barely keep up with the zoo on her own. In addition to her work as director, she ran a zoology lecture series at the Technical University and her voice could be heard on the *Friendship with Animals* radio broadcast once a week. When she wrote to the board asking permission to hire an assistant, several members advised her to withdraw the request so as not to open herself up to further attacks. But she was not the type to bow to pressure, and things could not go on the way they were. She was working sixteen-hour days and getting six hours of sleep at most. There were days when she "could hardly speak anymore," she wrote to her mother. When she finally settled down late at night, everything spun around in her mind. She still had so many plans: she wanted to establish an institute for behavioral science within the zoo, and a new hippopotamus house was already under construction. Together with Schröder she had managed to expand the zoo to seventy acres by exchanging land with the city. The zoo's collection was again up to nearly two thousand animals. In spite of all the enmity, she did not want to give up her position. She was too devoted to the zoo.

So she rejected the offer from Leipzig.

A Forced Departure

While Heinroth was in Leipzig, the supervisory board met in Berlin. All members concurred that it was high time for the woman to go.

A few days after she returned home, Heinroth was visited by a man named Fritz Schmidt-Hoensdorf. In the early 1930s, he had headed the zoo in Halle, and was now teaching parasitology at the Free University in Berlin. Even though he had served on the board of the Berlin Zoo for only one year, Heinroth sensed that he was already one of her fiercest opponents.

"Let's get right down to it," Schmidt-Hoensdorf said as he sat down across from her. "I have to tell you that the board has decided to part ways with you. It would be best for you to resign, so that you can be granted early retirement."

But Heinroth had no intention of stepping down, and she wasn't about to make things easy for him. Instead, she replied, "How in the world did the board arrive at that decision?"

Schmidt-Hoensdorf was cagey. "Of course we all know what you've done for the zoo," he said. "And we're very grateful to you for that. But the supervisory board cannot entrust the further construction oversight to a woman. If it were to go awry, we'd have to kick ourselves for having left you all on your own. It's easier to pin the blame on a man."

Heinroth sensed that any further discussion would be futile. The decision had been made. A few weeks later she got it in writing. "In order to ensure a steady implementation of the reconstruction of the Berlin Zoological Garden over an extended period of time, the supervisory board believes it will need to bring in a scientific director who is younger in years," the letter read, "by the beginning of the year 1957 at the latest." As compensation for all claims stemming from her contributions and those of her deceased husband, Heinroth would receive a monthly pension of 900 marks.

Katharina Heinroth was exhausted from struggling against so many obstacles, yes, but she had no wish to resign either; they would have to throw her out, she decided. Ultimately, though, it was not to be. Several months later, worn down by the opposition, she agreed to leave. She was allowed to name her successor and train him for half a year.

Her first choice was Heinrich Dathe, even though he had just opened the Tierpark in the eastern part of the city. However, hiring Dathe would have been politically problematic for the board, not to mention an act of labor piracy, according to the official version of the story. As a second option, she suggested Bernhard Grzimek, the director of the Frankfurt Zoo. But he turned her down.

In the 1920s and 1930s, Grzimek had studied veterinary medicine at Friedrich Wilhelm University, and had often visited the Berlin Zoo. The director at the time, Ludwig Heck, regularly supplied him with free entrance tickets. There were still animal keepers who had known Grzimek as a student, and who, he feared, would have no respect for him if he now returned as director. Besides, the political situation in the divided city made him uneasy.

A third candidate, Wilhelm Windecker, who had been running the Cologne Zoo for four years, also turned down her offer. Heinroth was starting to find the lack of interest distressing when she remembered a young man she had met a year earlier in Münster.

◆

In 1955 German zoo directors had come together, as they did every year, to discuss the latest perspectives on animal husbandry. As at all such meetings, the participants posed for a group photograph. This year, the photographer had chosen as the backdrop a statue of Hermann Landois, the founder of Münster's Zoological Garden. Like a mildly bored school class, the directors stood on the staircase in front of the bronze sculpture, gathered, it seemed, around

Katharina Heinroth. Everyone was smiling, or at least trying to, except for Werner Schröder, who retained his usual expression, a look that seemed to sum up all the travails of the postwar years. In the last row, Heinrich Dathe was grinning behind Heinroth's head.

In front of the staircase were two cast iron cannons. A man in a light brown tweed suit had swung onto the left one, his blond pompadour tousled from his hand running through it a bit too briskly. He looked markedly younger than twenty-nine. Even though one would not suppose so at first glance, the youngster on the cannon was an aspiring zoo director. Heinz-Georg Klös had assumed leadership of the Osnabrück Zoo in northwest Germany just a year earlier, becoming the youngest zoo director in either Germany.

Klös was originally from Wuppertal, where as a teenager he helped out in the local zoo, after most of the animal keepers had left for the front. At that age he was already certain that he'd become a zoo director someday. But before he was able to complete his schooling, the war intervened. When he was seventeen, he was drafted into the military and assigned to antiaircraft work, then reassigned to the mounted artillery division. While in Belgium near the end of the war, he wound up in British captivity. After his release in June 1945, he wasted no time in taking steps toward his intended career, starting with his college entrance exams. However, it was difficult to matriculate at German universities, which were admitting only a limited number of students; someone as young as nineteen-year-old Klös would have to wait.

He returned to work as a caretaker at Wuppertal's aquarium and aviary while biding his time. During this period the first animals were traded between zoos in different sectors. In 1946, Klös accompanied two Indian humped cattle to the Frankfurt Zoo, which had been restored just enough to reopen. The Wuppertal Zoo was located in the British occupation zone, Frankfurt in the American zone. Klös needed to be sure they avoided taking a route via Rhineland-Palatinate through the French sector; rumor had it that the French were confiscating everything they could get their hands on.

Because accommodations in Frankfurt were scarce, Klös stayed at the home of zoo director Bernhard Grzimek, where he would be a frequent visitor in the years to come. In the summer of 1947 Klös was finally able to begin his study of veterinary medicine at Justus Liebig University in nearby Giessen. He used the weekends to visit the Frankfurt Zoo. Grzimek was himself a veterinarian, which generally made it more difficult to advance in the field of zoo administration. Most directors were zoologists, who looked down somewhat on veterinarians, because the latter had to acquire more knowledge on the job.

Grzimek took the young veterinary student under his wing. Instead of having him work as an animal keeper, he let him tag along on his rounds through the zoo, introducing him to the responsibilities of a director.

During summer vacations, Klös returned to his hometown, where he worked in the zoo or picked up extra cash writing newspaper articles for the *General-Anzeiger Elberfeld-Barmen*.

The Elephant in the Suspension Railway

In July 1950, Klös was dispatched to write a feature story about the Zirkus Althoff, which would soon be giving several performances in the city. The circus director, Franz Althoff, was known for his spectacular advertising campaigns, so the young reporter decided to find out what was now in the works. Klös had had a bit of experience in the circus world himself; between semesters, he'd spent several weeks tending to the horses at Zirkus Hagenbeck.

Althoff's main attraction, and the highlight of his latest advertising campaign, was an Indian elephant named Tuffi, a four-year-old female who had been with Althoff since she was a calf. Even then she'd displayed no fear of people, and so she'd been used for publicity in a number of places where the circus performed. In the Bavarian town of Altötting, she drank up an entire holy water font, in Duisburg she took a tour of the harbor, and in Solingen she climbed up scaffolding to bring bricklayers a case of beer. In Oberhausen she rode to the town hall in a streetcar to pick up the mayor in his office on the fourth floor. That day, she departed somewhat from the planned agenda by eating a potted plant and urinating on the carpet.

Helma Vogt, Althoff's spokesperson, had already thought over what Tuffi could do in Wuppertal: she would visit her fellow elephants in the zoo. To get there, Vogt figured a streetcar stunt would surely go over well. "What do you think?" she asked Klös expectantly.

"In Wuppertal you ride the suspension railway," the young man explained in a patronizing tone.

To Helma Vogt, this objection came across not as condescending, but as the germ of a brilliant idea. She had never been in a suspension railway, let alone pictured an elephant getting into one—but if everyone in Wuppertal used it, Tuffi would have to do so as well.

On the morning of July 21, the intersection by the old market square in the Barmen neighborhood of Wuppertal was jammed with people, the police doing their best to push the masses of spectators and journalists back onto the sidewalk. The crowd could already see in the distance a single-file line of fifteen elephants adorned with white leather harnesses making their way to the station. At the very end of the line was Tuffi.

No one quite recalls who came up with the brilliant idea for a procession. As might be expected, both Franz Althoff and the head of the city's transportation services made public statements claiming credit. Whoever's idea it was, they hoped to draw attention well beyond the borders of the city to the circus, the zoo, and to Wuppertal.

While the herd waited at the bottom of the staircase to the railway station, Althoff made a big show of buying four tickets for Tuffi, each of which she took from the counter herself, by her trunk. Then he and she climbed up the stone stairs, accompanied by Althoff's twelve-year-old son, Harry, spokesperson Helma Vogt, an elephant keeper, and a throng of journalists, who took nonstop photos of the shoulder-high pachyderm as she climbed the steep staircase with astonishing agility.

The railway was suspended from a forty-foot-high steel frame that ran across the Wupper River, which snakes through the middle of the city. On the platform, Tuffi remained relaxed, displaying not the least fear of heights. Every once in a while she stuck her trunk through the netting that stretched across the platform's edge. Soon the train pulled in.

Car 13 was reserved for her. Althoff had planned for the journalists to ride with Tuffi in a circus bus along the route to the railway stop, where Tuffi would wave her trunk out the window for the cameras, then the journalists would join up with the elephant after her railway jaunt. But no sooner had the elephant boarded the railway car than some of the journalists pushed their way in. The others (including Klös), fearing that their colleagues would get better pictures, squeezed in as well. When passengers in the neighboring cars caught wind of the commotion, several of them quickly changed compartments too, so that car 13 eventually held not only the four circus people, but also about twenty journalists as well as numerous passengers and a fifteen-hundred-pound elephant. No one would—or could—get out.

The train whirred along toward the district of Elberfeld, home of the Wuppertal Zoological Garden. "Great advertising, isn't it?" Vogt gushed to Klös, who was standing beside her.

Up to this point, Tuffi had been the picture of serenity, but in the air things got far shakier. When the train screeched its way around the first curve, she trumpeted and flapped her ears in a clear sign of agitation. To make matters worse, she stepped on a passenger's foot, causing him to shout, "The elephant has gone wild!" Everyone crowded to the front of the car to see what had happened. Klös and the others at the front pushed back.

Elephants cannot look behind them. They have to turn around, which Tuffi promptly did. As people tried to clear out of her way, they fell on top of one another, and the seating area and journalists' camera equipment broke apart. There were screams. Tuffi gave Vogt a swift kick, and Vogt lost consciousness.

It was too much for Tuffi. She just wanted to get out, and banged her head against a window, once, twice, then broke the glass. She kept on banging—and the next thing she knew, she was in free fall. Franz Althoff planned to jump after her, but his son held him back. Klös, who was propping up the unconscious circus spokesperson, suddenly saw the chaos in slow motion. While Tuffi was plunging twelve meters down, all he could think was, "I can't picture the faces of passersby on the sidewalk if they're watching this."

Eventually the train, which had continued without interruption, got to Adlerbrücke, the next stop. Everyone who could still walk pushed through the door, rushed down the stairs, and ran back along the riverbank to where Tuffi had jumped. The Wupper is less than two feet deep in many places downtown, and the riverbed is rocky. But as luck would have it, it was somewhat deeper at this stretch, and the ground muddy. When the first journalists got there, Tuffi was having a wonderful time wading through the shallow water. As if by a miracle, she had not suffered any injuries beyond a couple of scrapes on her rear end from landing on her side. Helma Vogt fared worse. She was brought to the hospital with bruised ribs and gashes on her face. Klös went with her. When she came to, the first thing she asked him was, "What happened to Tuffi?"

It took some time for Franz Althoff to lure Tuffi out of the Wupper. People on the street and at their windows were astonished to see an unusual procession moving through the streets of Wuppertal: a dripping wet elephant with a sopping retinue of circus people and journalists, some of whom had ventured into the river up to their waists to take their pictures of Tuffi at long last. Pictures show her before, after, and even during the short trip on the suspension railway. But no photographer managed to capture her leap into the Wupper; they were too shocked by all the tumult. A picture postcard with a photomontage assembled afterward sold like hotcakes.

The planned zoo visit had literally fallen apart. But even though the stunt could easily have had a worse outcome, it was still effective publicity. No matter where the Althoff circus went from then on, people wanted to see Tuffi. Fans sent her sacks of mail, and the Cologne-Wuppertal Dairy named its products after her. Still, the two originators of the bungled advertising stunt—circus director Franz Althoff and the head of the Wuppertal transportation services—had to face charges in court. They were each fined 450 marks for recklessness resulting in traffic hazards and bodily harm.

Germany's Youngest Zoo Director

The story of Tuffi's jump from the suspension railway is certainly extraordinary, but Heinz-Georg Klös wasn't actually there for any of it.

The anecdote comes from a little-known book, *Noah's Ark—Steerage* by Martha Schmetz (pen name: Marte Smeets), an animal illustrator from Wuppertal. Fifty years later, Klös would adopt this passage almost verbatim for his memoir, *Friendship with Animals*. It fit with the image he wanted to create for himself. But at the time of the events in question, he was still at the very beginning of his career and doing everything in his power to achieve his goal of becoming a zoo director.

In 1952 he completed his graduate studies with a dissertation on the effect of heart medicine on the intestinal and uterine musculature of guinea pigs. For a while he worked as a veterinarian in Holstein and then as a research assistant in his hometown zoo. He was determined that one day he would take the reins of the Wuppertal Zoo himself. In the interim, however, he was given the opportunity to become director of the Osnabrück Zoo in the spring of 1954.

Osnabrück's "animal garden"was situated in a hilly beech grove. Like many small zoos of its kind, it was founded in the mid-1930s, during the rule of the National Socialists, who set great store by nature and one's place of origin, and so favored animal gardens featuring only creatures native to Germany. The new director, according to announcements placed in professional journals, would be expected to turn the facility, which had been destroyed in the war, into a modern zoo. Although Klös was one of more than fifty applicants, the ambitious young veterinarian had the good fortune of frequently having the right benefactor at the right time. This time, it was his acquaintance with Otto Fockelmann, an influential animal trader in Hamburg, that came in handy.

Fockelmann visited the young man one morning at the Wuppertal Zoo. He had known Klös when the latter was still a trainee at one of his companies, and had kept track of his career. He knew that Klös hoped to become director of Wuppertal's zoo.

"Herr Doktor Klös, do you really want this post in Osnabrück?" he asked, pausing briefly before adding, with a telling grin, "Or is it just a trick to make the Wuppertal administration see that you have other options?"

"Of course I want to be the boss here at some point," Klös replied. "But I think my chances will improve if I first show what I'm able to do somewhere else, the way an attending physician moves to a different clinic in order to be appointed to his old clinic later as chief of staff."

Fockelmann liked this self-assured attitude. "Then I'll help you," he said.

"How are you going to manage that?" Klös asked.

Fockelmann grinned again. "Just leave it to me."

Fockelmann presented the following offer to the Osnabrück board: he would bring the zoo two lions, two hyenas, two zebras, two lion-tailed macaques, two pelicans, six cranes, six vultures, ten flamingos, and some ducks and geese. They, in return, would *not* have to pay the full purchase price of 35,000 marks until they had earned it back through admission revenue. If an animal died before they had, Fockelmann would assume the loss. His only condition was that Klös be named director.

The board had an easy decision to make. The people of Osnabrück had never seen the kinds of sensational animals that Fockelmann was promising; the animal garden's most famous residents to date had been Teddy the brown bear, Tutti the badger, and a fox named Frecki. And so Heinz-Georg Klös started his new job in April 1954. He had just turned twenty-eight, making him the youngest zoo director in Germany.

Fockelmann would not have helped Klös had he not gained some advantage of his own from the appointment. Klös was added to his roster of customers with whom he could house his animals inexpensively while arranging to sell them elsewhere. Animal traders always have to figure out where to park their "merchandise" so they can create space for more.

In his first months on the job, Klös had to do many things by himself: calculate and purchase vast quantities of food, design enclosures, oversee advertising and public relations, and, most importantly, come up with new sources of revenue. In this, he was a trailblazer. He persuaded Osnabrück's public utility companies to donate polar bears and sponsor the animals so that their food would be paid for in perpetuity. He shook things up at the zoo, dividing the grounds into sections for predatory cats, hoofed animals, and birds, and bringing in special animal keepers to care for each. The newcomer's approach was sometimes a bit fast-paced for the board, who resisted his desire to turn everything upside down instantly. They denied his request, for example, to bring in elephants.

Reinhard Coppenrath, however, was fascinated by the new director. Although Klös was only ten years older than eighteen-year-old Coppenrath, and looked even younger than that, he did not take orders from anyone. Impressed, Coppenrath came to regard Klös as a role model. Coppenrath's father, Heinrich, was one of the founding fathers of the Osnabrück Zoo, and as a boy Reinhard had helped feed the animals. When one of the animals was about to give birth, or one of the animals escaped, his father generally sent him on ahead to check up on things. He savored the moments when Klös took him along on walks through the animal garden, told him about his plans, and gave him the feeling that he was letting him in on his musings. "Young man," Klös would say to Coppenrath, who would remember these words forever, "you always need to have a vision."

Klös, in turn, was flattered that the teenager listened so attentively and looked up to him—figuratively, at least, as the two were of roughly equal height. Klös may have been short and skinny, but he was able to stand his ground and get his ideas heard. He was persistent and well-spoken, and a fine strategist; he knew how to win people over and use them to his best advantage. If need be, though, he had no problem raising his voice to get his way.

Klös imposed order and hierarchy on the animal garden, as was evident during his morning rounds, which struck Coppenrath as remarkably similar to an attending physician's hospital rounds. The young director seemed like a doctor as he ambled through the park every morning with his flock of animal keepers and veterinarians.

Two years went by, during which Klös refashioned the animal garden into a full-fledged zoo. The number of visitors rose from 120,000 to 200,000, and word got around in Osnabrück and beyond. One day a man with the surname Schmidt-Hoensdorf from faraway Berlin introduced himself to Klös and together they strolled through the grounds. The young director thought nothing of it; an encounter of this sort wasn't unusual. After the tour, the two had lunch.

"By the way, Klös, I wanted to ask you," Schmidt-Hoensdorf said at some point, acting quite casual. "Would you like to come to Berlin? We could use a young man there." He conveniently neglected to mention that Klös was the fourth choice for the job in question.

Klös had heard that Katharina Heinroth had been imploring her supervisors for years to get her an assistant. But he had no intention of being second in command, and he told Schmidt-Hoensdorf so.

Schmidt-Hoensdorf had been expecting this reaction. "Herr Klös," he said, looking the man straight in the eye, "if you say yes now, you'll come to Berlin as the director."

Klös was taken aback; he had not been expecting *that*. It had been a major feat to get his appointment in Osnabrück at the age of twenty-eight. But what Schmidt-Hoensdorf was now offering him would be hard to beat. He'd had a similar offer from Leipzig sometime back, but had turned it down because of both the political situation and his fiancée, Ursula. He'd met her in Frankfurt, where she was the first woman to volunteer at the zoo. But she wouldn't have gone with him to Leipzig. "One doesn't go east!" his future father-in-law had insisted. And West Berlin was in the middle of the GDR.

"Of course I'll have to ask my fiancée," he replied, once he had taken a moment to gather his thoughts.

"Do talk it over with her," Schmidt-Hoendorf said as he rose— adding, as they parted, "But I'm quite sure we'll be seeing each other again in Berlin."

So West Berlin it was. When Klös told his friends, they advised him against going. "West Berlin," they would say, with furrowed brow, "that's almost in Siberia." But Bernhard Grzimek, whose advice he had always greatly respected, advised him to seize the opportunity. Ursula also agreed to the move, and so Klös asked the board of the Osnabrück Zoo to release him from his contract. The board members weren't happy to hear the news, but they knew that they couldn't match the offer, and so they gave their consent.

In late June 1956, when Klös traveled to Berlin to sign his contract, the general public took little notice of the young blond man. The International Film Festival was running at the same time, and media outlets were busy pouncing on actors staying at the Hotel am Zoo. Klös was "almost overlooked," the newspaper *Der Tagesspiegel* noted. Once he had signed the contract, he headed back to Osnabrück. His new job wouldn't start until the beginning of the following year.

◆

Katharina Heinroth had counted on being able to train the new director for half a year, as the supervisory board had promised, but now they withdrew their support. "The zoo doesn't have the money to pay two directors," Arno Weimann, the chairman of the board, told her.

Heinroth was miffed. Even though she knew that she would soon be departing, the zoo still felt like hers, and its future mattered greatly to her. "How shortsighted can you be?" she said to Weimann. "Herr Klös isn't even thirty years old. Do you actually think that a single one of the old zookeepers will suddenly agree to be bossed around by a newcomer?"

"Any zoologist fresh out of college ought to be able to run a zoo," Weimann snapped back. "But if it matters to you that much, you can coach him later. You still have the right to remain in your apartment."

Her contract gave her the option of staying on in her zoo apartment for another three months, but because so many buildings in Berlin had been destroyed and there were not enough apartments to go around, her move had to be delayed. It took her and her mother until the following July to relocate to an unfinished apartment in a high-rise building in the new Hansaviertel district, at the edge of the Tiergarten yet still in the West. Werner Schröder made space for her to store her books in the aquarium, but when the board found out, Heinroth was ordered to clear them out immediately.

The ongoing battles took a toll on Katharina Heinroth. She suffered through bouts of pneumonia, angina, and lumbago. Sometimes she regretted not having accepted one of the offers in years past from other cities because she was loath to part with her own zoo. The quarrels had done their damage. When she left the Berlin Zoological Garden after more than twenty years, she was a little relieved.

A Very Young Badger

When Katharina Heinroth said goodbye to the zoo staff on December 30, 1956, her successor had already been in Berlin for three days. Even during the move, Klös could see that this relocation was unusual. He and Ursula, who was now his wife, owned an extensive collection of reference works, each of which they'd had to obtain permission for before transporting their luggage through the GDR.

As long as Heinroth was still living in the director's apartment, the Klöses had to make do with a minimally revamped apartment in the newly constructed hippopotamus house. Klös had to haul the heavy moving crates himself, and he slipped and hit his nose on the corner of a crate.

At his first press conference with Berlin journalists, just under a week later, a scab adorned the bridge of his nose. To add insult to injury, the lion cub that a zookeeper had placed on his arm for the press photo shredded his new suit. With his short stature and boyish face, Klös looked like the epitome of an inexperienced whippersnapper.

Sensing that brash behavior wouldn't go over well, Klös held back any announcements of change. Instead, he stated modestly, not wanting to arouse false hopes, that he'd first "have to get to know every last inch of the premises. After all, the Osnabrück Zoo is quite tiny in comparison with the Berlin Zoo."

This wasn't the whole truth. Klös had already had a look around a few weeks earlier when he'd come for the opening ceremony of the aquarium's new crocodile hall. Even then he was struck by how many temporary enclosures there still were. It was particularly evident at that time of year, when the hedges and trees had barely any leaves and so could no longer conceal the haphazardly constructed postwar cages and stables. Needless to say, Klös already had plans for improvement in mind: he wanted to replace the emergency housing with modern buildings and enclosures and expand the collection of animals. His goal was to return the zoo to its former status as the world's most biodiverse.

But he preferred to keep all this to himself for the time being, along with something else he'd noticed during his visit the previous fall: one of the two giraffes, a female named Rieke, was suffering from tuberculosis. Other than Knautschke the hippo, Rieke was the most popular animal in the zoo. During the war she had been evacuated to Vienna, and was the only animal—apart from a few garpikes that were later moved back into the aquarium—to have been returned. Rieke had been a symbol of hope for Berliners in the postwar era. But as a veterinarian, Klös saw right away that she didn't have long to live. Instead of telling Heinroth, he hoped that Rieke would die before he took over as director. He feared the public wouldn't forgive the newcomer for the death of a favorite animal.

◆

People recalled little of Klös's first public appearance in Berlin, apart from his young age, and many associated his youth not with fresh ideas, but with a lack of experience. The next morning, Klös opened the newspaper to find an article stating that a "very young badger" was running the venerable zoo.

Things did not get easier. Two days after his arrival, there was an outbreak of foot-and-mouth disease, and shortly afterward, Rieke died. When the first offspring of the hippos Knautschke and Bulette died one day after its birth, Klös's debut was officially deemed a failure. Journalists, visitors, and shareholders doubted that Klös had been the right choice for director.

From the start, it had been difficult for him to gain the animal keepers' respect. The Berlin Zoo had traditions stretching back 110 years and rigid protocols; Klös couldn't simply turn everything inside out the way he had in the backwoods of Lower Saxony. And the animal keepers, some of whom had been working there since before the war, weren't about to be told what to do by some thirty-year-old newcomer with nothing but a diploma. Gustav Riedel, for example, who cared for the predators, had made a habit of driving his lions into their cage with a whip. When Klös raised the dangers of this approach with him, Riedel waved him off, insisting "Oh, they won't do anything to me!" Klös was even more dismayed to observe Gerhard Schönke at work. Schönke fed his seals and penguins by hand, and his brown bears too.

When Klös chided the animal keepers, they generally just whispered among themselves—but sometimes they griped right back at him. This took some getting used to. He'd never encountered this sort of behavior in Osnabrück, where the zookeepers, with their Lower Saxon upbringings, would think over what they'd say for a full half hour before opening their mouths. If he didn't want to make himself look ridiculous, he would have to come to an understanding with the older staff members, so he had Riedel and Schönke sign a waiver stating that they would assume responsibility for their actions.

Still, his long-term aim was to rejuvenate the zoo, so he was pleased when a gangling youth from Berlin's Moabit neighborhood dropped by to introduce himself a few weeks later. Ralf Wielandt had always wanted to work with animals. He'd already applied for a job at the zoo the previous year, but Katharina Heinroth had turned him down. She had no money to pay for his training, not to mention vocational school. For a while Wielandt trained as a painter to stay off the streets and contribute at least a little to his family's income. Then, a year later, he decided to try the zoo again.

"Well, why not?" Klös told the boy at his interview. "I'm young, and I want to have young people around me." He knew the old zookeepers would leave at some point. And with young employees there would be fewer problems—of this Klös was certain—because he'd be able to mold them himself. So Klös accepted without hesitation that Wielandt would have to miss one day of work a week to attend vocational school.

On April 1, just three months into Klös's tenure as director, Wielandt began his stint as a seasonal worker in a field officially termed "animal care." There was such a thing as state-approved zookeeper training in the GDR, but in the West older keepers were expected to pass along their knowledge and experience to new hires informally. Wielandt was sixteen years old, and Klös barely thirty, so Klös used the informal *du* form of address when speaking with him—most of the time, anyway. As he explained to Wielandt with a grin, "If you do good work, you'll be Ralf. If you mess up, you're Herr Wielandt."

◆

Klös's other source of support—apart from handpicked hires—was the zoo's supervisory board, the very group that had pushed out his predecessor. Now that they had the new man they'd been demanding for so long, they fawned on Klös in a manner very different from their dismissive treatment of Katharina Heinroth. They approved his request to hire a research assistant after just six months, something Heinroth had fought for in vain for years.

However, Klös couldn't take the liberty of making large leaps either. With no money for major purchases, his first acquisitions were various ducks and geese, which aren't especially pricey, nor sensitive to the cold, and have no special needs. The zoo had plenty of open meadows and ponds, which he fenced in for the time being, earning himself the punning nickname *Zaunkönig*, "the fence king." (The word also means "wren.")

In spite of the innovations he hoped to introduce, Heinz-Georg Klös was no iconoclast. He was well aware of the Berlin Zoo's heritage, and felt that any buildings that had withstood the war had to be preserved. Many in city hall—most notably Rolf Schwedler—weren't pleased by this embrace of the zoo's traditional edifices.

Schwedler was not a man inclined to handle ruins with kid gloves. As the head of the Department of Urban Development, he'd pressed ahead in recent years with the reconstruction of West Berlin. Under Schwedler, people muttered, more buildings were torn down than had been destroyed in the war. He hoped one day to rebuild the zoo from scratch. But in this Klös prevailed. He would succeed in preserving buildings like the historical stables for wisents and bison—two low-slung, richly ornamented wooden houses that had been constructed at the turn of the twentieth century in the style of an Indian longhouse—as well as totem poles and a Russian log cabin.

◆

Even though Klös sought publicity, the media circus in Berlin was very different from what he'd known in Osnabrück. At press conferences, one young journalist in particular asked questions for which Klös rarely had an answer, and could only shrug in response. And no wonder: Werner Philipp, who was only six years younger than Klös, had known the zoo since he was a small child. He'd once wanted to become a zoo director himself.

Since fleeing the Soviet sector with his parents in the spring of 1953, Philipp had eked out a living as a private tutor, and had recently begun working at the Associated Press, where he reported on the zoo, among other topics.

"If Philipp could be my spokesman, it would save me some work," Klös thought to himself before long. He instructed his business director, Hans-Joachim Wilde, to make the young man an offer.

"This would be an important stepping-stone," Wilde told Philipp, but the latter shook his head. "No, Herr Wilde," he said, "it would be the end of the line. I'm in my early twenties. All I'd do at the zoo is waste away."

Wilde was taken aback by such insolence, but he came to understand Philipp's logic and eventually admitted he was probably right. And so Werner Philipp remained on the other side of the desk, where he continued to observe Klös and the zoo with a critical eye.

In the years to come, Klös and Philipp would have an ambivalent relationship that went from jovial to tense, depending on how much Klös liked Philipp's most recent article or whether he wanted something from the man, in which case Klös could be quite charming. When he saw the journalist during his bicycle rounds through the zoo, he would call out hello from a distance before coming to a screeching halt and drawing him deftly into conversation. But if he was annoyed about an article—as he often was—he would ride by in silence.

Even so, the two young men had several things in common, including a shared passion for the zoo and the circus. Both even collected small plastic animal figurines and paintings by Wilhelm Kuhnert, the illustrator of *Brehm's Life of Animals*.

Western Donkey for Eastern Pig

One morning, Klös asked the chauffeur at the zoological garden to drive him to East Berlin. Before leaving, he signed out at the central office and told them where he was going, for safety's sake, in case he was detained at the border—one never knew. He went to Tierpark Friedrichsfelde to discuss an important matter with Heinrich Dathe, his counterpart there. Klös was visibly upset and felt he had every reason to be. His predecessor, Katharina Heinroth, had made an exchange with Dathe—a donkey stud for several Meishan pigs—without the knowledge of the West Berlin city government or the zoo's supervisory board. At some point, however, a journalist found out and published the story under a headline that Klös was now holding up to his counterpart. It read, "Western Donkey for Eastern Pig." Klös was worried that he could get in trouble with the board.

Neither of them suffered any consequences from this incident, but it does highlight the fraught nature of their interactions. Heinroth's departure fundamentally altered the relationship between the Berlin Zoo and the Tierpark. Gone were the days when animals could be swapped while bypassing both boards. And there was no love lost between Dathe and Klös. Dathe held it against Klös personally that he had profited from Heinroth's dismissal—all the more so because he had unhesitatingly assumed her post. Dathe felt that such a thing was just not done, that it was an indicator of Klös's bad character. He made his feelings abundantly clear to Klös, who at thirty was sixteen years his junior.

Officially, Dathe and Klös would continue to work together: in the fall of 1958 they would organize the annual meeting of the German Federation of Zoo Directors, and a two-day symposium of zoo veterinarians the following year. But behind the scenes, a competition had long since flared up between them.

Dathe tried to use the existence of the zoo to obtain advantages for his Tierpark. In a letter to Johanna Blecha, the East Berlin cultural councilor, he pushed for the construction of a heated enclosure. "I have no intention of getting involved in a building competition, because our strength lies in a different area," he wrote. Up to this point, the Tierpark had opted for species that could be kept outdoors year-round, getting by without heated stables. "But I would regret," he went on to say, "not having demonstrated with at least one building that we know how to feature heated enclosures as well." Dathe went to great lengths to gain approval for his request, and he succeeded. A few weeks later, when he learned no cement was available, he went directly to Walter Ulbricht, East Germany's head of state, and asked him for 1,600 tons of supplies "so that we don't fall behind the zoo in West Berlin, which at the moment has been putting in the utmost effort to compensate for its loss of prestige." Later in the letter he reiterated, "I would like to avoid the outcome, esteemed prime minister, of the West, which is watching our development like a hawk, noting triumphantly that after a year we are running out of steam."

There were already unmistakable signs that the new Tierpark was not just an innocuous supplement to the zoo in West Berlin: in 1956, the first year after it opened, 85,000 fewer visitors came to the old zoo than in previous years. Even though Dathe would continue to emphasize in public speeches and in newspaper articles that the Tierpark was not meant to compete with the Zoo, Klös knew that hadn't been the case for some time. He did not even need to travel to East Berlin to find evidence of this, but only to leave his office in the building next to the elephant house and walk a few steps across Hardenbergplatz to the nearest train station. Some three hundred feet away a billboard forty feet wide and thirteen feet high announced, "Visit Tierpark Berlin." Klös could do nothing to stop this publicity nor could he post advertising of his own there, because throughout Berlin, the train stations and the railway network were under East German control.

And as if that wasn't enough, Dathe was arranging an event for August 1958 that would bring masses of Berliners to Friedrichsfelde as never before.

CHAPTER 4

PANDAS AND PRESTIGE

With a show of nonchalance, Heinrich Dathe leaned on the nondescript round cage, his left hand on his hip, his right holding on to the bars. He was standing in front of his zookeepers like a schoolboy proudly recounting how he'd pulled off a prank. Behind him his latest acquisition was busily exploring its enclosure. This newcomer was such an extraordinary attraction that it needed nothing more than a simple cage with a concrete floor, a washing trough, a seesaw, and a tree stump in the middle.

Although an economic miracle was in full swing in the West, East Germany didn't do away with ration cards until May 1958, eight years later than the Federal Republic. After all the destruction and privations people had experienced, it was hard to shock them anymore—but fairly easy to ignite their interest, as long as there was anything at all to see that moved, that breathed, that *lived*. Thirteen years had elapsed since the war, and a new generation had grown up, but the zoos had lost none of their appeal, especially not the new Tierpark in the capital of the GDR. It was something special to see an elephant or a lion, but the animal now in the cage behind Dathe was far more intriguing—it was a sensation.

The children of the 1950s may have known this phenomenal creature as a drawing in *Brehm's Life of Animals*, or from the few existing photographs. But they had never actually seen one. Before the war, their parents recalled, there had been a panda in Berlin for just a brief time, over at the Zoo. Its name was Happy. You get to see an animal like that just once in a lifetime, they said. But now, after almost two decades, there was a giant panda in Berlin once again.

Chi Chi was the name of the one-and-a-half-year-old female who'd been causing quite a stir in the press in East and West. The summer before, Chinese animal trappers had captured the cub in the mountain forests of the province of Sichuan. Their dogs chased away her mother, and when the six-month-old couldn't follow quickly enough, she sought refuge up the closest tree; one of the men had no trouble getting her down. She was brought to the Beijing Zoo, where Heini Demmer, an Austrian animal trader, acquired her in exchange for a shipload of zebras, giraffes, hippopotamuses, and rhinoceroses and brought her to Moscow, where he housed her temporarily in a zoo. Demmer intended to sell Chi Chi to the Brookfield Zoo in Chicago, but at the last minute Secretary of State John Foster Dulles stopped the import because of a U.S. trade embargo involving 450 types of merchandise from the People's Republic of China, live animals included.

Chi Chi translates to "sassy little girl" if pronounced correctly; if the intonation is off, it can also mean "whore." But the name was the least of Demmer's problems. While he was waiting for a special permit from the United States to exempt the young panda from the embargo, he had to make up for the loss he had incurred in purchasing her. He also had to house her somewhere, so he offered her to several European zoos. She was sent to Frankfurt in a cramped wooden crate bearing her name and that of her owner, where she became the main attraction for the zoo's centennial celebration. Afterward she was shipped to Copenhagen.

Heinz-Georg Klös could have brought Chi Chi to the Berlin Zoo, which would have been an apt follow-up to Happy's stay there twenty years earlier. But Klös, who had held his position for just eighteen months, hesitated. He sensed something fishy about Demner's offer. Although in public he claimed that the problem was the trader's excessive fee, he confided to journalist Werner Philipp, "If the animal dies on me, everyone will say she died on Klös's watch at the Berlin Zoo. I'm not about to let that happen!"

Dathe, however, accepted the enticing offer on the spot. Although he was unable to pay the purchase price of 200,000 marks—no European zoo director could—he had known Demmer for a long time, and they quickly reached an agreement. In a guest contribution to the East German trade journal *Gärtnerpost*, Dathe wrote, "Quite apart from the fact that Heini Demmer is exhibiting the animal in the new Tierpark Friedrichsfelde to express his gratitude for the support he has received, his offer may also be regarded as a way of bestowing honor on the Tierpark. Despite being only three years old, the Tierpark has already achieved a reputation that extends beyond the borders of the GDR. Had it not, an offer of this kind would scarcely come our way."

Chi Chi arrived in Friedrichsfelde late in the evening of August 2, 1958. Unlike her predecessor, Happy, who apparently almost went through Germany's entire supply of bamboo on his journey through the country's zoos, she was used to dietary substitutions, and so was fed three times a day on cooked rice fortified with eggs, bananas, apples, oranges, carrots, powdered milk, dextrose, vitamin drops, salt, lime, yeast, or bonemeal, according to the time of day.

The lengths to which the zookeepers went to ensure Chi Chi's well-being paid off. Over the following three weeks, Friedrichsfelde drew 400,000 visitors, who crowded in front of the circular enclosure to catch a glimpse of the rare animal. Decades would pass before another bear attracted such a storm of visitors to the zoo.

In the Tierpark, every move that Chi Chi made was noted down. After all, when had people ever had the opportunity to study an animal like this in such detail? Fur samples were taken, individually or in tufts, and collected in small yellow envelopes. A research associate made drawings of how Chi Chi ate—in a sitting position and with both paws, almost like a human—and how she stretched, relieved herself, and licked between her legs.

On one occasion, a few men came to Friedrichsfelde from the Zoological Society of London to study the panda for several days. Then they took Chi Chi to London for a three-week trial, and eventually the zoo there purchased her from Demmer for approximately 120,000 marks. In England, too, the young panda became a crowd pleaser. Peter Scott was so taken with Chi Chi that he modeled the emblem of his new conservation organization—the World Wildlife Fund (WWF)—on her.

Dathe's Rise

Chi Chi's stint in the Tierpark only increased the zoo's—and its director's—already considerable prestige. In 1956, just one year after the Tierpark opened, a survey revealed that Dathe had quickly become Berlin's best-known resident. Every Sunday morning, just after 8:30, his weekly broadcast, *Overheard at the Tierpark*, had half of East Germans gathered around their radios. He was acclaimed abroad as well, having been accepted into the International Union of Directors of Zoological Gardens. He soon set up a zoological research center, affiliated with the German Academy of Sciences, on the grounds of the Tierpark.

The GDR had recently become the first country in the world to officially recognize the profession of zookeeper, as distinct from zoologist or veterinarian. Karl Max Schneider, the now deceased director of Leipzig's zoo, had instituted formal training courses for animal keepers in the 1930s, but it was Dathe who'd made the case for creating a specific university curriculum. The 1955 academic year started with six students enrolled to study the art and science of zookeeping at an institution in Saxony, several hours south of Berlin: two were from Leipzig, two from Dresden, and one each from Halle and Berlin.

As support staff for his Tierpark Dathe brought to Berlin two assistants he had known and admired for quite some time. Hans-Günter Petzold and Wolfgang Grummt had attended his lectures at the University of Leipzig in their student days. Grummt was an ornithologist, like Dathe, while Petzold focused primarily on lower vertebrates, although he'd written his dissertation on swans, and would, in the Tierpark, also work with bears. For Dathe, friendships were formed less on the basis of affection than on a shared professional outlook. As far as he was concerned, a friend was someone whose viewpoints in matters pertaining to zoos closely resembled his own.

By 1958 the Tierpark covered more than two hundred acres, making it the largest zoo in the world, and three times the size of the old zoological garden in the West. Since its opening three years earlier, extensive facilities for wisents, bisons, and wolves had been added to the first enclosures for deer, boar, and antelopes. The year 1956 saw the opening of a "snake farm," which housed tortoises, crocodiles, and poisonous snakes that were milked in order to produce serum from their venom. At the other end of the grounds, workmen had built a peninsula made of dark gray granite from the ruins of the city's central bank, a habitat for polar bears that was surrounded by a 280-foot-long moat. Some visitors joked, "The installation looks so grim because the Stasi financed it." Sure enough, the adjacent enclosure, housing American black bears, bore a discreet metal plaque that read: "The bear ravine was built with a donation by the staff of the ministry for state security"—in other words, by the secret police.

By and large, though, Dathe was successful at keeping the political slogans and banners that had become typical in East Berlin away from the Tierpark, something Western media noted approvingly.

The Tierpark was now the number one recreational attraction in the eastern part of the city and a popular destination for visitors from the West as well. Both the millionth and the two millionth visitors were West Berliners. In the first six months after the Tierpark opened in the summer of 1955, 550,000 visitors passed through its gates; by 1958 that number had swelled to 1.7 million—200,000 more than visited the Berlin Zoo and the aquarium combined.

These throngs from the western part of the city tended to annoy East Berliners. Municipal authorities noted that some East Germans complained that visitors from the West "snap up all the food and drinks," and that "the way the locals see it, West Berliners get to the Tierpark in the early morning hours in order to lay claim to most of the restaurant seats for themselves."

But not everyone in the West saw the Tierpark in such an exciting new light. In March 1959, a letter from the Berlin Zoo to the president of the West German House of Representatives stated frankly, "Tierpark Friedrichsfelde represents a danger for us." Heinz-Georg Klös had seen what had sprung up in the East out of the void. While he'd had to slowly clear his zoo of its many run-down and makeshift postwar solutions, Dathe appeared able to draw on ample resources to plan and build a modern zoo from scratch. Large sections of the huge grounds had barely been developed, it was true, but Klös saw volunteers and construction crews busily digging trenches and clearing out undergrowth to prepare for new enclosures. One construction site was particularly alarming: just a few years earlier, there had been nothing but a set of randomly placed bungalows, but now these had been replaced by a huge skeleton of concrete slabs and steel fins rising high into the sky. This huge predator house, on a patch of land more than fifty thousand square feet in size, was designed to offer space for as many as seventy big cats.

If Klös wished to outdo his competitor, he would have to add a feature that did not yet exist in the Tierpark. And he had something in mind. When the city's steering committee next visited the zoo, he suggested pressing ahead with the construction of a new ape house. "First of all, apes are hard to get without foreign currencies," Klös explained. "And second, iron bars are needed for their cages—and they might be even harder to come by than foreign currencies, given the current shortage of raw materials."

◆

Klös left no stone unturned in his hunt for rare animals. He had a particular soft spot for rhinoceroses and had long ago set his mind on buying a pair from India, the last one in Berlin having died fifty years earlier. However, Indian rhinoceroses, which are second in size only to the elephant among land animals, are rare in nature and difficult to obtain. There are only a few hundred living in nature reserves in India and Nepal, and a few more dispersed among zoos in Europe. Of these, only the Basel Zoo had been breeding the animals for some years, but the Swiss had no interest in handing over one of their rhinoceroses—let alone two. So Klös approached the Hagenbeck animal trading company, but soon received a letter of refusal. He then wrote to his old friend Otto Fockelmann, who had often helped him obtain all kinds of rare species (as well as his first job as zoo director). After a while, Fockelmann let him know he had an idea for how to come upon at least one rhinoceros.

As luck would have it, India's Kaziranga National Park had a young bull named Arjun who was available for transport to Europe. He'd be expensive, priced at 30,000 marks. But there was an additional, far bigger problem: the bull had already been promised to the Dresden Zoo. Luckily, Fockelmann was working with an animal trader from Turin who had good connections in India; one of his contacts was an Italian priest who ran a missionary school and had acquaintances in government circles. The clergyman was able to persuade the Indian authorities, with an unknown sum of illicit money, to sell the rhinoceros to Fockelmann. In the fall of 1959, Arjun was brought not to Dresden, but to Berlin. Klös actually got along quite well with the Dresden Zoo's director, Wolfgang Ullrich, and even considered him a friend. But a friendship can fall apart over a rarity like an Indian rhinoceros.

Trust among zoo directors was shaky at best. Klös had learned that the hard way when he acquired an antelope from Bernhard Grzimek, with whom he'd worked as a trainee in Frankfurt, without taking a close look at the animal in advance. Grzimek surely wouldn't take advantage of him, Klös thought; they were friends. When the antelope arrived, however, the animal was missing half its lower jaw.

Klös also vied for animals with Heinrich Dathe. Whenever Hermann Ruhe, the owner of one of Germany's premier animal trading companies, received new stock, German zoo directors from East and

West came running to Alfeld an der Leine, a town in Lower Saxony. After Ruhe returned from an expedition to East Africa (as was evident from his tan), Klös was provided a budget by the supervisory board to buy two zebras and a pair of ostriches. He had his tricks to get the exact animals he wanted. He always carried a stack of little nametags labeled "Klös—Berlin Zoo" with him. During the initial inspection he'd place them on all the most appealing animals so that his colleagues would see which he'd claimed for his own. In the end he would pick out only the two finest and healthiest ones.

Dathe, by contrast, had been given a free hand by the GDR Ministry of Culture—or at least that's what Klös believed. "If I arrive with a truck, Dathe comes with a whole railroad car," he once complained to journalist Werner Philipp. Klös had no other way to explain Dathe's methods; instead of choosing a few animals, he would simply say to Ruhe, "I'll take them all."

"A few of them aren't very healthy," Ruhe would warn. Although he was a tough businessman, he knew that Dathe could be sensitive and carry a grudge if anyone tried to foist sick animals on him.

"That doesn't matter," Dathe would answer. "We'll nurse them back to health."

Klös and Dathe differed sharply in their manner of conducting business. For Klös, a business transaction was good if he'd paid as little as possible. For Dathe, it was less a question of money than of acquiring distinctive animals. (It was fortunate that he was less concerned with finances, as owing to currency differences, Dathe and the other zoo directors in the GDR often had to pay ten times the amount that Klös and his colleagues were charged in the West.) Where the two men were alike was in their passion for collecting. Both would rather buy two new animals than forgo even one because of a lack of space. They took back to Berlin whatever they could get. Only afterward did they worry about how to accommodate their new charges.

Dathe in particular had a habit of bringing animals to the Tierpark before their enclosures were ready for them. The big cats were housed in a discarded railroad car, the elephants in an old stable dating back to when the noble Treskow family resided in the castle in Friedrichsfelde park. Once a week, the zookeepers took the elephants a few hundred yards to the European bison facility, where they bathed in the moat—all except one young female, Kosko, who enjoyed complete freedom of movement within the Tierpark. She had come to Friedrichsfelde as a gift from North Vietnam's head of state, Ho Chi Minh, but the old stable had been fully occupied when she arrived. Luckily, she was only two years old, and about as large as a bulky suitcase. She whiled away the time racing visitors' children through the park.

Homeless Man of the House

Even Heinrich Dathe had had to live elsewhere when he'd first arrived in Berlin. Until the new director's villa was completed, he stayed with the mother-in-law of his Leipzig deputy, Lothar Dittrich, who lived near the Tierpark. He saw his wife and their three children only on the weekends; they didn't follow until later, once the construction of their new home was complete.

It didn't bother Dathe that the director's villa was little more than an apartment. After all, who needed property in the German Democratic Republic? Besides, he regarded the Tierpark as his empire.

Dathe's residence was a few hundred yards away from the entrance to the park. When his children, Almut, Holger, and Falk, went to school in the morning, their route took them past the deer and the buffalo, whose sounds soon grew familiar: the bellowing of the red deer in the fall, the high-pitched calls of the Vietnamese sika deer, and the snorts of the dozing bison lying directly behind the garden fence, under the mighty oak trees.

From the outside, the villa looked like a socialist attempt to re-create a witch's cottage in Bauhaus style. The front featured a gray plaster facade and a pointed tiled roof, with a flat-roofed extension out back. The living room walls were lined with dark brown free-standing closets with frosted glass panes, and expansive garden-facing windows looked out onto turquoise columns depicting herons and pheasants. In Dathe's office, carved wooden orangutan faces hung on the wall, and a cabinet displayed white porcelain grizzly bears. A grandfather clock set the beat for his workday: tick-tock, tick-tock.

He took notes on every bit of paper he could lay his hands on—pages torn from vocabulary notebooks or the back of advertising leaf-lets. Mountains of files, towers of books, and stacks of documents rose from his desk, rendering the director almost invisible behind them. He kept only a small spot uncluttered for writing, about the size of a large sheet of paper. Over time, he found that one desk was not enough space to store the fruits of his devotion, and so his papers soon covered all the other tables in the house, even those of his three children. He used each table to tackle a different topic, and to collect the relevant literature. His children didn't dare create a mess themselves.

Dathe drew no distinction between working hours and leisure time. Starting at eight in the morning, he was out and about in the Tierpark. He gave himself a one-hour lunch break, generally at a quarter to two. But if a shipment of animals or a birth was immi-nent, lunch could wait, although it was hard for his wife to keep his meal warm. After lunch he went upstairs to his bedroom for a few minutes of napping. That refreshed him for the rest of his workday; he rarely came home before seven. After dinner he went to one of his desks. The Tierpark came far before anything else.

His wife even had trouble getting him to go shopping with her. If he needed a new suit, his driver, who luckily wore the same size, usually had to fill in for him. Dathe himself came along only for the final fitting, if at all.

Even when the family took its annual three-week vacation at the Baltic Sea, he gave at least one or two lectures on site. Unlike other fathers, who sat in beach chairs or built sandcastles with their children, he'd spend the day walking around with his Zeiss binoculars, on the lookout for birds. Every few feet he'd stop, look up at the sky, and pull his notebook out of his pocket if he noticed a rare species or a special pattern of behavior, so he could jot it down.

Dathe's children got used to structuring their leisure time on their own, as they knew they could spend quite a long time waiting for their father to come home. But life in the zoo had advantages: who else could tell the other children at school how a breech delivery works or how to give an infusion to an elephant? Falk, at ten years the youngest of the three, usually played soccer in the yard behind the house with his friends until it grew dark. Sometimes they marked off a playing field with sticks, grabbed an old tricycle tire that they turned into a discus, and pretended they were Olympic athletes. In the winter, when the driveway froze over, they skated until the icy surface was smooth as glass, making it almost impossible to get inside the house without falling. When his father came home, Falk got in trouble for making the driveway slippery; most of the time he was sent out again to spread something on the ice.

A great deal of their family life took place at home. Heinrich

Dathe did not like going to restaurants, and besides, there was no decent restaurant nearby to which one could bring visitors, especially not visitors from the West. He preferred to entertain his guests at home, where he had the added benefit of not being wiretapped. Falk would have picked up on any such interception; he was interested in technology and had long since inspected the sockets for bugs.

Every time Dathe spontaneously announced that guests would be coming for the evening, his wife, Elisabeth, had to hurry out to shop and put together a meal. The children were sent off to stock up on cigarettes or cake. Dathe himself did not smoke, and barely drank alcohol, but liquor and cigarettes were always in the house in case guests or workmen showed up; workers were typically given a drink and a cigarette or two when they finished for the day.

Dathe's preferred vices were chocolate and sugared milk, which Falk had to pick up with a tin jug from Mauers, the grocery store across the street from the Tierpark. Even though local transportation was good—streetcar line 69 passed by on its route from Johannisthal to the Walter Ulbricht Stadium—the neighborhood around Friedrichsfelde resembled less a bustling capital than a village in rural Brandenburg. On Schlossstrasse, which would soon be renamed "Am Tierpark," stood just a few old three- or four-story buildings. Aside from the grocery store there were two medical practices and a bar named Johnny, and to the south a nursery and then sheds and grain fields as far as the eye could see.

A Headstrong Deputy Director

The city of Leipzig took its time finding Dathe a successor. Several possible candidates turned the post down, including Katharina Heinroth back in 1955. So as Dathe had his hands full with the Tierpark, the day-to-day management of the Leipzig Zoo—which he had been left in charge of upon the death of Karl Max Schneider—was turned over to his former assistant, Lothar Dittrich, who was named deputy director. In spite of Dathe's heavy workload in Berlin, he asked Dittrich to keep him informed of any noteworthy developments.

Dathe called up Dittrich in the fall of 1956, when workers in Poland were taking to the streets to protest the Soviet system and students in Budapest were demonstrating for more civil rights. People across the GDR were reminded of the construction workers' strike of June 17, 1953, when, for the first time, the citizens of an Eastern Bloc country revolted against the state. At work, there was talk behind closed doors about whether something like that could happen again; the Tierpark staff barely spoke of anything else. Dathe had no use for this kind of distraction, so he phoned Dittrich to find out how the mood was in Leipzig. What Dittrich had to say was not to Dathe's liking.

"Here, too, the zookeepers are talking about this," Dittrich said. "Some of the staff have already hinted that they want to demonstrate if it should come to that."

"And what are you going to do about it?" Dathe asked.

"If they wish to demonstrate, I won't stand in their way," Dittrich said, although he assured Dathe that he would "of course, make sure that every section continues to be staffed." He couldn't resist adding, "Incidentally, they're right. Something does have to happen here. Things can't go on being so shortsighted and small-minded in this country. I've already given thought to how I can participate."

Dathe could hardly believe what he was hearing. "You will do nothing of the sort," he shouted through the telephone. "Not a single zoo employee will take part in any demonstration. Is that clear?"

That same day, he had his chauffeur drive him to Leipzig, where he ordered his deputy director in person that no one was permitted to leave the zoo. "You are to focus exclusively on the zoo, and on nothing else," he told Dittrich in a fury, "certainly not politics!"

Dathe's aim wasn't to protect the state—he wouldn't have been able to convince Dittrich of that anyway. Dathe simply wasn't a politically minded person. Since experiencing the consequences of his Nazi party membership, he'd avoided politics as much as he could. Always a confirmed pragmatist, his motto had become, "Render therefore unto Caesar the things which are Caesar's." He did what he had to for the good of his Tierpark. Anything beyond that didn't interest him.

Dathe's single-mindedness did not always win him friends. In the late 1950s, East Berlin mayor Friedrich Ebert wrote a letter to Johanna Blecha, the city's cultural councilor, in response to complaints about the zoo director from Erich Mielke and Willi Stoph, the ministers for state security and national defense. When Mielke's ministry had allotted money to build a new predator cage, Dathe wrote back to say that the sum was not enough, and asked for more. Mielke regarded his response as ungrateful and outrageous. With Stoph, Dathe seems to have been even brasher: he repeatedly insisted on starting up a call for donations among the soldiers in the National People's Army. Still, Dathe was so well known by then that he could get away with this kind of behavior without fear of serious repercussions for himself or his Tierpark.

Several years earlier, the Moscow zoo had designated the Tierpark the official reloading point for all animal shipments between the Eastern Bloc and Western Europe. Arriving animals had to spend several weeks in quarantine before they could travel on to the West or the East, and Dathe had enough space to accommodate entire herds. During their time in Berlin, animals from the Eastern

Bloc would receive an official stamp from GDR authorities identify-
ing them as "German," regardless of whether they came from the
Caucasus, the steppes of Central Asia, or the forests of Siberia.

Unlike Klös, who still stood in the shadow of Bernhard Grzimek,
the director of the Frankfurt Zoo and the German Federation of Zoo
Directors' new head, Dathe had long since become the key zoo director in East Germany. Nothing worked without him; he was running the most important zoo in the GDR, and so the centralized
state structure accommodated his wishes. Grzimek noted in a letter
to an American colleague that "the GDR government seems to be
building this new zoo for political reasons and prestige. At the same
time, the old zoos in the East—in Dresden, Halle, and Leipzig—
aren't getting any materials for reconstruction or modernization."

Several East German zoo directors shared this view. Hans
Petzsch, director of the Halle Zoo, was among the most vocal opponents of Dathe's outsized influence. When the Tierpark had opened,
his zoo had donated the first animals: a stork and a camel. But now
decisions as to which animals the other zoos got were being made in
Berlin. At one meeting, Petzsch is said to have banged his fist on the
table and shouted, "I don't need a Pope in Berlin. I'm the sovereign
Grand Duke of Halle!"

Lothar Dittrich in Leipzig also felt the effects of economic scar-
city, and he was unwilling to adapt to the difficult times. His ire was
not directed at Dathe, however. What bothered him most was the
small-minded bureaucracy of the GDR, and he clashed with party
officials. But the risks of opposition were clear: Hans Petzsch got
drunk one evening and declared somewhat loudly in public, "The
Goatee has to go!" The "Goatee" in question was Walter Ulbricht,
the GDR's head of state. Use of this nickname was regarded as defa-
mation of the state, and could result in a prison sentence. Petzsch

didn't go to prison, but the comment lost him his directorship of the Halle Zoo. He had to struggle along as a freelance writer from then on.

By 1960, Dittrich was still just the number two at the Leipzig Zoo; Ludwig Zukowsky, a native Berliner, had eventually been appointed Dathe's successor. But Dittrich remained under state observation. Unlike Dathe, he was neither politically unassailable nor willing to block out everything unpleasant going on outside the world of the zoo. This would soon result in problems that would eventually lead Dittrich to arrive at a momentous decision. But to understand how he got there, we first need to know a bit more of his story.

◆

Dittrich's problems began several years earlier, when Karl Max Schneider was still director of the Leipzig Zoo and he was Schneider's assistant. Schneider had agreed to exchange animals with the People's Republic of China: Siberian tigers would be sent to Leipzig from Beijing—Germany's first in the postwar period—and in return, Leipzig would deliver four hyenas and six lions from its world-famous breeding center.

In 1954, the first pair of tigers arrived by train, and the next year the second. Now it was Leipzig's turn, but before the exchange could be completed, Schneider died. Since Dathe was already in East Berlin, Dittrich was responsible for following through with the exchange—but how? Transporting the animals on the Trans-Siberian Railway would be too complicated; the easiest way would be to send them by sea. But the GDR's merchant fleet, established just a few years earlier, didn't yet have ships suitable for cargo of this kind. Czechoslovakia offered to ship the animals, but only if payment was made in Western currency, which was unavailable in Leipzig. Then one day at the Leipzig Fair Dittrich happened to strike up a conversation with a shipping agent of the Hamburg America Line, whom he told about his transportation problem.

"You know what?" the agent said. "If you have us do the transport, we'll move the merchandise for you at no cost."

"What luck," Dittrich thought. He had the lions and hyenas placed into shipping crates and sent them to Hamburg, along with a hundred sheep as food for the journey, which would take several weeks. Due to closing of the canal during the Suez Crisis, the ship would have to sail around South Africa.

On the day of departure, a great many journalists gathered at the harbor in Hamburg. After all, it was not every day that a West German company would be transporting East German animals to China.

"If you quote me, I ask that you quote me verbatim," Dittrich told the reporters. He was aware of the need for caution; in the GDR, business with companies from the capitalist West was frowned upon.

The very headline he'd feared appeared in big letters on the front page of a tabloid the next day: "Red Lions for Red China." Back in Leipzig, party representatives accused Dittrich of helping a class enemy, West Germany's Hamburg America Line, establish contact with the People's Republic. After Stalin's death two years earlier, tensions between the Soviet Union and China had peaked; bringing together the West and the Chinese now came across as an affront.

"The company provided the shipping free of charge," Dittrich tried to argue—not that it mattered to party officials. In their eyes, Dittrich had made a "severe political blunder." To him, the bigwigs were incapable of thinking in economic terms.

This was no isolated incident; another followed in 1958. For quite some time, the roof of Leipzig's nearly sixty-year-old great ape house had been in bad shape. One of the beams was almost completely rusted through. But it wasn't so easy to come by a new one in a rush. The whole city was low on consumer goods and raw materials—and if something *was* on hand, it was usually earmarked for the capital. Berlin came first; the rest of the GDR was more like an afterthought. By the time building material was allocated, the roof might have collapsed.

So Dittrich hired the master builder at the Leipzig Opera to get him a new iron beam from a mill in Hennigsdorf, just outside Berlin. When the builder arrived at the zoo with the beam, the Stasi was already waiting, and arrested him for "plan violation." When Dittrich found out, he called up the ministry's district administration office. "How could you detain that man?" he asked. "He was authorized. If you arrest him, you'll have to take me too."

The Stasi didn't buy that argument. "We arrest the one who did it," Dittrich was told.

The next day, Dittrich had the weeping wife of the builder sitting in front of him. "I'll do everything in my power to get your husband out," he promised her. "Of course he's innocent."

The next day brought another visitor, this time an opera director who was quite upset. In just a few days there was a scheduled performance of Carl Maria von Weber's *Der Freischütz*—but without the builder the scenery could not be completed.

"Wonderful," Dittrich said to the director. "Let's go together to the Stasi and say that without him nothing can move forward." Before long, the innocent man was free.

For Dittrich this incident was just one more confirmation of the government's idiocy. As the years passed, there would be more and more frequent occurrences of this sort. And with each of them, Dittrich's Stasi file grew thicker. Dathe could take the liberty of forbidding Socialist Unity Party posters in his Tierpark and needling politicians with appeals for funds, but Dittrich enjoyed an entirely different standing. He was well aware that he couldn't maintain a position of authority if he was unwilling to defer to the state.

There were other reasons the Socialist Unity Party wasn't kindly disposed toward the Leipzig Zoo. The party's youth organization had been unable to gain a foothold there, and none of the zoo apprentices had volunteered for military service. When at long last one did step forward, he was seen off with great pomp, but he soon defected to the West. Dittrich was blamed for this when the Stasi brought him in for questioning.

Dittrich could see that his file, which lay open on the table, already looked to be about two inches thick. When the interrogating officer briefly left his seat, he was able to peer over and make out one sentence: "D. is an opaque subject."

Flight Plan

Soon afterward, in early 1961, the government drew up a new—and, in Dittrich's view, senseless—budget, which came with further restrictions for the zoo. Dittrich decided that enough was enough. With his wife, who was six months pregnant, his six-year-old daughter, and his mother-in-law, he defected to West Berlin in April. From there he wrote a farewell letter to his colleagues in Leipzig, in which he outlined his reasons for leaving.

Since the GDR's founding nearly twelve years before, two and a half million people had fled to the Federal Republic of Germany. The majority of them, like the Dittrichs, headed to West Berlin. Once there, their first order of business was to report to the Marienfelde refugee camp in the south of the city, where they formed long lines in front of the reporting office to apply for asylum in West Germany.

They might wait for days. Twenty-five white three-story buildings provided temporary housing, but these were soon overcrowded. To create more space, bunk beds were set up in the kitchens.

Dittrich was able to persuade the Americans to let his wife, daughter, and mother-in-law stay with friends in Berlin's Charlottenburg district while he remained on site for interrogation; every refugee was considered a potential spy. U.S. armed forces commanders conducted their interviews with interpreters on hand if needed. But an interpreter was hardly necessary in Dittrich's case, as he spoke English quite well.

After a few days he received notification that everything was in order. He was given identification cards for himself and his family; they were now West German citizens. The next morning they were instructed to come to Tegel Airport at ten o'clock in order to be flown out. Dittrich headed to Charlottenburg, where his family was waiting, to tell them the happy news. No sooner did he get there, however, than the doorbell rang. It was a messenger from the refugee camp. "The flight plan has changed," he said. "Be at Tegel at eight."

◆

Shortly after the family took off, a car stopped in front of a Charlottenburg apartment building. Three Stasi officials got out, climbed the stairs to the second floor, and rang the bell. The Dittrichs' hostess opened the door. "Whom do you wish to speak to?" she asked.

"Lothar Dittrich," came the reply.

"I'm sorry," she said, "but we don't know anyone by that name."

The men were expecting this response. They pushed her aside, stormed into the apartment, and searched every room. But there was no trace of Lothar Dittrich or his family. Where could he be, they wondered. "Maybe he's at the zoo," one of them murmured, "saying goodbye to his colleagues in the West." The three men drove off in their car as abruptly as they had appeared.

At the Berlin Zoo, Heinz-Georg Klös was making his morning rounds, looking in on each section with his retinue of assistants and veterinarians. These rounds followed a fixed pattern: The section heads would start with updates, followed by questions from Klös. Until the director asked the first question, no one on his staff could speak. Klös generally found something that was not to his liking, such as cobwebs hanging over the visitors' area in the hippopotamus house. "Those were there yesterday," he chided the zookeepers. "You've got to get at them again with a broom." He was furious if the signs at the enclosures were not sparkling clean, and he had just as little patience for being disturbed at his morning ritual—as he was by three men in cheap shiny leather jackets who were lining up in front of him.

"What do you want?" he asked them fretfully.

"We're looking for Herr Lothar Dittrich," they said.

Now Klös was not merely annoyed, he was beginning to doubt their sanity. "Gentlemen," he replied, unable to resist slipping into a patronizing tone. "You would have to go to Leipzig for that. This is the Berlin Zoo."

Disgruntled and with no greater knowledge of the whereabouts of the man they were seeking than they'd had before, the three men departed.

Safe in the West, Lothar Dittrich learned of the incident and alerted the commander in charge in Marienfelde, where his men tried to reconstruct who had known about Dittrich's plan to leave—and who had betrayed him.

At about five in the afternoon, the next day's flight plan had arrived, indicating that the Dittrich family needed to be at the airport at ten the following morning. Shortly thereafter, the interpreter who'd been present at Dittrich's interrogations left for the day. From her home, she transmitted the flight data to her liaison at the Stasi, not knowing the plans had already changed. Lothar Dittrich had escaped abduction purely by chance.

◆

A new life in the West awaited Lothar Dittrich and his family, in an empty apartment in the town of Alfeld, in Lower Saxony. After their first week, Dittrich was already 10,000 marks in debt.

Lothar Dittrich had a university degree. He'd been deputy director of a major zoo. Now he would have to start over again. But that didn't matter; the main thing was that the family was finally out. He and his wife, who'd worked as a journalist, were full of hope that they'd be able to establish themselves again. They thought the future would be brighter, albeit different. But there would be other attempts to force their return to East Germany.

Dittrich soon found a job as a keeper with local animal trader Hermann Ruhe. One morning, as he was in the middle of herding young antelopes into their enclosure, a stranger appeared in front of the fence.

"Hello, I'm from the Alfeld detective squad," the man said by way of introduction. "I have a few questions for you. Would you kindly step outside?"

"Unfortunately that won't be possible," Dittrich answered. "As you can see, I'm busy."

"It won't take long," the policeman said with a smile.

"If I leave now, they'll all start fighting," Dittrich replied.

The policeman was not about to give up so quickly. "Believe me, it'll go very quickly," he insisted.

But Dittrich wouldn't give in either. "I'm sorry," he said. "It really isn't possible. It'll take me at least an hour and a half to round up all the animals and lock them in. But I can meet you at six thirty this evening at the Ratskeller, where I'll be happy to answer your questions."

The officer eventually agreed and left. No sooner was he gone than Dittrich began to lock up the animals. It took him only ten minutes to get them into their pen.

After his attempted abduction in Berlin, Dittrich had been given guidelines from the Federal Intelligence Service on how to behave in a suspicious circumstance like this. The first thing he did was call up the Alfeld police and ask, "Why did you send a detective after me?"

The police at headquarters were astonished by his question. "That's odd," they said. "We don't have a detective squad here. They're over in Hildesheim. But stay on the line for a second and we'll check with them."

In the background Dittrich could hear the policemen talking: Hildesheim? Didn't send anyone either.

"Did you hear?" an official said into the phone. "Our colleagues in Hildesheim don't know anything about this either. We'll have to ask our superiors in Hanover and call you back."

An hour later, Dittrich's phone rang. "Of course no one was sent to you," the policeman told him. "But please go to the appointment tonight and we'll have people on the scene. You needn't worry about any danger to your life."

That evening Dittrich made his way to the Ratskeller. When he arrived at the appointed time, he felt as though he were in a bad crime novel. Even from the door he could see that the men sitting at the tables, trying too hard to blend in, were all plainclothes policemen.

Dittrich sat down at a table and waited for a while, but the ominous visitor from that morning did not show up.

It wasn't until many years later that Lothar Dittrich learned his name had been placed on a list that Erich Mielke, the minister for state security, personally submitted to the central committee of the Socialist Unity Party. The list contained the names of refugees slated to be brought back to the GDR. Mielke's intent was not to return Dittrich to his old job at the Leipzig Zoo, but to incarcerate him in the Bautzen maximum security prison.

The Battle Lines Are Drawn

In early August 1961, a letter arrived at the Berlin Zoo's administration office. A visitor's annual pass had been taken away because she'd fed animals without permission. Not so very long before, feeding the animals had still been tolerated. Klös had hesitated before declaring it forbidden, perhaps because he was afraid of public outcry.

The zoo administrators agreed that the woman ought to get her pass back. She was an elderly East Berliner, and the zoo could not afford to lose the few remaining regular visitors from the Soviet sector. Far too many of them had gone over to the Tierpark in recent years.

It's not known whether the woman got another chance to visit the zoo. It seems unlikely though, as just a week later the zoo lost its remaining visitors from the eastern half of the city for good. In the early morning hours of August 13, something began that no one had anticipated, not even Lothar Dittrich when he'd fled East Germany four months before.

The relationship between the United States and the Soviet Union had continued to deteriorate over the years, with the status of West Berlin a particular point of dispute. Two and a half years earlier, the Soviet head of state had called on the Allies to withdraw their troops from Berlin. At a summit meeting in Vienna with President John F.

Kennedy in June 1961, Nikita Khrushchev declared West Berlin "the most dangerous place on earth" and threatened to excise the "malignant tumor." Kennedy insisted that the Allies would continue to control their sectors, and that they must still be allowed to enter the Soviet sector. (Soldiers had historially been among the only people allowed free movement between the two Berlins.)

It had been obvious to Lothar Dittrich that the GDR would have no choice but to do something—and soon—to stem the tide of refugees to the West. But when he heard the news on the radio in his kitchen in Alfeld the next morning, he almost fell off his chair. Less than half a year after he and his family had fled to the West, East German workers' militias and armed security forces had closed off the border crossings to West Berlin overnight and begun installing barbed wire along the border.

In the days that followed, concrete blocks were hauled from all around East Berlin to construct a structure that would define—and symbolize—the cityscape in the coming decades. The Berlin Wall ran right through streets and even houses. Wherever necessary the windows were filled with bricks and mortar. Families were separated, West Berlin sealed off. And block by concrete block, the front lines were drawn between the Tierpark and the Berlin Zoo.

In the years to come, their rivalry would become a proxy struggle, with each director an emblem of his city's politics. And as Dathe and Klös would, from their opposite sides of the wall, come to understand, victory in this war was no longer a matter of currying favor with visitors, but rather of pleasing the bigwigs in Bonn and East Berlin.

CHAPTER 5

THE ZOO OF THE FUTURE

Strange noises broke through the morning commotion on the streets of West Berlin. The gibbons in the Zoological Garden were singing like a jazz band gone wild. When the wind blew the right way, as it did that day, the sounds of the apes staking out their turf echoed past the Wall all the way to East Berlin, as though the city were still one.

But since that night the previous August, everything had changed. More than ever, fear hovered over West Berlin. Would there be an invasion by the East German National People's Army, or, even worse, the Red Army? The Americans stationed two hundred fighter planes in France as a precautionary measure in case of a Soviet attack. No Berliner wanted to picture what would happen then—a clash of the superpowers, a World War III.

By October 27, two and a half months after the Wall's first bricks were laid, danger seemed imminent. The gibbons making such a racket in the zoo that morning were oblivious to the turf wars of their human kin. They knew nothing about that treeless spot named Checkpoint Charlie, one of the few crossing points left between East and West. There, the hominids were not singing; they were standing across from each other, some driving tanks, ready for battle and waiting for their leaders to give the command to shoot. For them, war was nothing out of the ordinary.

The Checkpoint Charlie showdown never progressed past threatening gestures, and after sixteen anxious hours, the men on both sides stood down. But the greater showdown between East and West was far from over. From then on, it became a symbolic battle, rather than the type fought with tanks. The Allies continued to stake their claim to West Berlin, an "island of freedom" in the middle of a "Red sea."

Food supplies for three quarters of a year were stored throughout the western part of the city, in preparation for another blockade. The zoo began amassing supplies for its animals, building new barns and cold storage rooms. Fish were the only foodstuff not kept stored, which meant that the seals would have to be flown out in case of a food shortage. Still, they were luckier than the livestock. The zoo's domestic animals were designated a major part of the city's supply of meat, should the worst come to pass.

◆

On February 21, 1962, one year before President Kennedy came to Berlin, his younger brother, Attorney General Robert F. Kennedy, visited the Berlin Zoo. Far in front of the entrance a cluster of people had already formed around him and would not budge from his side, so the gatekeepers eventually had to open wide the gates of the zoo and let everyone in without charging admission—which greatly rankled director Heinz-Georg Klös.

Kennedy had brought with him a bald eagle, the emblem of his country, which he promptly named Willy Brandt, in honor of West Berlin's mayor—"without checking the eagle's gender beforehand," a journalist would chide. *Neues Deutschland*, the newspaper of East Germany's Socialist Unity Party, was soon providing exhaustive coverage "of the habits of Willy Brandt, [who] loves to eat dead rats" under the headline "Behind Bars." East German newspapers would continue to report on the namesake of the mayor of West Berlin for some weeks.

Official state gifts often come with another hitch: they tend to involve animals that the donor nations are eager to part with. Heinrich Lübke, the West German president, had a male leopard palmed off on him during a trip to Africa that was later discovered to have been castrated. Willy Brandt, the eagle, was barely able to swallow and his callused claws made it impossible for him to sit on a branch or grip his prey. The zoo's veterinarian called him "one creaky old bird." The eagle died two years later, but Klös had already acquired a younger one, "which had been passed off to the public as the real Willy Brandt whenever Kennedy's eagle suffered from rheumatism and could not sit outdoors," the Hamburg-based magazine *Der Spiegel* smugly reported.

This stunt may have stemmed from Klös's interest in winning over the politicians and other dignitaries in West Berlin—Mayor Brandt chief among them. And when he wanted to achieve his goals, he could be quite persuasive. Klös certainly kept coming up with new ideas to lure Brandt to the zoo. "Bring your son along. He'll surely like it," he'd say.

On one occasion he took Brandt and his eleven-year-old son, Lars, to see Kurt Walter, whom everyone in Berlin called "Ape Walter." The head of the primates section at the zoo was rearing two young chimpanzees, whom he fed from a bottle. Lars Brandt was impressed. He'd never forget the sight of the baby chimps lying in a cradle in Walter's home. Just eleven years old, Lars was still too

young to think about why he—of all children—was able to peek behind the scenes or to be gifted the skin shed by a poisonous Indian
chain viper by Werner Schröder, the aquarium director. But Willy
Brandt knew what Klös was aiming for, and he played along. He was
aware of the zoo's significance for the city and its people.

◆

The definitive division of Berlin meant that the Zoological Garden
had lost more than a million potential visitors in one day. Heinz-
Georg Klös therefore went begging to city hall for more subsidies.
He even suggested that the city's buses start and finish their routes
at the zoo so that more tourists would pass by. For him, the only
good to come of the new situation was that he no longer had to worry
about zoogoers drifting away to Friedrichsfelde. Berliners could no
longer choose between the Zoo and the Tierpark. It would take until
December 1963, two and a half years after the construction of the
Wall, for West Berliners to be allowed to travel to East Berlin.

Meanwhile, Klös annoyed the people of West Berlin by raising
the entrance price again. Shortly after he began working at the zoo
in 1957, the price of a ticket went up from one mark to a mark fifty.
Klös also did away with the zoo's popular Oktoberfest, which the
press—particularly the tabloids *Bild* and *Nacht-Depesche*—resented,
especially as this meant "spurning" a reliable source of revenue
(some 50,000 marks per year), as irate letters to the editor were
quick to point out. And soon a visit to the zoo would cost an adult
two marks!

His predecessor, Katharina Heinrich, and her colleague, Werner
Schröder, had begun celebrating Oktoberfest to attract additional
visitors during the cold half of the year, saving the zoo from financial
ruin. But that was in the late 1940s. Klös had taken a look at the re-

cent balance sheets: in past years, revenues had gone way down, and the zoo was no longer earning anything from the event. For him, the success of Oktoberfest was nothing but folklore. The festivities were disturbing the animals and putting a strain on the budget.

The World's Largest Animal House

The initial commotion about the new entrance price soon subsided. Berliners held their Zoo in too high a regard to keep protesting, and besides, they could see that it was being enhanced. In December 1962 Klös presided over the opening of a new aviary with a tropical hall where birds could fly about freely. Nothing this extraordinary had happened in Berlin since the opening of the aquarium's crocodile hall in 1913. Heinrich Dathe was invited to West Berlin for the grand opening, and had a good look around. His response to the aviary followed half a year later.

On that June day in 1963, East Berliners flocked to Friedrichsfelde in unusually large numbers—and not just to enjoy the brilliant sunshine. A positively gigantic event awaited them: the Alfred Brehm House for big cats would be unveiled. This was not just any building. At the opening ceremony, a banner above the entrance hall proclaimed: "A milestone in achieving socialism." With an expanse of more than fifty thousand square feet, the Alfred Brehm House was the biggest and "most modern animal facility in the world," as the press in East Berlin never tired of proclaiming.

Nor was the opening scheduled for just any day. Dathe had chosen this particular Sunday—June 30—because it was the seventieth birthday of Walter Ulbricht, the general secretary of the Socialist Unity Party's central committee, and chair of the Politburo and the state council. Ulbricht had never been to Friedrichsfelde, and didn't show up on his seventieth birthday either. His wife, Lotte, was a passionate zoogoer, but he didn't much care for animals, preferring to watch sports. Still, the symbolism was what mattered, and Ulbricht was given a gracious acknowledgment from afar. The occasion also gave Mayor Friederich Ebert a long-awaited chance to cut the ribbon for the opening ceremony.

East Berlin's mayor liked to visit Friedrichsfelde, especially because of Mao, a Chinese alligator who'd been living there for six years. Ebert had a soft spot for all species of crocodilians and had set aside city funds to purchase numerous other exotic animals to help Dathe outdo his rival in the West. Perhaps he also liked the Tierpark because children greeted him more euphorically there than anywhere else.

Dathe knew how much Ebert liked being recognized in public. When Ebert came to Friedrichsfelde, Dathe always made sure a school class was standing nearby to "run across" the mayor—seemingly by chance—and cheer and wave to him. He also kept a photograph of Ebert in the Tierpark guide.

Once Ebert had cut the ribbon outside the Alfred Brehm House and the applause had died down, the invited guests slowly made their way into the semidarkness, murmuring in amazement as they strode along the rows of cages lined with pastel tiles and filled with striped and spotted cats. They gaped at massive rock formations against which the lions and tigers looked like house cats on the set of an epic movie.

The cats had been temporarily housed in a converted railroad car near the castle. When the time came to convey them to their new cages, one big cat after another was tranquilized, pulled onto a door that had been taken off its hinges, heaved into the back of a small van, and driven across the Tierpark. Four animal keepers squatted next to each dozing cat, ready to spring into action if the tranquilizer wore off during the drive. Dathe was never present during these activities; he preferred to leave them to others.

The visitors streaming into the tropical hall were unaware of all this as they gazed in amazement at the flying foxes dangling upside down from slender palm trees. The building's construction had taken six years. Dathe was normally an eloquent conversationalist, but when he'd described the project on East Berlin's public broadcasting station, he outdid himself, his exhilaration shining through. He'd gushed about "a building in the shape of a lying sphinx stretching out its two paws" where "inside there are outdoor-style installations" and "in the middle a tall building, almost sixty feet at its highest point, that portrays a primeval forest in which birds can move freely, and people can go inside." He sounded like a boy recalling the biggest and most beautiful sandcastle he'd ever built. And indeed, as a twelve-year-old, Dathe had fantasized about a hall of this kind in an essay for school.

His European colleagues were impressed. Ernst Lang, president of the International Union of Directors of Zoological Gardens, would declare after a visit to Friedrichsfelde in 1965 that "in this zoo there is nothing to discuss, only much to admire." And for years to come, Dathe would include a quotation from Monika Meyer-Holzapfel, director of the Bern Zoo in Switzerland, in the Tierpark's promotional guide: "This is how we picture the zoo of the future!"

◆

Dathe welcomed zoologists from other countries quite openly, and made no secret of what he was doing. When questioned by the Stasi about his "contacts with nonsocialist economic territories," he stated that his contacts were "with places around the entire world and quite multifaceted as a result of membership in the International Union of Directors of Zoological Gardens and as the editor of the *International Zoo Journal*." Dathe was not about to narrow his horizons. International contacts were vital when running a zoo; he had seen what happened when Germany regarded itself as the center of the world.

When zoologists from the West stated at the border crossing that they wanted to see the Tierpark or Dathe, they were generally let through without further scrutiny. One of these visitors was a young officer in the U.S. Army. As a teenager, Marvin Jones had worked as a volunteer at the Bronx Zoo during World War II, where he'd begun to record the animals' family trees, something highly unusual for the time. After about a decade in the army, Jones put in a request to be stationed in a location with an interesting zoo. And Berlin, with its two zoos, offered twice the enticement. As a U.S. soldier, Jones was allowed to travel to East Berlin, but not to get into any East German car; the risk of abduction was too great. So when he wanted to visit Dathe at the Tierpark, he'd arrange to be picked up by Dathe's assistant, Wolfgang Grummt, at Checkpoint Charlie, and the two would walk the seven miles to Friedrichsfelde together. In the evening, Grummt had to bring him back again by foot.

Dathe's freedoms sometimes rippled well beyond the walls of the Tierpark. When he and his wife, Elisabeth, attended a parent-teacher conference at their younger son's school, they, like all the other parents, had to sign a paper stating that they did not watch Western television at home. Dathe refused. "I'm sorry," he told the flummoxed teachers, "but I can't comply with that. My profession requires me to keep myself well informed, and I can't do so without international magazines and television stations."

Dathe had once been skeptical about whether he'd need a television set at all. Back in 1958, he thought it would just be a distraction. But now the Tierpark had its own television program, *Tierpark-Teletreff*. In each episode, Dathe would take viewers on visits to the enclosures and share tidbits about the animals inside.

In any event, the other parents were delighted to hear his objection. "Then we won't sign either!" they announced on the spot. From then on, the whole class was exempt from the rule.

Into a Shipping Crate with a Moose

The formal division of Berlin barely restricted Dathe in going about his work, but his colleagues faced very different circumstances. Since the building of the Wall, many were no longer able to visit family and friends in the West.

Bernd Matern had been working in the Tierpark as a zookeeper since 1960, after completing an agricultural apprenticeship in cattle breeding. He was first assigned to the "outer ring," an area at the northeast rim of the Tierpark where rare species of wild cattle, antelope, sheep, and goats were housed in nondescript temporary enclosures.

Matern lived in the district of Berlin-Treptow, his front door some three hundred feet from the sector border. Another three hundred feet farther, his sister lived in the American sector; only five streets lay between them. For years, Matern had neither accepted nor avoided the border, and had regularly gone to his sister's for visits. But then came August 13, 1961—and suddenly the Wall was there.

Matern didn't want to spend even one more day in East Germany. But then Dathe offered him oversight of the deer section, one of the largest in the park. Matern was only twenty-one, but the director thought highly of him—and besides, the position had recently "opened up" when the previous section head, an amateur diver, had swum to the West across the Havel River. In retrospect, perhaps his escape shouldn't have come as such a surprise, as he'd earlier started up a diving group to which Dathe's older son, Holger, belonged. Once a week, the group held practices in the nearby Karl Friedrich Friesen swimming pool—oxygen tanks included—without anyone growing suspicious.

Several other animal keepers had already fled. Because the Tierpark was the central reloading point for all animal transports between East and West, nearly every day at least one shipping crate passed through—giving Gerd Morgen, who was in charge of the quarantine station, an enticing opportunity. Ever since the twenty-year-old had seen a movie about the zoo in Winnipeg, Canada, he'd fantasized about going there one day. His plan was to hide in one of the shipping crates and send himself to the West. The trouble was that only bears were shipped, and it was best not to stow away in a crate with a bear.

"If only a different animal were to come through," Morgen thought, "I'd give it a try."

In the fall of 1961, when a young female moose arrived from Russia on its way to a northern German zoo, Morgen saw his chance to flee. But the moose turned up in a filthy wooden crate that could be seen into from all sides. "We can't send that animal to the Federal Republic this way," he chided the zoo's carpenter and asked him to build a closed wooden crate. Only a narrow slit at the top of the front flap would stay open.

His colleagues wondered why he'd choose such a spacious crate for a moose until the day before the animal was to be shipped, when Morgen let them in on his plan. "When the train stops at the station nearest the Berlin Zoo," he explained, "I'll get out and go to my mother's, and I'll stay there." The others didn't ask many questions—even Matern. If he were to get an opportunity like this, he knew he'd seize it too.

Morgen's plan was to hold off on getting in with the moose until the crate arrived at the East Berlin railway station. There was only one problem: the customs office monitored the train platforms from a glass booth over the tracks. But his fellow zookeepers offered a solution: they knew of a blind spot that would block the customs officials' view. On the evening of October 26, they brought the shipping crate to the station and positioned it so that Morgen could get in unnoticed. He'd already used a bolt cutter to shorten the nails that held the front flap shut so that he'd be able to open it up from the inside. His colleagues made a show of hammering the too-short nails into the wood. Then they brought the crate to the front of the platform and heaved it into the first car. The train started up and headed west.

Inside it was dark and stuffy. Morgen settled in and covered himself with some hay, feeling the moose's warm breath on his face. He'd designed the crate to be long enough for both of them, but narrow enough to prevent the moose from turning around and kicking him. Luckily, the moose was used to spending days in cramped crates after her long trip from the Soviet Union. Shortly after the train departed, she lay down and paid no more attention to Morgen, as though his presence were the most natural thing in the world.

After traveling a few minutes, the train screeched to a halt. Friedrichstrasse Station: the border crossing. From a distance, Morgen heard the clomping of boots, which had to belong to the transit police, the *trapos*. The boots came closer. Through the wooden wall, he heard the muffled sounds of the railroad car door being opened wide and several men talking loudly as they approached. The *trapos* stopped in front of the moose crate; one peered through the slit at the top. This was the reason Morgen had had it installed, or else the policeman might have tried to peer through a crack in the side panels. Through the slit in the front, the officer couldn't see the stowaway, who was lying in a blind spot right below. In the semidarkness the policeman saw only the animal's long ears.

"Get up, you old donkey!" he growled at the animal.

Morgen had to bite his lower lip so as not to burst out laughing.

Luckily, the officials went on to the next car and soon the train continued on its way into West Berlin. Morgen felt sweat streaming over his face. The moose stayed calm.

When the train arrived at Zoo Station, Morgen waited until all the West German passengers had gotten in and their suitcases were in place before standing up, pushing aside the front flap, and climbing out with great difficulty. Only then did he realize that his legs had fallen asleep. He closed up the crate and looked for a way to get onto the platform, but the nearest door to the railway car was locked. Morgen tried again—no luck. He ran down the corridor, found an open side door, and voilà: he was outside.

"This heat!" Morgen thought, peeling off his leather jacket. He was still wearing his dark green Tierpark uniform underneath.

The tracks directly behind the station were laid out in a wide curve, so the concourse was slightly off-kilter, making it impossible to get a view of the whole platform. No one saw Morgen get out of the first car, not even the *trapos* who were suddenly coming toward him. West Berlin's train stations were run by the East German railway system, and trains were checked for refugees. Morgen knew that, but still, he hadn't anticipated so many *trapos*. He counted about twenty of them, along with eight West German policemen, standing every few feet along the platform.

During the whole trip he hadn't been afraid, and he wasn't now either; he was thinking about what he had to do. "If anyone stops me, I'll jump down into the track bed and run across," he thought as he walked past the first *trapo*, then past the second and the third. Morgen had the feeling they were scrutinizing him skeptically, but no one asked him to stop or show his papers. Maybe the Berlin bear on his uniform's chest and sleeves made them think he was a railway worker. He passed by the two last *trapos* and a train conductor, who looked equally fierce, and arrived at the staircase that led down to the entrance hall.

He'd have to change money somewhere so he could buy a ticket to Kreuzberg, where his mother lived. "Won't she be surprised," he thought.

But it was already after ten at night. The currency exchange offices had closed hours earlier. Having no better idea in mind, he went to the travelers aid desk where, fortunately, one of the railway employees gave him twenty pfennigs.

"Why are there so many police upstairs?" Morgen asked him.

"Someone escaped," came the reply.

◆

When Gerd Morgen failed to show up for work two days in a row, the excitement in the Tierpark mounted. All the animal keepers were questioned, but none let on what they knew. His apartment was searched, without turning up a thing. Eventually Bernd Matern and the others were summoned to the Stasi's district office, which was located right next to the Tierpark. They were grilled for hours, then let go. The officials learned nothing.

Matern wasn't sure why they'd gotten off so lightly, but he and others assumed that Dathe must have interceded. He'd probably said something along the lines of: "These men are indispensable. I can't do without them for one more day." And Dathe's word carried weight. He wasn't a member of the party, but he had the freedom to do as he liked. Otherwise Matern would have landed in prison.

Matern was aware that Dathe had to outmaneuver party bigwigs to preserve what freedoms he could. But Matern no longer wished to have any restrictions placed on him. He wanted to read newspapers from the West and listen to AFN, a broadcast network for Americans overseas. Like so many others, he'd grudgingly made do with his new circumstances for a time, but that would change in 1964, when he was drafted into the National People's Army. After half a year he decided to make his escape. Still, he knew what was at stake; three years earlier, his friend Günter had been caught.

Eleven days after the Wall had gone up, twenty-four-year-old Günter Litfin tried to get to Lehrter Station in the western part of the city by crossing over some train tracks. When the *trapos* discovered him and fired off warning shots, he jumped into a canal. He'd nearly made it to shore when he suddenly stopped swimming. Two days earlier, the Politburo had issued orders for the GDR's border guards to shoot anyone who tried to flee. A bullet pierced Günter's neck and lower jaw. He was the first to be shot and killed at the Berlin Wall.

Even so, Matern took the risk. He'd been planning his escape for some time, down to every detail. He and a few friends made arrangements for a boat, using his contacts in the West. They planned to cross a lake—the Wannsee—to the district of Grunewald, in West Berlin.

They were caught even before they could cast off. The contacts were working for the Stasi. Matern was sent to prison for three years, but he got lucky. Since 1963, the Federal Republic had been buying the freedom of East German political prisoners in exchange for foreign currency. Matern was released from custody after two years and allowed to settle in the West.

He later learned that Dathe was exasperated not to have known in advance about his plans to escape. Dathe apparently thought he could have saved him from serving time in prison and gotten him back to the Tierpark. But Matern had no interest in returning to East Berlin.

◆

In the meantime, Gerd Morgen had settled down in West Berlin, where he introduced himself at the Zoological Garden. He'd gone there regularly before the Wall went up, so he knew some of the animal keepers, including primate section head Kurt Walter. Morgen would have liked to get a job in the zoo, but Klös had made Dathe a gentlemen's agreement not to employ animal keepers who'd escaped from the East. Morgen stayed in West Berlin for eight months, and had found a job in an equine clinic at the Free University when Klös asked him to come by again. "Could you picture going to Basel?" he asked. "My colleague Dr. Lang is looking for another keeper for his apes." Morgen didn't hesitate.

Rivals on Their Own Turf

Dathe kept up with his counterparts in West Berlin. Werner Schröder, the director of the aquarium, was a friend, someone with whom he could toss around technical terms in Latin and share a hotel room at international conferences. Klös found it harder to get along with his colleagues. But for some time now he had been troubled by a growing rivalry within his zoo—not with an introverted, offbeat fellow like Schröder, who kept to his aquarium, but with a man whose very presence must have struck the director as dangerous.

Wolfgang Gewalt was fresh out of college when he came to the Berlin Zoo as a research assistant in 1959. He was the complete opposite of Klös: a giant with an angular, bearded face, who at six foot two jumped so effortlessly and nonchalantly over every railing that women visiting the zoo swooned at the sight of him. Any comparison with Gewalt made Klös seem even stiffer and more awkward.

Klös's six-year-old son, Heiner, enjoyed taking walks with Gewalt, a passionate hunter who shot at wild foxes, crows, and pigeons on zoo grounds without asking permission. To him, they were simply pests. The boy was impressed by this man so very different from his father, who hadn't touched a gun since the war.

Gewalt was two years younger than Klös, but two heads taller and twice as garrulous. And he didn't shy away from contradicting Klös, even in front of colleagues. On morning rounds, which some said made physician's rounds seem like a democratic discussion group by comparison, Gewalt refused to adhere to the unwritten rule that no one was entitled to ask a question until Klös had done so first.

One morning, in the rhinoceros house, the group surveyed some newly arrived Malayan tapirs. Captured in the wild in Southeast Asia, the creatures were real treasures. One female had already been living in the zoo for two years, and now two additional females and a male would be joining her in three cramped crates, even though tapirs are shy loners by nature.

"Say, Herr Doktor," Gewalt blurted out. "Don't you think it's a bit crowded in there?"

Klös let out a quick snort. "If I get another three, I'll put them there too!" he said.

Everyone—zookeepers, inspectors, and veterinarians—looked over at Gewalt expectantly. He grinned. "Well, I'd certainly like to see that, Herr Doktor," he said.

Wolfgang Gewalt was a Berliner through and through. He'd attended the renowned Französisches Gymnasium, a public high school in the Tiergarten district, before enrolling at Humboldt University in the East in 1948 to study zoology. He later transferred to the Free University in the West, where he received his doctorate in 1959. His dissertation was on the visual faculties of martens, a family of small, furry animals with bushy tails.

Even as a student Gewalt was a daredevil who'd go swimming in the ice cold Baltic and climb pine trees to pluck young long-eared owls from their nests. During those years he wrote scientific articles about squirrels, raccoons, curlews, and great bustards, one of the heaviest flying birds and already extinct in large parts of Central Europe. At his parents' home in Frohnau in the northern part of Berlin, he hatched and raised several chicks. When guests came to visit, they were astonished to find a tame bustard strutting around the table and being hand-fed kitchen scraps.

In time, the animals grew larger: At the Berlin Zoo he hand-raised two young gorillas, which made him even more popular with visitors, especially women. Klös cast a wary eye, displeased to see his assistant getting more attention than he did.

Even though Gewalt greatly enjoyed being in the spotlight, he also helped his fellow zookeepers whenever he could, including Dathe's former right-hand man in Leipzig, Lothar Dittrich. After escaping to the West, Dittrich had worked his way up in the Ruhe animal trading company. First he captured gazelles in East Africa. Then he served as head of the Hanover Zoo, which Hermann Ruhe ran as a place to exhibit his animals for resale.

Before the Wall, when Dittrich was still working in Leipzig, he'd have to make a special trip to West Berlin whenever he wanted to travel to "capitalist countries." Western Europe had yet to recognize the GDR as a sovereign state, so Dittrich first had to apply for a temporary West German passport and then get a visa at the embassy in question. All of this needed to happen within one day. Dittrich could not afford a taxi, and these errands could not be accomplished on foot, so Gewalt would drive him back and forth in his own car. During the trip they'd chat about the latest developments at the Zoo. Whenever Dittrich asked why Gewalt did things the way he did, Gewalt would reply, "Well, I arranged that with blond Heinz." By "blond Heinz," he meant his boss, Heinz-Georg Klös.

◆

In the long run, having both Gewalt and Klös made for one director too many. Gewalt saw no path for promotion, and so he left Berlin after seven years. Several versions of the reason for his departure made the rounds. According to one, an antelope was killed while he was on duty, which turned the tabloids against him. Another claimed that during his morning foxhunt he shot a woman in the leg while she was on zoo grounds. The third, and correct, version was that the two men were heading for a major clash. Gewalt was upstaging Klös on his own turf.

Gewalt began looking for new employment and on April 1, 1966, was named director of the Duisburg Zoo. His predecessor, Hans-Georg Thienemann, had opened a dolphinarium there the previous year—the first in Germany and one of few anywhere in Europe. But just a few months later, Thienemann unexpectedly died of a stroke, at the age of fifty-six. The zoo could no longer keep pace with the one in Berlin, and the drab industrial city at the confluence of the

Rhine and Ruhr Rivers was not what could be described as anyone's dream destination. "Gewalt will not be heard from again," Klös told journalist Werner Philipp contendedly.

Rarely had Heinz-Georg Klös been so wrong, and he'd soon come to realize as much. Duisburg turned out to be the best thing that ever happened to Wolfgang Gewalt.

White Whale in the Gray Rhine

On New Year's Day of 1966 the series *Flipper* began running on German television. Throughout Germany, both East and West, children spent every Saturday afternoon glued to their TV screens from the moment the theme song came on. They all wanted an animal like Flipper for their friend—and for the lucky children of Duisburg, this new friend was just a few streetcar stops away. At the zoo they could watch bottlenose dolphins perform their tricks, and with any luck they might even be chosen to climb into a boat and be pulled by the dolphins through the pool. Spectators came to the little zoo in droves. By the end of the year the number of visitors exceeded one million.

Gewalt's predecessor couldn't have chosen a better time to build a dolphinarium, and zoo directors in East and West did not look idly on. Dathe had intended to include a dolphinarium in his first sketches for the Tierpark, and now Leipzig started making plans. The coastal city of Rostock came closest to building one, but shortly before construction could commence, East German head of state and sports fan Walter Ulbricht rejected the plan. "Before we build swimming pools for dolphins, we should be building them for humans," he said, or words to that effect. Not for another half decade would Klös be able to bring a dolphin show from Florida to Berlin for performances during the summer months.

Then Gewalt had another amazing stroke of luck: two months after he started his job in Duisburg, an animal unlike anything seen in the almost thousand-year history of the city turned up in the waters of the Rhine.

On the morning of May 18, two Rhine skippers were on the river aboard the tanker *Melani* when at kilometer 778.5 something white appeared in the gray water next to the boat, ten or maybe twelve feet long, spouting air and snorting water. The sailors immediately radioed the river police to report, "There's a white monster swimming here." The officers assumed the two men had had one too many drinks the previous night. When the police arrived, they first had the men take a blood alcohol test. Negative. Then they saw it for themselves: a white back, rutted by scars and welts, surfaced from the water, and air spouted out.

But if this truly was a whale, the police reasoned, how did it get into the Rhine? Three days earlier there had been a report of a whale sighting near Rotterdam, where, at the mouth of the Rhine, things like that had been known to happen. But here, almost three hundred miles upstream, in the largest inland port in Europe? Weren't whales supposed to live in salt water? The officers wasted no time in calling up the Ministry of the Interior, whose staff at first took the call to be a prank. "Who is this anyway?" one official asked, annoyed.

The next day, Wolfgang Gewalt was notified. He was familiar with these kinds of calls. Concerned citizens or firefighters often called up the zoo in springtime claiming to have found an abandoned eagle chick on the roof, and when a keeper went to have a look, it turned out to be nothing but a young swift. Now there was supposedly a white whale swimming in the Rhine. Gewalt figured it was probably nothing but a drowned and bloated pig floating in the water. He grudgingly arranged to have a police boat drive him to the spot where the animal had last been seen. But this was no false alarm. The young zoo director could hardly believe it—there was actually a whale. And a white whale, no less, also known as a beluga, an animal that can measure up to twenty feet long and weigh more than a ton. When Gewalt saw the animal—this one thirteen feet long and more than 1,600 pounds—he blurted out, "Man, that is some creature!"

Gewalt had already been planning to build a new, bigger pool for his dolphins. And he was not going to stop there. He wanted to use the old pool as a whalearium. And now here, right in front of his nose, his very first resident was swimming—a creature so rare that even many of his zoo colleagues had never seen one. It would therefore be "grotesque for the Duisburg Zoo to leave alone the whale that was wandering about in front of our door," Gewalt explained to the public, only to "procure a specimen of this sort from Alaska."

Thus began the hunt for the whale, which the media named "Moby Dick," after the title character in Herman Melville's novel. But the fishers on the Lower Rhine weren't prepared for whales, so Gewalt had to get creative. The zoo director and his assistants put together a trap made of fence posts and nets from a nearby tennis club. They tried to use boats to force Moby Dick into a shallow basin and catch him there, but their attempts were unsuccessful. The whale kept diving under the nets.

Gewalt brought in a national champion in archery to affix a small round buoy to the whale to prevent it from diving below the surface and disappearing. Animal rights activists responded by renting a helicopter and pitching oranges into the water to throw off the hunters, certain that they were doing the right thing. Gewalt was equally sure that in the sludgy waters of the Rhine, the whale wouldn't survive for even a week.

While the Ruhr region's coal and steel had propelled the German postwar economic miracle, the environmental consequences had largely been ignored. The Rhine became a cesspool, contaminated by tons of chemicals and industrial wastewater; sulfur dioxide from the steel mills scorched the fruit trees and garden plot vegetable beds. Ground Thomas slag, a waste product of steelmaking, settled on windowsills like pink and gray snow. The 1960s were the heyday of steel production in Duisburg, which achieved prosperity as one of the largest steel manufacturers in the world. But the "City of Coal and Steel," as residents proudly called it, was far ahead of other cities in air pollution as well. Its poor air quality had long since acquired a new, alien-sounding name: *smog*.

◆

In the GDR, any mention of environmental pollution was taboo, and reporting on it was forbidden. Economic progress was the top priority and so, according to the government, socialism simply had no smog. Only capitalism produced such a thing.

"Products from Leuna bring bread, prosperity, and beauty. . . ." The advertising slogan could be read on the wall of a building in East Berlin. But Leuna Works, located south of the city of Halle, was also spewing tons of sulfur dioxide into the air; a black fog that burned in people's eyes and noses was making its way through the streets. Wastewater full of mercury and lead from the so-called chemical triangle (the cities of Halle, Merseburg, and Bitterfeld) was contaminating the Elbe River and its tributaries. A popular ditty went like this: "Bitterfeld, Bitterfeld, its dirty air is unexcelled." In 1970, the GDR would pass a comprehensive conservation law, one of the most progressive environmental protection acts in Europe— but the only real change was the introduction of higher chimneys,

which meant that factories would now spread their toxins even farther. For many years state propaganda created the impression that
smog came to a halt at the "anti-imperialist protective wall." But
over time the air pollution in the GDR increased so drastically that
it could no longer be denied, and so a harmless-sounding phrase,
"industry fog," was coined to describe the mess, in the press and on
the radio.

In the smog-plagued West, Willy Brandt, who was running for
chancellor as a Social Democrat, had decried pollution as far back as
1961, insisting, "The sky over the Ruhr must become blue again."
At first he was showered with what he'd later term "bucketfuls of
scorn" from within his own ranks. His party reproached him for
promising "the blue of the sky" while standing in front of two hundred power plants, blast furnaces, and refineries. *You can't make an
omelet without breaking eggs*, went the conventional wisdom in the
region spanning Dortmund and Duisburg; economic progress was
well worth a little smoke in the skies. Hardly anyone really knew
what fine dust was, anyway—if anything, it was what housewives
wiped off the cupboards once a week. It wasn't until public interest
in cleaner air was aroused that the federal government also took up
the cause.

But in spite of some changes in the law, the situation did not
improve. There was still hardly any talk of an environmental movement, even though people had streamed into movie theaters just a
few years earlier to watch Bernhard Grzimek's nature documenta-
ries *No Place for Wild Animals* and *Serengeti Shall Not Die*. To many
West Germans in the mid-1960s, conservation was something that
happened off in Africa.

And so, to some people, it seemed like an act of divine provi-
dence that this white, innocent creature had turned up out of filthy

floods, in the shadow of the blast furnaces. It swam up the Rhine, and came to them! To help them become aware of just how badly the river stank.

◆

Throngs of onlookers formed along the shores of the Rhine each day of those weeks to catch a glimpse of Moby Dick. "Why is a whale in the Rhine having such a nice time?" the *Süddeutsche Zeitung* wondered on its front page, while the newspaper *Bild* sent out a blimp to get aerial shots of the whale.

East German newspapers also made mention of Moby Dick. On May 20, the *Neue Zeit* ran the sighting of a white whale outside of Duisburg above accounts of sexual offenses against an eleven-year-old girl in Erlangen, anti-Semitic graffiti in Munich, and a typhoon in the Philippines. As long as the hunt for the whale went on, the GDR carried coverage of it. As the days passed, the whale's reported length increased, from thirteen feet in the early articles to twenty in later ones.

Meanwhile, Wolfgang Gewalt was standing on a ship in the middle of the Rhine, attempting to use a Cap-Chur pistol to shoot a tranquilizer through the whale's skin. The gun's long barrel recalled the weapon that Sean Connery used while chasing villains as James Bond in *From Russia with Love*. What Gewalt didn't know was that the cannula of the tranquilizer dart was far too short to penetrate the whale's blubber, a layer of fat roughly eight inches thick.

Friends started taking bets about the outcome of the hunt, and a waterfront restaurant owner joked to his diners, "If the catch is successful, we'll have white whale cutlets." But when Moby Dick suddenly plunged into the depths after a hit from Gewalt's pistol and remained out of sight for days, the mood shifted. Tranquilizing the whale had been a risky move, because the animal would have to come to the surface eventually to breathe. Many were already starting to fear that Moby Dick had drowned. One newspaper demanded: "Arrest Dr. Gewalt!"

For his adversaries, Gewalt's name—which translates to "violence"—said it all. But the target of their hostility didn't ignore their criticism; he actually reveled in it. He savored his edgy image. In his apartment, he displayed all the headlines calling for his head, as though they were trophies of animals he'd hunted down.

In late May, however, Gewalt called off his hunt for the whale temporarily so that the animal could regain its "faith in mankind," as he explained, with more than a hint of mockery, to the magazine *Der Spiegel*. "It's certainly not normal for a whale to swim inland," he reminded readers.

◆

Moby Dick's odyssey most likely began on the east coast of Canada in early 1966, when a young beluga was caught in a shallow bay at low tide. The whale was put on a freighter and sent off to a zoo in England, but shortly before the ship reached its destination, it encountered a storm in the English Channel. A wave flushed the whale overboard and into the North Sea. All traces of the creature were lost, until a few months later, when Moby Dick turned up in the Rhine.

After his adventures in Duisberg, the whale was purportedly sighted again in Holland, where he was dubbed "Willi de Waal." There, hunting him was prohibited; Frits den Herder, the founder of Europe's first dolphinarium, railed in the press about Germany's "barbaric trapping methods." Still, those methods left less of a mark on Moby Dick than the toxic Rhine water, which gave the whale brownish spots on his skin.

Hollanders tried to get the whale back into the ocean, but at a fork in the river he missed the branch to Rotterdam and instead swam to the dammed-up Ijsselmeer, where a lock was opened for the express purpose of getting him to the North Sea. He didn't find that either, and swam back toward Germany, where Dr. Gewalt and thousands of curious onlookers awaited him at the banks of the Rhine.

◆

Not everyone was excited to see Moby Dick back. Bernhard Grzimek, director of the Frankfurt Zoological Garden and Germany's preeminent zoologist, griped in *Der Spiegel* that "hundreds of thousands of people are fretting about this one beluga" and yet "no one cares that the Norwegians virtually wiped out these same white whales near Spitsbergen in a bloody, brutal way, because Spitsbergen is far away." Grzimek didn't publicly criticize Gewalt's conduct, but in a personal letter to the younger zookeeper he expressed doubts about his intentions to house the whale in his zoo. Duisburg's dolphinarium—a concrete basin 33 by 33 feet and 10 feet deep—was probably too small.

In early June, Gewalt took to the pages of *Die Zeit* to justify his actions to readers. "If a giraffe were to get lost in the forest outside Duisburg, we would seek to capture it," he wrote, because it wouldn't be able to find its way out. Besides, he continued, "in our enclosure, surrounded by others of the same species, it would be extremely well cared for."

Others weighed in too, and as state elections approached, the whale's plight took on political dimensions. The Christian Democratic Union called for Moby Dick to be left alone, while the Social Democrat Party recommended capturing him and bringing him back to the open sea. Meanwhile, Moby Dick kept on swimming, against the current and unperturbed, leaving behind his hunter as he passed by Duisburg, Düsseldorf, and Cologne.

On the morning of June 13, a meeting of the Federal Press Conference filled every last seat in a Bonn assembly hall. Government spokesman Karl-Günther von Hase had just opened the session, which would be addressing important NATO concerns, when suddenly a man rushed into the hall and announced that Moby Dick had turned up in front of Parliament. In an instant, world politics lost any interest it might have held. Politicians and journalists crowded outside. At the banks of the river, people were throwing sandwiches and pickled herrings into the water, but the whale spurned these offerings. He displayed his spotted, scarred back one last time and headed south.

He swam close to four hundred miles upstream, leaving almost half the Rhine behind him, before turning around near the town of Remagen and swimming back the entire distance. This time, Wolfgang Gewalt let him do as he wished. The beluga spent one night outside Wesel before crossing the border into the Netherlands on June 15 and heading toward the mouth of the Rhine. During the final miles he was accompanied by two Dutch police cars on shore and three boats on the river. The next evening, at about twenty to seven, Moby Dick, the white whale who had cast his spell over Germany for an entire month, was spotted one final time before disappearing for good.

In the years to come, the people living near the Rhine would keep his memory alive. An excursion boat was named after him, and the music group Medium Terzett composed a folksy song about him the following spring:

What is the white whale wishing for, the white whale on the
Rhine?
He's heard the Rhine's made not of water, but of fine Rhine
wine.
What is the white whale wishing for, it's easy to divine,
The white whale's wishing for Rhine wine as he settles
down to dine.

It would still take more than a decade for the contaminated
river to begin to recover, but the appearance of a whale in the Rhine
helped environmental protection become mainstream.

◆

Duisburg zoo director Wolfgang Gewalt may not have been popular,
but by June of 1966 he'd become famous. His failure to catch Moby
Dick didn't stop him from continuing to try to acquire whales; indeed, he soon redoubled his efforts. In 1968, Duisberg's dolphins
were moved into a bigger pool, and the old pool was reclassified as
a whalearium. The following year, Gewalt traveled to Canada's Hudson Bay, where he caught two white whales with the help of First
Nations people and brought them to his zoo. Additional excursions
followed: one took him to Argentina's Tierra del Fuego, where he
caught black and white Commerson's dolphins (also known as jacobitas), another to Venezuela, where Orinoco river dolphins ended up
in his nets. By the 1970s, there were as many as six different species
of whales and dolphins in the Duisburg Zoo, the most anywhere
in Central Europe. But the related expenses were high, as were the
losses. Of the first six imported jacobitas, only one survived the first
few weeks, and three of the five river dolphins died within three
years.

Still, Gewalt's expeditions to capture animals served as promotional campaigns for his zoo—and for himself. He was out to cultivate his image; otherwise, it would have been more cost effective to leave the trapping to others.

Gewalt may have been extreme in his passion for collecting animals, but he wasn't alone; zoos throughout the world had begun breeding endangered species to save them from extinction. Heinz-Georg Klös boasted to newspapers about releasing eagle owls back into the wild of the Harz Mounains, while the GDR hoped to return beavers to their natural habitat in the Elbe River. For many rare species, however, there were only one or two animals in captivity at any given time, not enough to breed effectively, meaning that the animals required to realize these breeding projects would first have to be captured in the wild.

For animal trappers, these were golden times.

Communist Tigers for Capitalist Tapirs

The zoos on both sides of the Iron Curtain profited from the animal trade. Every fall, numerous trappers—exclusively West Germans—were permitted into the GDR to collect surplus offspring to resell to West German zoos. The East German zoos were given rare species in return. Sometimes, however, the exchange of animals was conducted on circuitous paths that bypassed the government—and weren't always legal.

Since the 1950s, trappers had kept up-to-date lists of those animals most sought after by zoos. Gerd Morgen, who'd briefly found work as an ape keeper in Basel after fleeing East Berlin, soon left the zoo to hunt gorillas and chimpanzees in southern Cameroon, while a young Bavarian, Martin Stummer, was making a name for himself in Ecuador. Like everything in Stummer's life, this had been a matter of coincidence. The twenty-four-year-old had stumbled into this line of work quite simply because he was an adventurer.

As a teenager, Stummer rode his bicycle from Munich all the way to Greece. His later travels took him farther afield, and his destinations to greater heights. He skipped school to climb a six-thousand-meter mountain in Pakistan with a friend. After graduating, he headed first to Africa, where he visited doctor and theologian Albert Schweitzer in Gabon, and then to South America, where he took up residence.

In the villages of Ecuador he discovered that the indigenous people catch piglike mountain tapirs and keep them as a living meat supply; the young animals lived side by side with other household pets, only tied up with ropes. Even though they were still growing, the ropes weren't loosened over time, and they eventually cut into the animals' flesh, leaving most with bloody necks. Stummer figured the animals would surely fare better in European or American zoos—and even if he earned money in the process, he was convinced his actions would be honorable.

He founded an animal trading company and named it Amazonian Animals. At first he bought animals from indigenous people, saving them from winding up in a cooking pot. But he was drawn to the unknown, and before long he was taking trips to the Pacific coast, to the rain forest of the Amazon, and to the highlands of the Andes to catch pumas, snakes, and macaws. He established contact with government agencies to facilitate getting export documents, and set up several animal collection sites.

He was successful, especially at capturing mountain tapirs—mysterious creatures that lived in the inaccessible forests of the Andes at altitudes of more than two thousand meters. It was rare to even glimpse them in European zoos. Only a single specimen had spent a short time at the Berlin Zoo, back at the turn of the twentieth century.

Stummer's helpers had their dogs track down the shy tapirs, which were lassoed before the good swimmers could escape into the torrential Río Palora. The young ones—easier to transport and still adaptable—were tranquilized with a weak dose of curare, a poison used on arrowheads. From the Andes Stummer brought the animals to his headquarters in Quito, where the sensitive folivores spent several weeks getting used to the plants they would be fed in captivity. Word of the German's hauls got around quickly, and he delivered the rare animals to several zoos in the United States and Europe. A single pair brought him $5,000.

Then, one day, Stummer received an invitation from Siegfried Seifert, the new director of the Leipzig Zoo, to come to East Berlin.

It was a cold winter day when Stummer met Seifert in the capital of the GDR, at an Interhotel on the corner of Unter den Linden and Friedrichstrasse. Once they'd sat down at a table at the back of the lobby, Seifert came to the point: "We need a couple of mountain tapirs."

"No problem at all, Herr Direktor," Stummer said. "I've recently been authorized to capture and export ten pairs."

"Very nice," said Seifert. He hesitated briefly, then added, "The problem is we don't have any Western currency."

"That's not good," Stummer replied, starting to get annoyed that he'd bothered to make the trip.

"I know, I know," Seifert said, soothingly. He leaned forward and said, almost in a whisper, "But in exchange I'll get you one male and three female Siberian tigers, all guaranteed purebred. We'll get the authorization from our government and fill out the complicated paperwork. You won't have to do a thing."

"Even so, we'd have to proceed cautiously," Stummer said, a little too loudly, and still clearly miffed.

The director waved his arms up and down. "Please, Herr Stummer, lower your voice," he said. "The hotel has eyes and ears. There are bugs hidden everywhere, and the Stasi is always watching. We'll be in trouble if they think an exchange of communist tigers from Siberia for capitalist mountain tapirs can't be reconciled with socialist interests."

Eventually they came to an agreement: Seifert would also order several boa constrictors, which Stummer would tuck away in a shipping crate with the tapirs, per Seifert's instructions, since he wouldn't be able to get papers for the snakes. (The snakes were likely placed in burlap sacks to keep them from strangling their traveling companions.) At the end of their meeting, Seifert shook hands with Stummer and said, as he left, "Don't trust anyone besides us. We're not interested in politics. We deal only with animals."

On the flight back to Ecuador, Stummer grew increasingly nervous at the thought of what he would do with four Siberian tigers in the tropics. Luckily the world's largest big cats were in high demand in the West, as they weren't easily found outside the Eastern Bloc. Stummer offered the animals to several West German zoos; Wilhelma, a zoological and botanical garden in Stuttgart, took them off his hands, along with a pair of mountain tapirs and some other wildlife from Stummer's collection. Stummer had built a veritable mini-zoo in Quito and gained a reputation as a specialist in hummingbirds.

The animal trappers he had come to know were generally shady individuals, all riff-raff in Stummer's eyes. Still, he told himself that anyone who bad-mouthed trappers was sure to bad-mouth zoo directors as well, as they had seemingly insatiable appetites for new additions. The esteemed Bernhard Grzimek publicly called for bans on exporting endangered species, but wanted to secure exclusive rights to rare animals from Stummer. Stummer was willing to catch anything on a zoo's wish list if the money was right.

He got commissions from West Berlin as well, where Heinz-Georg Klös was determined to acquire northern pudus—the world's smallest deer. Also known as "rabbit deer," they live in the Andes, four thousand meters up. "Get me pudus, whether or not it's legal," Klös wrote in a letter to Stummer. He later followed up with the necessary applications and forms.

But by the late 1960s animal trapping was already experiencing a decline. For traders like Hermann Ruhe, it became increasingly difficult to sell animals for a profit when zoos were breeding species themselves; stricter quarantine regulations certainly didn't help. Still, it would take years—well into the 1970s—for criticism of animal trapping to become mainstream and for international laws, such as the United States' Endangered Species Act of 1973, to limit trade in wildlife.

By then, Gerd Morgen had already stopped hunting great apes; the effort no longer paid off. He left Cameroon and spent the following decades at sea as a cook. As a young man, he'd dreamed of traveling to Winnipeg, but Canada was too cold for him. Never again did he see the moose in the wooden crate that had unwittingly helped him escape from the GDR.

In 1976 the GDR signed the Convention on International Trade in Endangered Species of Wild Fauna and Flora; the Federal Republic followed a year later. And yet, at least at first, these laws applied only on paper. Zoos continued to find creative ways to acquire rare and protected species.

As the 1970s gave way to the 1980s, Duisburg's zoo director,

Wolfgang Gewalt, would become an increasingly frequent target of criticism on account of his numerous trapping expeditions, while protests against keeping dolphins in captivity grew more vocal. As people became accustomed to seeing the creatures in zoos, a new concern for their well-being developed. Dolphins and whales were suddenly glorified as friendly and intelligent. Gewalt was baffled by this kind of mythologizing. "Just let them be animals, the way seals are," he said in one interview.

Martin Stummer would continue to capture animals in Ecuador for a few more years; in 1972, Klös finally got his northern pudus from him. Unfortunately they survived less than half a year in Berlin, the male dying of pneumonia and the female succumbing to food poisoning shortly afterward. Some zoologists call animals that neither reproduce nor survive for long in captivity "nails in the coffin." The mountain tapir, which spent only a brief period in European zoos, was one of these.

Eventually, even Martin Stummer left South America, first for Papua New Guinea, where tribes of headhunters were said never to have seen a white man before, then to the Philippines, where he became the king of a small island nation. He was a man who kept on going, on to the next adventure.

CHAPTER 6

BIG PLANS, LITTLE FISH

Jörg Adler headed down the autobahn toward Berlin at 60 miles an hour. The young animal keeper had started his trip at the Leipzig Zoo an hour earlier. At this rate he'd arrive at Tierpark Friedrichsfelde in two and a half hours. Unless he had engine trouble, nothing could stop him now. An accident was almost out of the question—that morning, there was only one other driver on the road; in the early 1970s hardly anyone in the GDR owned a car. If Adler were passed by another vehicle along this drive, it would be quite a sensation.

The sure part was the trip's duration. Three and a half hours of monotony, no more and no less. There was no shorter or faster route. Adler needed three and a half hours each and every time, pretty much on the dot; the motor of his Trabant couldn't manage any faster. Each of these trips to Berlin seemed to Adler symbolic of the state of the GDR: no matter how hard you tried, things in this country couldn't be rushed, and destinations could be reached only by specific routes.

Adler had long been painfully aware of this state of affairs. In

1964 he'd graduated from high school with mediocre grades. Instead of studying, he'd opted to clean syringes for his veterinarian father or go with him to visit patients. His father, whose specialty was horses, also taught at Leipzig University. Jörg wanted to become a veterinarian as well, but the problem was that Jörg Adler's father was neither a laborer nor a farmer, which put Jörg at a disadvantage in admission to a veterinary medicine program. He needed better grades, or he'd have to use the national fast track by enlisting in the army or joining the party. The latter two options were out of the question; Adler came from a Christian-minded dissident family. There would be no fast track for him.

As was customary in the GDR at that time, Adler had to complete an apprenticeship in addition to his secondary education. The course of study was assigned to him: he would train as a mason, as would all of his classmates. Along with his high school diploma, Adler received a certificate of proficiency as an installer, and the central university bureau designated him a student of structural engineering.

He spent a year torturing himself in an academic field he found exceedingly dull, until he broke off his studies and applied to several zoos and stud farms as a laborer. His first response came from the Leipzig Zoo, and he began working there in 1966. Two years later, he completed his training as an animal keeper. He quickly rose through the ranks, becoming section head for the hoofed animals, then for the apes. The next thing he knew, he was responsible for everything under the sun. Adler was one of only three licensed drivers at the zoo, and the only one with actual driving experience, so director Siegfried Seifert often sent him to the capital on delivery runs to the Commission for Zoological Gardens or to oversee an upcoming shipment of animals from the Tierpark.

In politics as in zoos, all roads led to Berlin—and in the latter case, straight to Heinrich Dathe, who was by then the undisputed patriarch of East German zoos. In 1976, the *Süddeutsche Zeitung* wrote, "Dathe is for the GDR what Grzimek is for the Federal Republic."

Adler first met the "Grzimek of the GDR" while on vacation with his parents sometime in the late 1950s in Ahrenshoop on the Baltic Sea. The little town was a gathering spot for the GDR's artistic and intellectual elite. Gerald Götting, the future president of the People's Chamber, East Germany's unicameral legislature, was staying in the hotel room next door, and Wolfgang Ullrich, the director of the Dresden Zoo, had his beach chair three places away. Karl-Eduard von Schnitzler, the most popular commentator on GDR television, put in appearances at one of the local restaurants—unless barred from the premises for misbehavior, as he frequently was.

The young Jörg Adler had already noticed a short stocky man back then, not because of his stature, but because of his behavior: he never lounged on his beach chair or in the bar, but was always walking with his binoculars. Every few feet he would stop and look up, hoping to spot a bird. Adler couldn't imagine that one day he would interact with the great Dathe, who could be heard on the radio and seen every week on TV. Life doesn't move along as predictably as a monotonous trip from Leipzig to Berlin.

Even before turning off the autobahn, Adler could see the signs: "Visit Tierpark Berlin." Dathe had had them mounted along all the access routes leading into the city. He'd even arranged for parking spaces at the entrance to the castle when the Tierpark was first built, although hardly anyone had a car in the 1950s. Even now, Adler's was generally the only one parked there.

Those summers at the Baltic, young Adler had never attracted

Dathe's attention; after all, the zookeeper was absorbed in looking up at the sky. But he'd come to think highly of the young man from Leipzig, or at least that was Adler's impression. Every time he came to the Tierpark, Dathe took a few minutes to spend with him—sometimes even half an hour—no matter how much he had to do. Dathe began by asking how Adler's family was faring, before the conversation quickly moved on to technical matters: how to restore sick animals to good health, how to improve the animals' living conditions, how best to feed species with limited diets . . .

Adler was at times surprised by the interest the director showed in him, as Dathe and Adler's boss, Seifert, were not exactly the closest of friends—in a way they were even rivals. The Tierpark had a say in which of the country's zoos got which animals, leading to frictions. When the Leipzig Zoo had wanted to import mountain goats from Canada a few years earlier, a good deal of squabbling had ensued, with Seifert ultimately prevailing. Still, the Tierpark could also be quite helpful, like when three elephants destined for Leipzig were impounded at the Port of Rotterdam. It took help from Berlin to get the animals into the GDR.

Perhaps Dathe's fondness for Adler was due to the zookeeper's special relationship to the city in which he'd launched his career. Or perhaps it was simply that Dathe set great store by achievements—and Adler was certainly ambitious.

"Write some more for *Der Zoologische Garten*," Dathe would suggest to the young man as he left Friedrichfelde for the three-and-a-half-hour journey home.

Still, it was Seifert, not Dathe, Adler had to thank for having advanced this far in his career. The director of the Leipzig Zoo was, like Adler, a devout Christian, and he supported the young animal keeper in whatever way he could. He even helped him begin a degree in veterinary medicine and become a technical assistant in the Leipzig veterinary clinic, which served the zoo.

Seifert may not have been especially close to Dathe, but he did get along with Dathe's rivals in West Berlin. When Heinz-Georg Klös visited Leipzig, Seifert usually sent for Adler and asked him, "Please show Professor Klös around." Klös had known Adler's father well, but his conversations with the son were usually limited to chatting about the weather and the health of Adler's children. Even so, they spent hours together strolling through the zoo.

Klös had a good relationship with people in the East—in Leipzig, Prague, and Wrocław. The Leipzig Zoo in particular often benefited from this relationship. On one occasion the West Berliner even helped them get bananas for a sick orangutan; an assistant passed the fruit off to Adler at a border crossing one night. (Bananas were hard to come by in the East.) Such sharing would have been inconceivable between the zoos directly on either side of the Berlin Wall.

Divided Gardens

In 1968 it became even more difficult for zoologists and veterinarians in East and West to gather and share information. Until then the pan-German zoo association had held an annual East-West summit meeting. The organization's leadership had for years been allocated evenly between the two countries; if the president came from the Federal Republic of Germany, his deputy would hail from the German Democratic Republic. In response to government pressure, however, the East German zoo directors were forced to to withdraw from the association, which they did by issuing identical, stiffly worded letters that made it clear to their colleagues in the West that this was a dictated statement.

The East German zoo directors established their own Commission for Zoological Gardens the following year, and appointed Dathe its chairman. They deliberately opted to call the new group a "commission"—rather than an association—in hopes of avoiding the suggestion that the coerced separation was permanent.

After the split, the annual Symposium on the Disorders of Zoo Animals and Wildlife, which was organized by the GDR's Center for Vertebrate Research, assumed much greater importance as a place for veterinarians and zoo directors from both sides of the Wall to stay in touch and share their experiences. The trade magazine *Der Zoologische Garten*, edited by Dathe in East Berlin, also continued as a joint publication, while textbooks published in the GDR stayed in use in West Germany, Austria, and Switzerland. Still, the forewords to these books created problems for Western zookeepers, with their praise of running a zoo according to socialist principles. Lothar Dittrich, Hanover's zoo director, prepared a new foreword better suited to the Federal Republic, which would later be pasted in.

In other respects, though, good communication between zoo directors in East and West continued, the Iron Curtain notwithstanding. They corresponded, visited one another, and socialized. All, that is, except those in Berlin.

The Wild, Wild East

Zoos had a fixed place in GDR state ideology: in accordance with paragraph 67 of the 1965 law regarding the uniform socialist educational system, zoos, like cultural centers, museums, theaters, and botanical gardens, were "to support the educational process at all levels and to give all members of the public the opportunity to expand and enhance their education."

As cultural establishments they were under the purview of the ministry of culture, whose goal was to establish a zoo in each of the fourteen districts of the GDR. In addition to the three zoos already in existence in Dresden, Leipzig, and Halle, six new facilities were created by the mid-1960s. Besides the one in Berlin, new zoos were built in Rostock (1956), Erfurt and Magdeburg (both 1959), and Cottbus (1960), with a later addition in Schwerin (1974). Moreover, all over the young German Democratic Republic, a series of small domestic animal gardens known as *Heimattiergärten* were set up. In towns that had no major zoo, these *Heimattiergärten* were designed to introduce people to the country's varied fauna and ignite their interest in the world of zoos. At the beginning domestic species were kept there, but later they were expanded to include individual exotic species. The significance of the *Heimattiergärten* for local residents was particularly evident in Hoyerswerda.

This town in Upper Lusatia had grown rapidly in the 1950s and 1960s, attracting more and more people, who found work at Black Pump, a nearby industrial combine. Prefabricated housing developments proliferated on the outskirts of town and into the countryside, and before long a handful of residents constructed enclosures for deer and swans at the castle moat in the Old Town. By the mid-1960s more than 260,000 people visited its *Heimattiergärten* annually, at a time when the city itself had a mere 46,000 residents. The region had hardly any other recreational facilities, and vacation getaways were rare. At most people went to the Baltic, but even that was far away—so families went to the local animal park five or ten times a year.

By the early 1980s, zoos were the country's most popular leisure destinations, welcoming sixteen million visitors annually— meaning that there were as many zoogoers as citizens of the GDR.

The number of *Heimattiergärten* swelled to 125. Even though there was a clear hierarchy in the East German zoos landscape, with the Berlin Tierpark at the apex, the zoo commission stipulated in 1974 that the big zoos had to help out the small *Heimattiergärten* in their regions. Each of them served an assigned territory, which generally extended over several districts. The nine zoos provided veterinary guidance to the smaller animal parks and *Heimattiergärten* in their territories; they also supplied new animals and trained apprentices.

Despite this support, zoological gardens across the country felt the effects of the GDR's structural problems. In the Leipzig Zoo, the workday usually began at seven in the morning and rarely ended before eight at night. The keepers, who faced shortages of virtually everything, had to chip in to keep things afloat. During their breakfast break, they'd discuss the schedule for the day: some took care of the animals and mucked out the stables, while others went to town and spent hours waiting in line to get ham, wallpaper, or other goods for themselves and their colleagues. This mentality created a bond—and the staff in Leipzig was an especially tight-knit bunch. After work they'd head to a pub and indulge in drinking and singing, before roaming the streets. After all, there was nothing worth watching on TV, there were few opportunities to travel, and hardly anyone owned a car.

Jörg Adler felt that in spite of all the problems, it was a fantastic era, in which the "Shit Party" took quite some time to gain a foothold. Until the late 1970s, there wasn't a single Socialist Unity Party member in the entire zoological senior management, but there were several active Christians. The zoo could be regarded as a small oasis of subversion. This had to do in part with the special character of the city itself. Because of the trade fairs, which took place twice

Barely anything was left of the Zoo's aquarium after the bombing of Berlin. Only remnants of the dinosaur frieze on the exterior wall can be made out here. It would take close to a decade for the building to be reopened. *Archiv Zoo Berlin/Heinroth.*

RIGHT: Berlin Zoo director Katharina Heinroth at the opening ceremony for the new hippo house in May 1956. TOP: The hippos Knautschke and Bulette (smaller one) later became the parents of a blossoming family. Visitors to the Zoological Garden did not care that they were father and daughter.

Top: bpk/Friedrich Seidenstücker. Right: Archiv Zoo Berlin/Lassberg.

Tierpark director Heinrich Dathe with a masked palm civet at his desk, while he and secretary Irene Engelmann try to sort out his piles of paperwork. The civet looks on attentively.

Archiv Tierpark Berlin/Hans Meissner.

In the early years, Dathe and his staff relied on the help of volunteer construction assistants, seen here during the construction of the camel enclosure in 1958.

Archiv Tierpark Berlin/Gerhard Budich.

Many of the new animals for the Tierpark—such as these Bactrian camels from the Moscow Zoo—were brought by foot from Lichtenberg station to Friedrichsfelde.

Archiv Tierpark Berlin/Mielast-Bade.

With no enclosure yet ready for a young elephant when she arrived, Kosko was allowed to roam the Tierpark grounds—to the delight of the children of Berlin.

Archiv Tierpark Berlin/Zimmer.

At his official introduction in January 1957, Heinz-Georg Klös, who was only thirty years old, looked boyish, not like the director of the oldest German zoo. *Landesarchiv Berlin/Gert Schütz.*

When U.S. attorney general Robert F. Kennedy brought a bald eagle with him on his visit to Berlin in 1962 and named the bird Willy Brandt, after West Berlin's mayor, the East German press gleefully picked the name apart. *Landesarchiv Berlin/Johann Willa.*

With spears, nets, and stun guns, Duisberg Zoo director Wolfgang Gewalt (second from right) and his assistants tried to catch their Moby Dick in the Lower Rhine. *Stadtarchiv Duisburg.*

"Like Noah's night lodging." The Russian writer Daniil Granin was greatly impressed by the sight of camels and flamingos roaming through the Tierpark past German oak trees. *akg-images.*

A touch of Siberia: visitors to the Tierpark could observe the tigers at their outdoor installation without bars getting in the way. *Archiv Tierpark Berlin/Günter Henning.*

The "Kuhdamm" (literally: cow dam) of Friedrichsfelde, a pun on the Kurfüstendamm, the leading commercial street of West Berlin, which was popularly known as the Ku'damm.
Landesarchiv Berlin/Herbert Kraft.

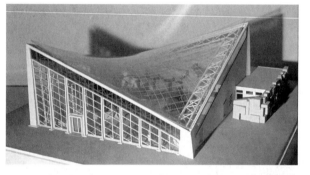

Work on the Tierpark's tapir house went on for about a decade; the construction site then lay idle for years. In 1979 the edifice finally burned down.
Middle: Archiv Tierpark Berlin/ Werner Engel. Bottom: Archiv Tierpark Berlin/Martin Mosig.

West German chancellor Helmut Schmidt at the official welcome of pandas Bao Bao and Tjen Tjen in November 1980. *picture alliance/AP Images; photographer: Edwin Reichert.*

Tierpark director Heinrich Dathe (left) and his Berlin Zoo counterpart Heinz-Georg Klös at a meeting in Friedrichsfelde, East Germany, in 1984. In the background (from left) are Rudolf Reinhardt, curator of birds at the Berlin Zoo; Falk Dathe, curator of reptiles at the Tierpark; and Hans Frädrich, who spent many years at the Berlin Zoo as Klös's number two.
© *Klaus Rudloff.*

In September 1989, the Tierpark's new pachyderm house finally opened. Nineteen-year-old Patric Müller (second from right) and his colleagues presented the elephants to the public. Just seven months later, the elephant keepers' fears came to pass when Dombo, the matriarch, died in the moat. *Top: Archiv Tierpark Berlin/W. Scherf.*

Right: Clipping from Neues Deutschland, *September 4, 1990.*

The professor and the beloved beast: Heinz-Georg Klös in his element.
Landesarchiv Berlin/
Thomas Platow.

a year in Leipzig, this city, along with East Berlin, was arguably one of only two places in the GDR with even the slightest bit of cosmopolitanism.

◆

The Berlin Tierpark had a staff of more than four hundred, yet Dathe still had to improvise to get all the necessary work done. He relied on people who were "somewhat outside the normal work process," as he wrote in his diary: unskilled workers from prisons, mental institutions, and homes for the disabled were brought in to perform simple tasks. These helpers tended not to be the least bit squeamish. Some tried to catch ibises by whacking the slender, crescent-beaked birds from tree branches with a broom.

Within the confines of the zoo grounds a subculture developed, a refuge for people who didn't fit into the social mold—political nonconformists, oddballs, outsiders. The animal keepers gave them nicknames. In Leipzig there was the "chain woman," whose entire face was pierced at a time when there was no fashionable term for her look. There were also the "bookworm" and the "mushroom picker." In the Berlin Tierpark, the "rhino masturbator" would hang around waiting for the rhinoceroses' next attempt at mating. The animal keepers would crack jokes about these regulars, and call to one another, "Look who's standing in front of the enclosure again!"

The occasional visitor asked outright whether the keepers could call them over when the next mating was getting underway. Others just wanted a few slivers of elephant toenail clippings to use as fertilizer for their gardens.

The other side of the Wall had these kinds of characters as well. One elderly woman who regularly visited the Berlin Zoo was able to differentiate each individual animal in the huge baboon clan on the monkey rock, and she gave each of them names. One morning, a young temporary worker found the woman placing ten candles on the wall of the enclosure and lighting one after the other.

"What are you doing there?" the baffled worker asked.

"Well, today is Bodo's birthday," she replied, her eyes shining.

The young worker was taken aback. "Who's Bodo?" he blurted.

The old woman's face, which had been beaming, now looked annoyed. "What's this, young man?" she asked. "You claim to care for the apes yet you don't know Bodo?" Before he could answer, she grabbed his sleeve and pulled him toward her. Bending over the wall, she pointing to a baboon perched on one of the huge rock's lower ledges, partly hidden from view. "That's Bodo," she shouted, "and he's turning ten today!"

Another character was a man the zookeepers called "Hyena Heinrich," because he made a habit of standing in front of the hyena cage and trying to kiss the fur of one of the animals as it made its way along the bars. However, the zookeepers also profited from these strange regulars, who knew each creature so well. In the sprawling hoofed animal section of the Berlin Tierpark, it was a great help to be able to ask them when which bull had mated with which cow.

Friedrichsfelde's vast size was a problem not only for the keepers, but also for those monitoring the grounds. Some children took advantage of the expansive premises by swiping flowers from the flowerbeds and selling them for a few pennies to passersby. When the Tierpark closed at sunset, visitors could stay as long as they wanted, because there were no guards to make them leave.

The spacious grounds and available buildings also enabled the animal keepers to meet with colleagues from the West without facing bureaucratic snares. Dathe's younger son, Falk, was following in his father's footsteps; his speciality was reptiles. When a snake expert from the West announced his intention to visit to mount a slide show about his recent excursions, Falk Dathe could call up a couple of terrarium hobbyists the morning of the event and be confident they would spread the news. By evening, the hall would be filled. Spontaneous events of this kind could never have taken place at universities, which deferred to the state.

The Stasi left these gatherings alone, because animal lovers were considered innocuous. Even if the Stasi were to intercept their conversations, the secret police wouldn't be able to make sense of shop talk about "sheltopusiks" and other creatures. Any officials who did recognize the Russian origins of the word and wondered who this "yellow belly" might be would soon learn it was a four-and-a-half-foot-long reptile that feeds primarily on insects and small animals and can live as long as fifty years. Talk of a legless lizard from southeastern Europe didn't exactly sound like the stuff of conspiracy.

The Stasi received very clear statements about a variety of other matters, however. Several Informal Collaborators (as the state termed them) reported on the staff's dissatisfaction "with the paucity of building activity in reconstructing the existing installations and constructing new ones," in the words of one.

A shortage of raw materials, which had bedeviled the GDR since its establishment, was the major cause of these delays. Back in 1950, the Federal Republic had imposed a steel embargo on the GDR. Then, in 1964, a price reform shot the cost of raw materials up by as much as 70 percent. Ever since, what construction materials there were went to East Berlin first, and when more workers were needed in the capital, they were delegated there from other districts. The country's other zoos suffered the consequences.

As one of the city's top attractions, Tierpark Friedrichsfelde was relatively well provided for. The Soviet writer Daniil Granin had praised the zoo exuberantly in his travel report "Look and See," which appeared in *Die Neue Welt* in 1969. "The day was drawing to a close, the Tierpark was emptying out, and it seemed even more gigantic," he wrote.

> Wild boars ran past us, ducks flew up above, flamingos strutted about, along with peacocks. Llamas pulled up grass, and young deer romped around. I have never seen so many birds and animals in freedom. They were not afraid of people; the Tierpark called to mind an expanded green version of Noah's night lodging. You could stand there and observe the animals for hours. All these fowl, twittering, running about, fluffy, their eyes flashing, this life was living and expressing itself in the most natural way, almost in freedom, which made it seem even more beautiful, and more diverse. . . . There may well be zoological gardens in the world that are richer than this zoo in Berlin, but it is not a matter of the number of animals or the equipment; the most beautiful and astonishing aspect was the sensation of creativity.

But even in the capital, construction would soon grind to a halt. While zoo director Klös was dedicating a new rhinoceros house, expanding the great ape house, and building new bear compounds, Friedrichsfelde was basically at a standstill. The Tierpark's second entrance, with its small ticket booth and wooden lattice fence, more closely resembled the entry to a set of garden plots than a gateway to the world's largest animal park.

In the early years of the Tierpark, Dathe had been promised everything possible—animals, construction materials—but since the opening of the Alfred Brehm House in 1963, those heady days were gone. The stench of cat urine had eaten its way into the building's masonry. When a Tierpark zookeeper came down with a head cold, his co-workers would suggest, "Go to the predator house for half an hour. The ammonia will clear your sinuses!"

The elephants were still living in the old horse stable, where rats had settled in under the floorboards; at night, when the elephants slept, rodents nipped at their feet. A new home had been planned for some time, but kept being postponed. In the hoofed animal section, the so-called outer ring, many walkways were neither paved nor graveled, but little more than footpaths. In the summer they were dusty, in the winter either soaked from rain or frozen solid. Makeshift fences frequently had to be replaced or reinforced after animals ate through the wooden beams and broke out. Once two Canadian elks got as far as the train tracks that ran behind the Tierpark. Another time, a couple of muntjacs—small Asian deer—couldn't be caught until they'd reached Karl-Marx-Allee in the city center.

These makeshift solutions were a consequence of the Tierpark's hasty opening in the summer of 1955—and of Dathe's preference for spending his allotted funds on collecting. Some visitors got the feeling that they'd wound up not at the much touted "zoo of the future," but at an agricultural production cooperative—and that they were unwelcome there.

Even so, Dathe went to great lengths to ensure that the Tierpark continued to be an exemple to other zoos. He arranged for the construction of smaller aviaries and installations, and always invited the media to the openings, to create the impression that things at the Tierpark were moving forward. But as the years passed, plans and reality continued to diverge—and the ill-fated tapir house became the most symbolic of all the stalled construction projects.

Tapir or Not Tapir

It all started back in 1961, when the Building Academy in Berlin offered Dathe plans for a futuristic structure. The drawings showed a hall that measured 80 by 80 feet. Its roof would be held up by steel cables, like a hammock, dispensing with the need for supporting columns on the inside. Architects call this form a "hyperbolic paraboloid." It was an experimental construction, without precedent. "Could you use this?" Dathe was asked.

"Yes," he replied, pleased to finally have the opportunity to implement one of his favorite ideas. "We'll make a tapir house out of that."

A tapir house had been included in the first site plans for the Tierpark in the mid-1950s. The black-and-white Malayan tapirs from Southeast Asia were already living on zoo grounds, behind the old stable that housed the elephants and rhinoceroses and inconveniently away from visitors' paths.

The following year, the foundations for the new tapir house were laid and the first steel girders erected. The newspapers ran articles about it, complete with sketches showing tapirs and hippopotamuses bathing in the shade of palm trees. The construction site displayed a sign announcing: "A tapir house is being built here." Even the route maps in the Tierpark guide sketched in the scaffolding, which looked like an oversized, bulky letter "M." Erich Schmitt, the caricaturist for the East German *Berliner Zeitung*, nicknamed it the "grasshopper building."

Heinz Tellbach was asked to supervise the project. The young architect had designed pens, cages, and fences for the Tierpark in its early years, before moving on to drafting small houses for GDR VIPs in the secure and luxurious Waldsiedlung housing development north of Berlin. After work, Tellbach sketched buildings for various zoos. When the Tierpark started planning its next batch of construction, his former mentor, zoo architect Heinz Graffunder, brought Tellbach back onto his staff.

Tellbach was authorized to accompany Graffunder to West Berlin to gather ideas at the Zoological Garden. Director Klös took them around personally, proudly showing them the new buildings that had been added over the years. Tellbach had expected more. He found the architecture too plain. The aviary was particularly disappointing, its nondescript low-rise building about as attractive as a shoebox. Buildings of this kind needed to stand out, he thought, like the Tierpark's Alfred Brehm House and the tapir house he was going to build. He refrained from saying this aloud to Klös, who ended their meeting with the patronizing gesture of slipping Tellbach two marks so he could visit relatives in West Berlin.

Several more years went by, but while the tapirs had had offspring, they'd yet to emerge from their temporary stable. After the house's steel framework was completed in 1967, work came to a halt. The Berlin municipal authorities were running out of construction materials, and needed them more urgently at Alexanderplatz to spruce up the central square downtown.

Shortly thereafter Heinz Tellbach attended one of the popular Tierpark balls, which had become a lively part of the East Berlin social season, where he met Erich Schmitt. As a loyal Tierpark visitor, the caricaturist had already heard that construction had been stopped. On the reverse side of Tellbach's invitation he drew a sketch of the unfinished steel building, with a father and son in front of it.

"Daddy," the son asks, "is that the framework where the tapirs are hanging?"

Tellbach grimaced. He didn't know whether Schmitt was trying to cheer him up or taunting him. It was probably a combination of both.

While the massive framework rusted away, the sign at the construction site continued to announce: "A tapir house is being built here." In the Tierpark guides little flowers were drawn in to entwine the shell, as though it had fallen into a deep sleep, like Sleeping Beauty, and was waiting to be awakened with a kiss. As the years went by, the "M" grew smaller and smaller on the page, until it disappeared altogether.

In the late 1970s what were now ruins were finally torn down. The foundations would remain in the ground for decades to come, until they, too, were removed, and there was nothing left to remind Germans of the failed experiment.

◆

In many other zoos, the country's economic troubles were even more pronounced. Sometimes all it took for grand goals to go awry was something small.

In the mid-1970s, the director of the Magdeburg Zoo appealed to the local building authority for authorization to create a penguin enclosure with a swimming pool. Too eager to wait until the agency had granted permission, he had his workers start digging, figuring that the approval would soon be on its way. Not long after, however, the mayor announced that he would be coming for a visit, and the illegal construction pit was quickly covered over with foliage to avert any suspicion. Over the following years, a great deal more foliage would be added, because the director had overlooked a very different, basic problem: in no other district of the GDR was it as difficult to get fresh sea fish, and without fresh sea fish the penguins could not be fed. The dream of penguins at the Elbe River came to naught for a lack of mackerels.

A Dream in Gray

Meainwhile, in Leipzig, Jörg Adler was distressed by the state of the great ape house. Something or other was always broken, even if it was just a wobbly door handle. The building had been constructed in 1901, and had grated on Lothar Dittrich's nerves back in the 1950s because the iron girders were rusting through. Even though the roof had been patched several times, there were frequent leaks, and since the cage doors didn't close properly, now and again one of the apes would break out.

And so Adler could hardly take his eyes off the pictures he'd discovered in *Der Zoologische Garten*. He sat enthralled in his study, staring at the black-and-white photos of enclosures in the newly opened zoo in Münster, West Germany. Adler felt as though they had come from another world.

In 1974, a new zoo had been built on the outskirts of Münster after its original site in the city center was claimed by Westdeutsche Landesbank. The head of the bank had threatened to relocate to Dortmund if his demands weren't met, and so the hundred-year-old zoo was moved to the suburbs.

On a new site of almost seventy-five acres, the "all-weather zoo"—as it was called because the large animal houses were joined together by canopied paths—was five times larger than the old one. It had been planned in advance, on a drawing board, like Tierpark Friedrichsfelde. But while the latter had to be put together bit by bit, with Berlin's residents pitching in, the installations in Münster arose all of a piece. In the photos, Adler saw small black bears climbing around on a lone bare tree in a terraced concrete landscape, like teenagers in an apocalyptic fantasy.

This design, considered progressive at the time, was used for both inner-city pedestrian zones and zoo installations for apes and bears. But just one year after the all-weather zoo opened its gates, the nearby Krefeld Zoo set a new standard in keeping apes. There, gorillas, chimpanzees, and orangutans lived in family units in a tropical hall with a warm, humid climate and jungle plants, separated from visitors by only a narrow moat.

Krefeld's tropical ape house was a pioneering structure in modern animal keeping, but it remained the odd building out for quite some time. Concrete, tiles, and bulletproof glass continued to define zoos for decades to come, mainly for reasons of hygiene: roundworm infestations were still a major health problem, and in some zoos apes' cages were scrubbed twice a day. Tiled walls were easier to clean, and bulletproof glass was more attractive than bars because they didn't evoke thoughts of prison cells. The glass also prevented visitors from feeding the animals.

All that concrete monotony didn't bother Jörg Adler. He marveled at the solid structure, thinking, "At least they don't need to worry the ceiling might come crashing down." The all-weather zoo remained to him a fantasy, a promise in black and white. The idea that Adler might actually visit Münster and get to know the zoo firsthand was as likely as the prospect of a leakproof roof atop Leipzig's great ape house.

CHAPTER 7

GOLDEN TIMES IN THE GOLDEN CAGE

Every morning at ten o'clock, Werner Schröder, the director of the Berlin Aquarium, left the realm of fish and reptiles and strolled down Budapester Strasse, past the zoo's graffiti-covered outer wall, past the gate, past the gray ticket booths, and over to the world of real estate sharks and snaking lines. All around the ruins of the Memorial Church a new city center—City West—had been arising slowly over the past twenty years. After the Wall was built, West Berlin needed a downtown shopping center, a counterpart to Alexanderplatz in the East. Its striking centerpiece turned out to be a clunky glass and aluminum colossus, twenty floors of offices plus a movie theater, swimming pool, and shopping mall, with an ice rink in an inner courtyard. At more than 280 feet high, it was the tallest building in West Berlin. At least zoo director Klös was able to secure the major concession he fought for: the design was rotated by 90 degrees so as to cast less of a shadow on the adjacent zoo.

The Europa-Center, which opened its doors in 1965, was intended to introduce a hint of America into the walled-in city. But now, in 1977, it was just another staid office tower in a strip mall of souvenir stores.

Whenever Werner Schröder didn't feel like strolling along the Kurfürstendamm, he'd stop to spend his breakfast break there. He sat down in a café, ordered a cup of tea, and would watch the young women skating in circles next to him on the ice rink, the loudspeakers droning out lyrics of the song "Movie Star" by Swedish pop star Harpo: "And you think you will look like James Bond . . ." Schröder lit a cigarette and turned up the collar of his overcoat to shield him from the breeze.

At six o'clock each morning he'd get up and feed his pets—a gray parrot, a greyhound, and several chameleons. He and his zookeepers would complete their morning rounds through the aquarium, and then he'd have a look at the mail and make his way here.

Schröder had headed the aquarium for a quarter of a century. When he began working on the building's reconstruction—it had been destroyed in the war—the site where the Europa-Center now stood was nothing more than an abandoned lot. The local press called it a "blot on Berlin's calling card." Now decals and posters proclaimed, "This is where Berlin does its buying. This is where the world meets up." But the spot that truly ought to have been called the Europa-Center was on the other side of the street.

Schröder had turned the aquarium into one of the most popular cultural institutions in the city, and the most biodiverse place on the continent. The great public aquariums of Europe could still be counted on two hands, and Berlin's was clearly one of them. Seven hundred thousand visitors—from the city and beyond—came every year. Unlike at a zoo, tourism wasn't dependent on the seasons, because visitors weren't exposed to the elements. When it was as cold and gloomy as it was this time of year, not quite yet spring, it was easy to forget how pleasant Berlin could be in the summer, although the previous summer had been somewhat too hot, with temperatures regularly rising to 95 degrees as early as June. All of Europe had suffered from a heat wave that had dragged on for months. In Hanover, zoo director Lothar Dittrich had to house the South African jackass penguins in a cold storage facility; in Duisburg, Wolfgang Gewalt had a canopy roof put up over the whalearium so the snow-white belugas wouldn't get sunburned. Werner Schröder and his staff had been kept busy cooling the aquarium's water and placing damp moss in the amphibians' habitat. With the exception of a few sensitive animals, most survived the heat unharmed.

Schröder was especially proud of his crocodile collection, which comprised twenty-six species and was the largest in any European zoo. His friends in the East could only boast that Friedrichsfelde had the second-largest number.

Recently two of Schröder's keepers had discovered a clutch of American crocodile eggs buried in a sandhill in the crocodile hall. While one of them used a long iron rod to keep the ten-foot-long parents at bay, the other removed three eggs and placed them in an incubator. Breeding crocodiles isn't easy. American crocodiles don't become sexually mature until they're ten to twelve years old. And even then everything has to be just right: the environment, the climate, and above all the chemistry. Female crocodiles are picky and in no rush. If their suitors fail to impress them, they can wait. They have plenty of time; they can live up to eighty years, and are fertile past the age of fifty. But this time everything had worked, and with any luck, the next few months would see baby crocodiles born in Europe for the first time.

Among his colleagues, Schröder was esteemed beyond the borders of West Berlin. He had just as close a friendship with Heinrich Dathe as he'd had with Katharina Heinroth and Austrian animal behavorist Konrad Lorenz. When Lorenz came for a visit, they'd sit together into the evening hours in Schröder's fourth-floor apartment, next to the insectarium. They drank tea, talked shop, and if they disagreed on some matter of fact, all they had to do was go down two floors to the aquarium and take a look. In zoology, everything had its proper place—just as it did in West Berlin.

For Schröder, the city was like one big living room. Everyone knew him. He counted many prominent artists, including expressionist painter Max Pechstein and actors Hans Söhnker and Viktor de Kowa, among his friends. He sometimes played Ping-Pong with the boxer "Bubi" Scholz. Life was reasonably pleasant on the island of West Berlin—the only problem was the Wall.

Schröder considered himself an optimist for the present and a pessimist for the future: he was sure that things would never again be as good as they were that day, so each and every day needed to be put to good use. He also sensed that not many days remained.

Siting in the café in the Europa-Center, he drank his last sips of tea before making his way back to the aquarium. On the way there he passed by the theater where the Stachelschweine cabaret group, whose name translates to "porcupines," held their shows. Since the opening of the Europa-Center, the group had performed there every evening on a small stage on the ground floor. In 1949, when the artists had been looking for a rehearsal space, no one had wanted to help them because young people like the theater troupe were thought to do nothing but smoke and make a mess. Schröder, who was a smoker himself, had made an empty room available to them under the condition that they would keep it clean.

Close to thirty years had gone by since then. Schröder had witnessed the post-war reconstruction, and the division of Berlin. West Berlin was now itself a kind of aquarium, a microcosm that depended on supplies from the outside. Just as the animals in their tanks could survive only as long as the filters and heat kept working and the food kept coming, West Berlin was being fed intravenously by the Federal Republic and the West.

The people of West Berlin were making the best of their lives, suppressing any fears of latent danger from the East; the Americans, French, and British would take care of that. The animal keepers had talked themselves into believing so too. They didn't know how their colleagues in the Tierpark were faring because there was little way of contacting them. They could communicate with colleagues in Leipzig, or in Breslau, Sofia, or Prague, but not East Berlin, where people invariably jumped to the conclusion that everything was an attempt at espionage. All the Zoo staff knew about the Tierpark was what they could learn on individual visits to Friedrichsfelde and from the stories that circulated about Heinrich Dathe and his rivalry with Klös. People were saying that when one acquired a new species, the other was immediately envious. In the West, Dathe was said to make his entire staff stand at attention, military-style, every morning. Could he really be even stricter than Klös?

Schröder's friendship with Dathe put a strain on his relationship with Klös. They limited their contact to the essentials—press conferences or receptions that required them to appear in public together—and had nothing to do with each other outside of work.

Klös had been searching for a successor for Schröder for quite some time. Schröder predated the director in Berlin and had overseen the rebuilding of the zoo and the aquarium, securing quite a bit of authority for himself. In Klös's view, this left him too little room to exert his own influence on the running of the aquarium. He wanted Schröder out of the way, but it wasn't so easy to find a capable replacement.

Of Antelopes and Aquariums

Zoo directors and scientists had recently joined forces for the first time, under the authority of the West German Federal Ministry of Food, Agriculture, and Forestry, to establish general guidelines for the care of zoo animals. The resulting document, the 1977 Assessment of the Humane Treatment of Mammalians, addressed an array of issues including the size and furnishing of enclosures, climate, social conditions, nutrition, and shipping practices. Heinz-Georg Klös was, naturally, a member of the commission, as was zoologist Wolf Herre, who taught at Kiel University in the country's north. The experts would gather at a different zoo each time they met to talk and so of course Klös invited the group to Berlin; he did everything possible to expand his influence and that of his zoo.

Klös had previously tried to host a meeting of the German Society for Mammalian Biology, but had had to cancel on short notice, which Herre couldn't resist bringing up. "He'll uninvite you all again," he supposedly joked to his fellow committee members.

Herre was one of the most highly regarded zoologists in Germany, but he didn't want to antagonize Klös. The West Berliner may not have had the influence that his rival Dathe enjoyed in the East, but since Frankfurt's Bernhard Grzimek had retired, he was the leading voice among West German zoo directors. It could be advantageous to stay on his good side. So when, shortly afterward, Klös asked Herre whether he knew of someone who could serve as head of the Berlin aquarium, Herre came up with a candidate on the spot: his former doctoral student Jürgen Lange, whom he called up right away.

"They're looking for a successor for Dr. Schröder in Berlin," he told the young man. "You should meet with Professor Klös." But Lange wasn't taken with the idea.

"You don't have to accept the position," Herre insisted. "But please do me the favor and at least meet with him or he'll never talk to me again."

Lange was no stranger to Berlin. In the mid-1960s he'd spent several months at Humboldt University studying antelope skulls. A West German student at an East German university was quite a rarity at the time. Lange lived with relatives in West Berlin and worked as an animal keeper in the zoo on the side. When he left, Klös told him to come back once he'd graduated. But no job opened up.

A position did, however, become available elsewhere. In 1970, the Wilhelma Zoo in Stuttgart was seeking a new head for its aquarium after the man in charge was named zoo director. The facility had opened only three years earlier and was considered the most modern aquarium in Europe.

Fish were actually the last thing Lange was interested in. As a child he'd owned guppies, and he minored in marine biology in college, but he hadn't found it very stimulating. He wanted to continue working with mammals, preferably antelopes. "Take the job at the aquarium for now," he told himself, somewhat naively. "You can always make the switch later."

Lange soon figured out that running an aquarium was far more complicated than keeping antelopes or other mammals. Many of the aquatic animals that came to Stuttgart from the wild had never before been kept in captivity. He had to pore over textbooks to find out the most basic information—sometimes even their species' names.

He also became fascinated by tank design. Antelope enclosures all looked pretty much the same, but re-creating a riverbank in a tank only six and a half feet long entailed far more than simply copying six and a half feet of shoreline. Everything had to be right. Visitors had to think, "That looks just like our brook back home." Lange was intrigued by the creative challenge. And even the most brutish aquarium fish didn't wreak havoc on their habitat the way hoofed animals or elephants did; no matter how big their sections were, after a few months they'd turn into dusty wastelands. There was also all the ingenious technology the fish needed to survive. Before long, Lange couldn't imagine anything more exciting.

◆

Zoos had unwritten laws, just like free enterprise. When people made a career change, it was either to take a step up or because more money was coming their way.

But Lange had no desire to make a change. He'd been in Stuttgart for close to seven years, and was content there. Still, he did his dissertation adviser the favor of contacting Klös and arranging to meet with him in Berlin.

Klös invited him to his office in the zoo's administration building for their discussion. Klös's assistant, Hans Frädrich, and a member of the zoo's supervisory board were already waiting there. The four spent a long time talking about this and that before turning to the job itself, which Klös praised to the skies. But Lange had a plan: the way to get out of this as quickly as possible was to make excessively high demands, at which point Klös would have no choice but to reject him.

"How many staff members does the aquarium have?" Lange asked.

"At the moment, ten," said Klös.

"That sounds like too few to me. At least five or six more would need to be hired," Lange said, his voice resolute. "How old are they on average?"

Klös thought for a moment. "About forty."

"Then at least four new people in their early twenties have to join the staff. The older ones are already too stuck in their daily routines."

That made sense to Klös. He'd seen things the same way when he came to Berlin as a young director. But he couldn't make this sort of decision on his own. "I'll have to discuss that with the board," he said, looking embarrassed.

"You do that," Lange said contentedly.

This sequence of questions and answers repeated itself several times that day. Every time Lange came up with a new demand, Klös asked him to step outside so he could work things out. Whenever Klös asked him to come back in, a different board member was sitting at the table. After countless rounds of negotiations, which extended over two days, Lange had the feeling that he'd met the entire board.

"We'll need to talk about your salary," Klös said at some point.

"What can you offer me?" Lange asked.

When Klös named the sum, Lange raised his eyebrows. "If I'm to come here, you'll have to offer me substantially more than I earn in Stuttgart now," he said. "And every year I would like to have 7 percent more, to keep pace with inflation." Friends in Stuttgart who were freelancing for TV and theater had given him this advice.

Klös, who was infamous for his negotiating skills among West Berlin's politicians and leading business figures, began to sweat. He hadn't sat across from such a hard bargainer for quite a long time. He didn't suspect that Lange's only goal was to make himself unaffordable.

◆

Jürgen Lange was prepared for any eventuality except one: that Klös would give him everything he asked for. He hadn't known how desperately the director had been seeking a successor for Schröder. Lange had played his cards all wrong.

He was aware that he couldn't turn the offer down; word would soon get around. If he were to back out now, any time he applied for a job, the person doing the hiring would say, "That Lange's not for us. He didn't even take the offer from Berlin." So he said yes to Klös and, with a heavy heart, left Stuttgart.

Lange did have to agree to one compromise: although he'd be head of the aquarium, he would not be its director, as Schröder had been, but only a research assistant. With Schröder out, Klös would no longer have to work alongside a competitor.

Schröder had been assured, even quite recently, that he could stay at the aquarium as long as he liked. But at a meeting of the supervisory board he learned that his contract would not be renewed and that his successor had already been identified.

Schröder would be turning seventy at the end of the year. He'd already given thought to his departure—at his age it was time to think about retiring. But he hadn't expected to be dismissed. The worst part was that he'd have to move out of the apartment he'd been living in for thirty years. At night he began receiving anonymous phone calls warning, "If you aren't out by the end of the year, we'll leave your things in front of the door." Schröder was reminded of what had happened to Katharina Heinroth. But unlike her, he wasn't a fighter. The stress wore away at him so much that he fell ill and had to spend several weeks in the hospital.

In October of 1977, while Schröder prepared to depart by year's end, his successor, Jürgen Lange, started work in Berlin. After visiting the aquarium, Lange once again wished he could cancel his contract. Aquarists have a saying: after ten years you refurbish the tanks, after twenty years you tear them down. Some of the technical installations at the Berlin aquarium were even older than that. In the early 1950s, when Schröder was rebuilding the aquarium, high-quality construction materials were in short supply, so he'd had to make do with what was available. In the decades since, the pipes and insulation had begun to crumble. The building was falling apart.

The Berlin Zoo was the oldest in Germany, and the institution's age was evident to Lange every day. Many things struck him as oddly formal and antiquated, and the atmosphere was much sterner than what he was used to in Stuttgart. Some of his early interactions were downright troubling. It wasn't long before Schröder warned him, "You can't believe anything Klös tells you over there at the zoo. He lies from morning to night."

The next day, when Lange stopped by the administration building, he ran into Klös. "Ah, you've just been at the aquarium, haven't you?" Klös asked. He took Lange aside and said in a quieter voice, "Listen, you can't believe a word Schröder says. He lies from morning to night."

◆

Lange went about things differently from Klös. He took on only apprentices who were in the third year of their rotation through the zoo, so that they could stay on at the aquarium as soon as their training ended, not up and leave for another temporary position. He entrusted these new hires with running the insectarium or the amphibian division. Elsewhere in the zoo that would have been inconceivable. Under Klös, only staff members who'd been working for at least ten years could be promoted to section head.

In the evenings, Lange often made the rounds of West Berlin's discotheques, not to dance, but to examine the generators and ceiling lights to gather ideas for more effective lighting for his tanks.

He also brought events to the aquarium—fashion shows and theater performances.

Klös thought this was far too much like the carnival atmosphere of the Oktoberfests in the 1940s and 1950s. When Lange was on vacation or a business trip, Klös seized the opportunity to tighten the reins at the aquarium, but the keepers refused to take orders from him. Disputes arose, with one word harsh leading to another.

"Tomorrow you can pack up your things!" Klös would shout.

"I quit!" the staff member would fire back.

When Lange returned, he would generally find one or two letters of resignation on his desk. As he heard his staff's stories, he would shake his head and ask, "Couldn't you keep your mouths shut for two weeks until I was back?" In the end he was always able to change their minds; none of the resignations went through.

Golden Times in the Golden Cage

West Berlin was a special place. Because it was isolated from the rest of the Federal Republic, its economy lagged several years behind that of "mainland" West Germany. Bullet holes could still be seen on the fronts of buildings, traces of urban military operations during World War II. At some street corners people could easily get the sense that the weapons had only recently fallen silent.

The "island in the Red sea" had to be buoyed by the Federal Republic. There was no free competition; everything was highly subsidized, from the construction industry to culture to nightlife to the zoo. Nepotism ruled.

Within this world, Klös had risen to a position of considerable power. He was the undisputed lord of the most popular recreational facility. He knew how to make patrons of the arts, men of independent means, and owners of department stores scramble to finance the next lion or elephant. Lange never failed to be amazed by how the director got so much money. When Klös first started working at the Zoo in 1957, he was sometimes underestimated. Now, people would whisper to each other, "Here comes old Klös. This will be expensive."

Local politicians were also aware of the importance of Klös's zoo. People said that anyone who picked a fight with the Berlin Zoo was done for. The director was not a party man, but he had the backing of the "Zoo Party," which had more members than any other. Klös told the newspaper *Die Zeit* in 1978 that he had "the world's best zoogoers." There were just about two million people living in West Berlin, and yet the zoo and the aquarium welcomed three million visitors annually, only a tenth of whom were tourists. West Berliners were impressed by the diligence and shrewdness with which Klös cared for their zoo, this one spot in the walled city that offered a hint of wilderness.

Klös's influence was not limited to West Berlin. When the sitting president of the Federal Republic visited the divided city, his agenda included not only the obligatory opening of hospital wards, but also a walk through the zoo. Klös planned to entice every president to the zoo at least once, although these outings didn't always go off without a hitch.

Theodor Heuss, the first man to serve as president of West Germany, had visited the zoo when Katharina Heinroth was still there. Heinrich Lübke, his successor, dabbled in microbiology in his spare time and was eager to make the trip. However, he was also known for making unfortunate remarks. When he saw the zoo's parrots gnawing on the branches in their cages in order to trim their growing beaks, he asked Klös, "How can you let the animals get so hungry that they eat wood?" Klös tried to laugh off the criticism, but Lübke wasn't finished. "Your parrots have such ruffled feathers," he continued. "Haven't you ever heard of trace elements?" When Klös took issue with the allegation that he wasn't feeding his parrots the right vitamins and minerals to promote healthy feather growth, Lübke replied, "You can't talk your way out of anything with me. Don't forget that I was once the minister of agriculture."

Lübke's successor, Gustav Heinemann, balked at the idea of visiting the Zoo, but the chief of protocol for Berlin's mayor insisted it was a must. So Heinemann agreed to go, although he did so sullenly. He had a better time there than he had expected, however, and when the chief of protocol started looking at his watch and reminding the president of his next appointment, Heinemann answered, "Oh, I like it here so much that I'd enjoy staying a little longer." Mayor Klaus Schütz, who was scheduled to join Heinemann in dedicating a new hospital in the neighborhood of Urbanhafen, had to wait three hours until the president wrapped up his visit to the zoo.

◆

Klös's ancestors came from a farm in central Hesse, in the rural middle of Germany, and he ran his zoo in the hands-on way a patriarch would oversee his lands. He could be quick-tempered and shout at the slightest provocation. But he could calm down just as quickly and act as though nothing had happened. The "Elder," as he was reverently referred to by the animal keepers, was always there—mornings, afternoons, evenings, and nights. He knew about everything: who was pitching in at which section, who was married, who had children and who did not.

His own children, though, rarely saw him. Like Dathe's, they had learned early on that their father's most important child was the zoo.

Klös managed his household the way he did his work, always believing that he was doing what was best for his family. As long as his children were still at his table, he wouldn't tolerate any dissent. His daughter Susanne put up a sign on the door to her room that read, "This place is hell." And whenever a fight broke out between Klös and his son, Heiner, Heiner would declare, "I never want to be like you!"

Heinz-Georg Klös would have loved for his son to take over for him at the zoo one day. He dreamed of the kind of dynasty the Hecks had enjoyed in Berlin for three generations—more than eight decades—which left an enduring imprint on Germany's zoos.

Klös tried to portray the history of the Berlin Zoo as a continuous and uninterrupted tradition dating back 130 years. An establishment of this sort had to be scrupulously built up and maintained—not plucked out of thin air like the Tierpark over in the East. In this spirit, he tried to patch things up with Katharina Heinroth, who was still living in Berlin and lecturing occasionally at universities. Heinroth, for her part, suspected he had something quite different in mind. "Klös just wants to get his hands on my inheritance," she told Werner Schröder and his wife, actress Inge Sievers-Schröder. Many elderly women in West Berlin remembered the zoo in their wills.

Heinroth happily played along, pretending in public to be reconciled with Klös and the board, and accepting rides in the zoo's chauffeured Mercedes. "They should keep clinging to the belief that they'll get my inheritance," she told her friends, "but my brother Lollo will get it no matter what." She called this her "little act of revenge." Her contented grin as she said it made her wrinkles look even more deeply etched into her face.

Klös also wanted to publicly recognize Heinroth's predecessor, Lutz Heck. At the 1977 convention of the German Federation of Zoo Directors, he proposed making the former director an honorary member of the group, as though that man's friendship with Hermann Göring, his use of forced laborers during World War II, and his expropriation of the shares of Jewish stockholders had never happened. Horrified, several members of the association threatened to resign and alert the press. This response surprised Klös, not because he had any affinity with National Socialism—quite the contrary—but because he regarded Lutz Heck first and foremost as a great zoologist who had helped the Berlin Zoological Garden attain world renown. Klös was also willing to overlook the fact that Heck had disappeared when the war ended, and then had the temerity to sue the zoo for outstanding pension payments.

Klös was pragmatic—or naive—about political matters in much the same way Dathe was: everything was fine as long as it worked to the benefit of his beloved zoo. They were the alpha males, and they had little tolerance for criticism. When Klös believed that someone had it in for his zoo, he took extreme action—especially when the threat came from someone like journalist Werner Philipp.

Klös had been following Philipp's career at West Berlin's *Der Tagesspiegel* for over a decade, since well before he'd tried to make the reporter the zoo's press officer. At times Klös would have loved to forbid Philipp to write his articles, which tended to be critical—and what Philipp had recently come out with had finally gone too far. A few small panes had cracked in the aquarium, Philipp wrote, and could easily have been replaced, except that, as was typical in sluggish West Berlin, things seemed to work according the principle "Never do today what you can put off till tomorrow."

When Klös next saw the journalist bicycling through the zoo, he rode up to him and braked sharply, so close to Philipp that gravel flew up from the ground. "You've written something bad about the aquarium again!" he shouted.

"So what?" Philipp snapped back. "It was true, wasn't it?"

"Yes," Klös answered, snorting with rage, "but you can't write something like that. From now on you're banned from the premises."

Philipp had no intention of accepting this ban, so he bought one of the Zoo's four thousand shares for 1,900 marks, reasoning that Klös couldn't keep a stockholder out of the zoo. Before long, they ran into each other again.

"What are you doing here now?" Klös asked in surprise.

"I'm a stockholder," Philipp answered. "At the next shareholders meeting I'll make sure we get a new director."

Klös didn't reply, but Philipp sensed from the director's face what he was thinking: "Philipp, you've got nerve!"

The zoo's alpha male wouldn't put up with dissension from his direct subordinates, but it seemed to please him that the journalist hadn't caved.

Schmidt's State Gifts

Klös aspired to make the Berlin Zoo the world's most biodiverse. But missing from his collection was a giant panda. In the mid-1960s, after passing on the opportunity to take in Chi Chi and watching as people flocked to Friedrichsfelde by the hundreds of thousands to see her there instead, he put out feelers to Willy Brandt, the city's former mayor who had become foreign minister—but to no avail. Apart from a pair that went to North Korea, China was no longer exporting pandas at that time.

Not until the early 1970s did the People's Republic gradually open up to the West, with so-called panda diplomacy playing a major role. Pandas were handpicked to be presented as state gifts to carefully selected countries. Japan was the first recipient, accepting a pair in 1971. The following year, Richard Nixon received two of the rare animals, which he had placed in the National Zoo in Washington, D.C. Two more went to Paris, and another two to London. In 1975, when West Germany's new federal chancellor, Helmut Schmidt, made his first visit to China, Klös couldn't help but get his hopes up—but Schmidt came back empty-handed. Klös had to look on as zoos in Mexico City and Madrid were given preference over Berlin.

When the Chinese premier, Hua Guofeng, announced that he would be visiting Bonn for a week in October 1979, Klös wrote a letter to Schmidt's wife. Loki Schmidt was a friend of Ursula Klös, so Klös made the bold suggestion that her husband should request "not vases or silk carpets, but rather pandas."

In early November he received a reply from the chancellor himself: "For you personally—but truly only for you! I wish to say the following: if we should get the panda bears, I will give them to Berlin."

Schmidt asked Klös to keep quiet about this promise. The federal election and several state elections were approaching, and other German zoos were hoping to get the pandas for themselves. But Klös, ever the optimist, had an enclosure designed, and was left scrambling to explain to the zoo's board what he intended to do with a glass annex to the predator house that would run up a bill of 750,000 marks. "This will be a play area for the baby animals," he fibbed. "We absolutely have to have one in case our big cats cast out their young and we have to hand-raise them." The board considered that plausible enough and approved the funds.

In the spring of 1980, Chancellor Schmidt at last instructed his spokesman to announce that pandas would be coming to Berlin. Schmidt intended the gesture to send a signal to the Soviets that West Berlin was a full part of West Germany. Vladimir Semyonov,

the Soviet ambassador, understood—and was affronted. He pro-
tested that West Berlin was ineligible to receive a state gift as the city
was not a part of the Federal Republic, but rather a "special political
entity." Berliners cared little about this semantic argument—they
were brimming with panda fever.

Klös's assistant, Hans Frädrich, took an extended trip abroad to
visit several zoos and learn what their pandas ate besides 20 kilo-
grams of bamboo per day. He discovered the animals' fondness for
chocolate, chopped meat, honey, spinach, rice, and gruel. The bamboo for Berlin's pandas would be imported from the south of France
twice a month and kept in the zoo's cold storage facility at 39 degrees
Fahrenheit.

Meanwhile, Berlin's journalists speculated about how to pro-
nounce and spell the names of the two pandas, who were already
accustomed to life in captivity from their time in the Chengdu Zoo.
The German press referred to the female as "Quan Quan," "Tschüan
Tschüan," "Tian Tian," or "Tjen Tjen," which translated to "the flaw-
less one," "the divine one," or "little heaven." The male was called
"Bao Bao," which meant "sweetie" or "darling."

The summer of 1980 gave way to fall, and still the pandas' arrival
kept being put off. First, the planned flight from Beijing was postponed when Lufthansa found out that the animals would have to be
looked after continuously. When the Chinese government started
wondering why things were taking so long, Schmidt instructed the
West German air force to fly the pandas to Germany. Defense Minister Hans Apel, however, objected that spending 150,000 marks
to transport two bears was just too much, whereupon negotiations
were taken up again with Lufthansa. Eventually it was decided that
three Chinese zookeepers would accompany the pandas on the
flight, and a departure date was set for October 1. But these arrange-

ments also came to naught. This time it was the Chinese authorities who balked; October 1 was a national holiday.

More than a month later, on November 5, at 2:05 p.m., the moment finally came. When the plane landed three hours late at Tempelhof Airport, the pandas were received as though they were state guests. A "Welcome to Berlin" sign was illuminated on the display board at the gate. Countless journalists were standing by, cameras flashing, as the pandas' metal crates were loaded onto a green VW bus and driven to the zoo, where several hundred visitors were already crowding around the bulletproof glass and singing the German equivalent of "For they are jolly good fellows!"

The new open-air enclosure looked like a cross between a solarium and a dog park. Bright blue tiles oozed all the charm of a hospital, yet in the papers the dwelling was touted in terms that suggested a lavish preschool. The pandas "can tromp across the sod that has been laid out for them, they can luxuriate in two swimming pools, they can climb up artificial trees and have fun on a swing," the *Hamburger Abendblatt* wrote. "Each panda has a sleeping area that measures 65 square feet, and a lounge 550 square feet in size, with a play corner and dining table, of course."

The pandas had three days to settle into their new home before Chancellor Schmidt stopped by for a visit. When he signed the zoo's guestbook, his wife added, underneath his entry, "The 'godmother,' Loki Schmidt, is especially delighted."

When the Schmidts and the Klöses gathered at the zoo restaurant for a celebratory drink, journalists asked the chancellor what he liked best about the pandas. "They're so wonderfully silent," he quipped. "We ought to vote them into the party executive committee."

Like so many zoo animals before them, the pandas quickly became Berlin celebrities. A picture of the two soon embellished decals alongside the text "Berlin does you good."

Little more than three years later, however, in February of 1984, Tjen Tjen's health declined rapidly. Over the course of several days she wasted away as one organ after the other failed. Veterinarians were baffled. When the zoo reported her death, the media coverage ran the gamut from sarcasm to sympathy. The left-leaning newspaper *taz* wrote a sneering piece about the "most tragic event since the death of Ernst Reuter," Berlin's former mayor who died in office of a heart attack, while the tabloid *B.Z.* ran a seven-page report, and a commentator on the broadcasting station *Sender Freies Berlin* mockingly called for a period of "national mourning." Even the outgoing mayor, Richard von Weizsäcker, commented on Tjen Tjen's death, calling her "a city VIP." In Berlin—and perhaps only there—this was nothing out of the ordinary. "In the walled-in city, a yearning for nature and a proverbial love of animals are at an all-time high," the magazine *Der Spiegel* wrote.

While veterinarians and pathologists were still investigating the cause of death, the public had already started speculating about whether it was the smog-laden Berlin air at fault or the KGB, seeking to snuff out the symbol of German-Chinese friendship. It turned out that the female panda had died of a viral infection. But whatever the cause of death, the era of panda diplomacy was over.

Eastern Stones for West Berlin

Paying his respects to Tjen Tjen was one of Richard von Weizsäcker's final acts as mayor. In May 1984 he was elected president of the Federal Republic and moved to Bonn. Before leaving West Berlin, he saw to it that one of the final makeshift arrangements from the postwar years disappeared from the Berlin Zoo.

Two years earlier, in August 1982, Weizsäcker had spent an evening in the Klös family's living room. He frequently visited the zoo, and the director usually invited him in afterward for a glass of red wine or a cheese sandwich. When Klös later walked with the mayor to the exit on Budapester Strasse, it was already growing dark. The two ticket booths with their gray-sprayed concrete facade and a wrought iron gate between them now looked even more dreary than they had during the daytime.

"This is where that lovely elephant gate once stood," Weizsäcker said to Klös somewhat hesitantly, as though he couldn't even imagine it while staring at the blocks of concrete.

"Yes," Klös echoed pensively, "that's where the elephant gate once stood."

Weizsäcker had fond memories of the old gate. In 1937, on the day before his college entrance exams, he'd gone to the zoo. Two stone elephant statues, almost life-size, had held up the expansive red entrance archway with a green tiled roof. Constructed in 1899, in Siamese style, the magnificent gate was designed to herald, even from afar, "that a realm of the exotic opens up here," as Lutz Heck, the former director, once wrote. Weizsäcker passed his exams the following day; the way he remembered it, the elephant gate brought him good luck. Six years later, in November 1943, the gate was destroyed by bombs.

Klös had often thought about how this area could be improved. It could be turned into an enclosure for African hoofed animals, with only a moat to separate it from the downtown neighborhood of City West. Even a dolphinarium was discussed, although Klös rejected that idea as financially imprudent.

Lost in thought, he gazed at the two wretched ticket booths.

"Why haven't you rebuilt them?" Weizsäcker asked.

"Zoo funds are earmarked for specific purposes," Klös explained. "I have to build more animal houses before I can worry about entryways."

Weizsäcker examined the gate, grabbing the wrought iron bars with one hand. "But surely it would be nice if there were a stately entrance here again, instead of something like this."

Klös grinned. "Well then, Mayor, how about you try to get us a gate?" he said. "Although I don't know whether the Class Lottery would make money available for that."

Many of the zoo's structures had been paid for with funds from the German Class Lottery, an authorized betting ring that raised money for the state, but Weizsäcker was well aware that this money could only be used for animal housing. "No," he said. "It has to be something involving animals. But if it is, the sum could easily go higher."

It hadn't occurred to Klös to think of combining the gate with a new enclosure, though he'd wanted to replace the nondescript pens directly behind the entrance for a long time.

"I'll figure something out," he promised the mayor as they parted.

A few weeks later, Weizsäcker had a design for an "Asia enclosure with elephant gate" on his desk. Klös had even found the original plans for the old elephant gate, although the zoo archive had been destroyed in the war; former director Lutz Heck had saved them. Construction was projected to cost a hefty 16 million marks. Hardly anyone knew that the gate was not an add-on, but the very reason for the project. The city gave the green light to invite competitive bidding.

Two West German companies submitted bids for the project.

There was only one problem: the columns of the original elephant gate had been made out of Elbe Sandstone, and the only place to get that was from a quarry in the Elbe Sandstone Mountains, outside Pirna—in the German Democratic Republic.

Shortly before Klös could decide which bid to accept, a man with a Saxon accent showed up at the zoo. He introduced himself as the general director of the State-Owned Enterprise for Elbe Natural Stone in Dresden.

"Why don't you order the gate directly from us?" he asked.

"I already have two bids from companies in the Federal Republic," Klös replied.

"They always come to us anyway," his guest said. "They don't lift a finger. All they do is rake in money."

The director of the State-Owned Enterprise for Elbe Natural Stone eventually made Klös an offer that was markedly lower than those of the two West German companies—and whenever Klös could save money, he was happy to pounce. But this time was somewhat more complicated, because it would entail doing business with an East German company.

No sooner had the visitor gone than Klös called up Weizsäcker and told him about the new bid. "They're only half as expensive," he said.

"Well then, let's take them," Weizsäcker answered happily.

The Dresden company got the commission, and the West Berlin city government quietly drew up a contract with the GDR.

◆

The dedication ceremony for the reconstructed elephant gate was held in October 1986. The Saxon stonemasons who'd faithfully re-created the gate were invited to the event. Only Richard von

Weizsäcker was not in attendance; by that time he'd left West Berlin for Bonn. At first Klös worried that Weizsäcker's successor would object to the contract with the GDR, but the new mayor, Eberhard Diepgen, also approved. In his opening remarks, he praised "the pan-German achievement that is now enriching the center of our city."

The only shadow that fell over the zoo's stone guardians came from the adjacent Europa-Center, as the afternoon sun slowly set behind the towers of City West.

The End of an Era

Two years later, the people of West Berlin would bid farewell to one of their favorite animals. Knautschke the hippopotamus had been injured so severely in a fight with his son Nante that he had to be put to sleep on June 20, 1988.

With the death of Knautschke, the Berlin Zoo lost its most prominent resident of the postwar era. Generations of children had grown up with the hippo; for many people, he was one of them. Knautschke had been born in 1943, a war baby who stayed put on the island that was West Berlin his entire life. The hippo had lived in the city for forty-five years and sired thirty-five calves during that time. (Berliners were unperturbed by the fact that almost all of these calves were a result of inbreeding.)

Knautschke was an integral part of the zoo in much the same way that the actor Harald Juhnke was an integral part of his favorite bar on nearby Savignyplatz. Only in West Berlin, where an exaggerated love of animals and local patriotism combined to form a kitschy sort of hero worship, could a hippo become a symbol for an entire city.

A few days after Knautschke's death, the tabloid *B.Z.* published a
letter to the editor in the form of a poem:

> I'm standing here beside your pool
> And that you've died just seems so cruel.
> Although the age you reached is high
> It's still so hard to say goodbye.
>
> Forty years ago I came to you
> My dad and I, off to the zoo.
> Our stomachs empty, feet so chilled
> Alone this whole big pool you filled.
> The warmth here was quite a reprieve
> No one would ever want to leave.
>
> Now you're gone, you're not within,
> And we have lost some of Berlin.

The most popular animal on the island was gone—and before long
the island itself would be too.

CHAPTER 8

THE GRAY GIANT COMES TUMBLING DOWN

One evening, early in 1986, Heinrich Dathe came home even later than usual. When his wife asked him if he'd had something to eat, he said that he hadn't, adding, "I really didn't have the time." He was grappling with a major problem, and had had to meet with several prominent men from the agricultural sector to talk them into providing two greenhouses. Greenhouses were in short supply in the GDR, as they were urgently needed to grow vegetables. But Dathe needed two to build a long-planned tropical hall for his crocodiles, which were still being housed either with the snakes or in an outbuilding behind the Alfred Brehm House. Some had already grown so large that they filled out their glass tanks completely and adapted their shapes to fit the space. Several of their snouts had actually grown vertically, making it impossible for them to eat on their own; they had to be hand-fed.

Dathe had to go to great lengths to get any new facilities at all; other construction sites kept taking precedence. A new high-rise building had recently been added to the Charité university clinic, an ostentatious showcase of a hospital not far from the Wall that could be seen from West Berlin. The Lichtenberg train station had opened a new entrance hall, and even the city's French Cathedral had undergone renovations.

As usual, improvisation was called for. In 1984, Dathe had received a barred dome-shaped structure from an agricultural production cooperative that had been designed for housing tractors. He was happy to get it, as he could put pretty much anything to good use. A team of laborers spent months of after-hours work transforming the dome into an aviary for seagulls.

Dathe was exasperated that the Tierpark's expansion was moving so slowly. It'd been like this for years. The unfinished tapir house had been torn down rather than completed, and while a new pachyderm house was supposed to have been built by the beginning of the decade, all there was to show for it were plans gathering dust in some drawers. The elephants were still living in their makeshift stable. When the first two females, Dombo and Bambi, had moved in in 1955, the shelter was supposed to be a temporary measure, but "temporary" had turned into three decades. In the following year, Berlin would be commemorating its 750th anniversary. Dathe imagined it would be embarrassing if there were no new building to mark the occasion. Sometimes he thought it might be better for there to be no celebration at all.

The zoo staff was unhappy too. One Stasi Informal Collaborator bemoaned the lack of exacting anniversary plans; there was little to report other than "that the painting and locksmith guilds will help overhaul the existing enclosures."

Most of Dathe's visions fell victim to the GDR's flagging economy, but one did succeed. For a long time he'd been planning to construct buildings on a mountain of rubble in the northeastern part of the park. He already had definite ideas about what should go there.

In 1984, when his counterparts in West Berlin came for their yearly visit, Dathe brought them down muddy paths and up to the landfill. The wind whipped around their ears while Dathe spoke in the pouring rain about the future. With a big sweep of his hand he pointed down the hillside. "Over there we'll soon have spacious enclosures for mountain animals," he said. Klös's eyes widened in surprise. He couldn't imagine how a dreary slope with bits of birch trees and brushwood could be turned into an attractive animal enclosure. But before Klös could get a word in, Dathe continued trudging up the hillside to a rough area at the top. He stopped at the edge of a puddle and said, "And here there will be a café where we'll sit on the terrace and look out over the entire city!"

Dathe's neighbors had done everything they could to foil this plan. At the foot of the hill, behind a gray concrete wall, stood the Stasi district administration building. If there was anything the secret police wanted to prevent, it was coffee-drinking Tierpark visitors watching their every move.

But the Stasi also knew by now that it was not so easy to talk Dathe out of his plans. Several Informal Collaborators kept the police in the loop about the director's intentions for the café—and time was on their side. The minutes of an Informal Collaborator meeting in the spring of 1986 noted that even if Dathe were eventually permitted to build his café, at least five years would elapse before construction got underway, and another five before it opened. Even the Stasi counted on the slowness of the state.

Not that the Stasi had it in for Dathe's zoo. Quite the contrary—the Tierpark was an asset that could be used to present the GDR in a positive light, and so the secret police sought to maintain its international renown. When an informant from the Tierpark's senior management reported that West Berlin's zoo director was trying to divide the annual Symposium on Disorders of Zoo Animals and Wildlife, which had always been held in East Berlin, between the city's Eastern and Western halves, the Stasi jumped in to prevent this from happening. "Tierpark Berlin has many friends in various countries, including the United States," an internal memo noted, "and they are informed by these friends about the actions of Prof. Dr. Klös."

Greedy Gifts

While Dathe focused on getting materials to develop his spacious site, Heinz-Georg Klös was running out of ideas for where to put his animals. The biggest problem was a lack of space. He'd recently expanded the zoo by seven and a half acres, and yet the director's passion for collecting still led to double occupancies. In some enclosures the animals had to use the space in shifts. The hyenas, for instance, could be let out onto the large outdoor installation at the predator house only at night, when the lions were asleep in their cages.

All the same, Klös tried to use the city's upcoming anniversary to get even more animals. He'd already been pestering the mayor, Eberhard Diepgen, for some time. "Have the guests of honor bring along animals for our Zoo," he wrote, enclosing a wish list: cranes and pelicans from Australia, fallow deer and red deer from Denmark, spectacled bears from Ecuador, okapis from Zaire, elephants from Thailand, Sumatran rhinoceroses from Indonesia, and Indian rhinoceroses from Nepal and the United States. Los Angeles, Berlin's sister city, had a full herd of rhinoceroses in its zoo, and he was eager to get a female he could breed.

Few of his wishes were fulfilled. Some turned him down, or cited export restrictions; others didn't even bother to reply. Although the mayor of Los Angeles brought two animals with him when he came for a visit in May 1987, they were a pair of fishers, weasel-like mammals found in large numbers on the West Coast of North America.

Klös was underwhelmed by these unwanted gifts, yet he had no choice but to accept them with a show of happiness. He could, of course, understand that his American colleague didn't want to hand over any of his more valuable animals, preferring to send ones he could easily do without. After all, Klös had done something similar back when Willy Brandt was mayor in the 1960s.

When Brandt had gone on business trips, he'd enjoyed taking along a young brown bear as a present for the local zoo, whether or not the recipients had need of one. He thought there was no more suitable gift than a living specimen of Berlin's mascot. Before leaving on his trips, he always called up Klös and said in his rather hoarse voice, "I need another bear."

The director had been happy to oblige. Breeding bears wasn't very difficult, and Berlin's were reproducing so abundantly that they were sometimes given birth control pills. Of course the young bears grew up quickly and would soon look less cute and take up precious space. Thanks to Brandt's lack of imagination when it came to gift giving, Klös no longer had to worry about what to do with the adolescents.

While brown bears were a sure crowd pleaser, fishers were rarely kept in European zoos, as the nocturnal predators could hardly ever be seen; they spent most of the day sleeping indoors. Even Klös seldom caught sight of one. Every time he asked the animal keepers about their whereabouts, he got the same terse response: "They're always inside the building when you come, boss."

At one point, a few weeks went by during which only one of the fishers was seen. Deaths in the aviary were also growing more frequent. Several geese, a cockatoo, and two rare cranes had already been killed. The keepers couldn't explain what had happened. The culprit wasn't a fox; it had to be something larger. Eventually, Klös thought to have the fishers' lair examined. When a keeper opened the lid of the wooden crate, he found only one of the two animals, gazing up at him sleepily.

Klös was beside himself with anger. "I don't care how you do it," he hollered at his staff, "but bring me back that damned fisher!"

Luckily, the escaped animal was found shortly, holed up in a shed near the petting zoo, having a nap.

◆

Meanwhile, at the Tierpark, construction was—shockingly—moving ahead. Dathe had finally been able to obtain two greenhouses for his crocodiles' tropical hall, as well as authorization to build a new pachyderm house. Architect Heinz Graffunder, who'd drawn up the plans for the Alfred Brehm House for big cats, oversaw the design. Graffunder was by now well versed in crafting housing for humans as well, and had made a name for himself in the GDR. Since his last work for the zoo, he'd received a commission to design the Palace of the Republic, the seat of the East German government.

By early 1987, construction on the pachyderm house was well underway. It would be even larger than the predator house, with 65,000 square feet, enough space to breed African and Asiatic elephants as well as rhinoceroses and pygmy hippopotamuses.

Sadly, Dathe had little time to relish this triumph. On April 16, his wife died of heart disease at the age of sixty-eight. Elisabeth had been unwell for quite some time, but had never thought to go to the hospital. Without her, the Dathe household ceased to function. She had freed her husband from many responsibilities, taking care of the house and their children and even typing his manuscripts, which enabled him to devote himself completely to his scientific work. All of a sudden, he was on his own. The children had grown up and moved away, and Heinrich Dathe was not the sort of person who'd be comfortable alone. To blunt the pain, he did what he did best: he threw himself into his work.

Luckily there was plenty for him to do. In August, the crocodile house opened, and in September he hosted zoo directors from every corner of the world for a five-day conference on "Zoos and the Environment." He guided the visitors through his Tierpark as though nothing was amiss, giving one speech after another and trying not to let on about his recent loss. Although he would soon be turning seventy-seven, he had no desire to stop working and the municipal authorities gave no indication that the time was coming for him to step down. He barely gave any thought to what retirement might be like. There were still a good number of manuscripts piled up on his desk that he wanted to publish and a great deal else to get done.

While the shell of the pachyderm house was growing rapidly, the building wasn't yet habitable—but already four young African elephants had arrived from Zimbabwe, and two Asian elephants were on their way from Moscow. The old elephant stable was getting more and more cramped, and the keepers needed all the help they could find, even if that help came in the form of Patric Müller, who was still in training.

In 1986, sixteen-year-old Müller had begun his apprenticeship as an animal keeper. The program rotated him through almost all the sections of the Tierpark, but from the outset he much preferred working with the elephants. The older keepers soon noticed that he had a knack for dealing with the most challenging animals, unlike most of the other trainees, who lacked the levelheadedness and natural authority to show an elephant—who could weigh a good three tons and have the intelligence of a five-year-old child—who was in charge. Sometimes the elephants would stage mock attacks, only the keepers wouldn't know until afterward whether it had been a mock attack or a real one—assuming they even survived. In 1963, the West Berlin zoo's eleven-year-old bull, Salim, gored his keeper in front of horrified onlookers. Müller soon learned the trick in these situations was to stand still, but even so, he sometimes went weak-kneed; he knew that what might feel like a gentle push to a playful or irritated elephant could be lethal for him. For this reason, many elephant keepers regarded themselves as a kind of elite among zoo staff, with the most dangerous job of all. A predator keeper has only to open a sliding gate to let lions, tigers, or leopards in and out of their cages; there's no way to avoid direct contact with an elephant. When the visitors left the Tierpark in the evening, some elephant keepers even rode their charges through the grounds to the construction site, so that the elephants would get used to the route to their new home.

Müller was living in a housing cooperative that required him to spend a certain number of hours doing construction work each week, so he figured he might as well pitch in at the pachyderm house. He and his colleagues quickly noticed a flaw in the design: the doors were mounted in a way that prevented the keepers from getting their wheelbarrows through. There was also another far more worrying flaw.

Dathe had asked for the new section to be designed according to the "Leipzig principle" of a raised enclosure surrounded by a deep moat. It was the old model of the zoo as a stage, an analogy he'd gotten to know during his time in Leipzig and had been using ever since the Tierpark had opened. But this construction method was now considered outdated, because it posed too many risks. The moat was shaped like a funnel, and with no fence or rope to get in the way of the visitors' view, there was a risk that an elephant might fall in. If one did, there was no easy way into the moat to rescue it.

The keepers couldn't just go to Dathe and register their complaint; there were fixed protocols to be respected. So they pointed out the problem to the zoo's inspectors. Some minor faults were corrected, but the moat's basic design remained unchanged. Dathe planned to keep the elephants chained up at night to keep them from falling into the water in the dark. The keepers tried not to imagine what would happen if one of the animals managed to break free.

In the late summer of 1989, the elephants moved into their new home. Tall palm trees, creeping figs, rubber and eucalyptus trees planted inside the building gave the space a junglelike atmosphere. The only thing still missing was the doors. Until they were installed, the keepers would have to stay for night shifts to ensure the animals' safety. Patric Müller took advantage of the opportunity to impress his new girlfriend, whom he invited to tag along. Where else in the East could you spend the night beneath palm trees? A vacation in Bulgaria might afford the opportunity, but certainly nowhere else in the GDR. As it turned out, however, the night was less romantic than Müller had hoped. The elephants kept rustling loudly with bales of hay—and farting.

With its sixteen-meter-high roof, gray prefab walls, and large, mostly empty interior, the pachyderm house looked like a combination of concrete slab, greenhouse, and factory. It was outmoded by the time it opened. The long planning and construction periods posed a particular problem for zoo design; by the time an enclosure was finally complete, standards had often evolved. In the West, six or seven years could elapse from planning to completion; in the East, a lack of materials and skilled workers could double that time. Dathe had had to wait almost fifteen years for this new elephant house, only three of which were spent actually building the thing (quite nearly a speed record). At least the new building, however unfashionable, was an improvement over the old elephant stable.

The pachyderm house officially opened in late September 1989. Dathe proudly announced in front of East Berlin's mayor, Erhard Krack, Politburo member Günter Schabowski—an inveterate animal lover—and numerous colleagues that this was "likely to be the biggest building that will ever stand in the Tierpark."

It would also be the last building that he and architect Graffunder worked on together, and the very last one to be constructed in the Tierpark while Dathe was in charge.

News of the new attraction quickly got around, and people streamed into the Tierpark in record numbers—3.2 million visitors as the year drew to a close, a record that would never be surpassed. Protests were slowly gaining strength throughout the country, and soon there would be more important matters on people's minds than new houses for big animals.

On the Go

Thousands of East Germans traveled to Hungary in the summer of 1989, as they did every year. But now everything was different. This year, the goal was not to take a vacation, but to get to the West.

In May, the Hungarian government, loath to spend money on renovations, had issued an order to dismantle the rotting border fence between Hungary and Austria, putting the first gap in the Iron Curtain. When horrified GDR leaders prohibited travel to Hungary, people went by way of Poland and Czechoslovakia, flooding into West German embassies in Warsaw and Prague.

The keepers at East Berlin's Tierpark continued feeding their animals and mucking out stables day in and day out, but many of them found their thoughts drifting in a very different direction. On October 2, the Stasi learned from an Informal Collaborator that "topic no. 1 among the animal keepers is leaving the GDR."

Three days earlier, Hans-Dietrich Genscher, West Germany's foreign minister, who'd been born in Halle (now part of East Germany), appeared on the balcony of the German embassy in Prague, looking like a silhouette against the floodlights. Genscher had given many speeches, and often talked quite a lot without really saying anything new. This time, he said little. "Today, your departure . . ." he began, addressing the hundreds of people waiting down in the embassy garden. He couldn't get any further. The sounds of rejoicing drowned him out.

Those who'd stayed home didn't want to wait any longer either. Resistance took hold. One of the centers was the Gethsemane Church in East Berlin, where members of the opposition held vigils for political prisoners and kept tabs on other protests throughout the country by telephone. One of the elephant keepers at the Tierpark was among the regulars there. Müller and his colleagues covered for him to keep him from getting into trouble, doing all his work.

In Leipzig demonstrators had already been gathering every Monday evening for months to call for reforms, including the freedom to travel. Over the course of the year, their numbers swelled from a few hundred to several thousand. Jörg Adler was among them. He'd worked his way up at the Leipzig Zoo from a simple animal keeper to head of the primate section, studying both veterinary medicine and agricultural science. He was authorized to travel all the way to Vietnam to bring lions to the country in exchange for native elephants. Even though there were three research assistants technically above him in the zoo's hierarchy, he was director Siegfried Seifert's right-hand man.

Outside the walls of the zoo, however, things had become increasingly dangerous. Since the early 1980s Adler had attended Monday prayer meetings at Leipzig's St. Nicholas Church, where he'd witnessed the Stasi and the People's Police arresting people. The rear window of his Trabant sported a sign boasting of another Leipzig parish in such large print that anyone driving behind his car could read it: "Leipzig-Grünau—the first new church in the GDR." Since he'd stuck up the sign, he was constantly being stopped by the police for questioning on all kinds of trivial pretexts. On one of his trips to Berlin someone even tried to force him off the road. When his daughter was rejected from a music program for political reasons, he decided it was high time to apply to emigrate.

Three years passed. In mid-September 1989, Adler was finally summoned to the Department of Internal Affairs, the cover name for the regional Stasi. Scores of would-be Leipzig emigrants were beating a path to its door. Adler had to wait for a while before he was called into one of the offices, where a gray-haired official sitting behind a gray desk told him, "If you don't engage in political activities on October 7 and don't appear in public on that day, you can assume that you and your family will be able to leave the GDR by the end of the year."

On October 7, the GDR would be celebrating its fortieth anniversary. Few suspected that this would also be its last—not even Adler, who made his way home and said to his wife, "Here goes." She knew what that meant: any day now, they could be gone. They began to prepare for their departure, packing their bags, giving their friends everything they couldn't take with them. But the hardest task of all for Jörg Adler still lay ahead: to explain himself to Siegfried Seifert, the man who had shaped his career more than anyone else.

With a queasy feeling, he went to see the Leipzig Zoo director in his office the following morning. "Herr Professor," he said in a hoarse voice, "I need to talk with you."

"Not here," Seifert interrupted, pointing to the walls. They went outdoors and strolled through the zoo until they came to a park bench where they could speak without being monitored.

Adler felt like a traitor to his mentor, without whom he would never have risen so high. Seifert was the one who'd urged him to continue his education. Seifert had even found a way for Adler to get around joining the party.

One day in the early 1980s, two Socialist Unity Party representatives had come to Seifert to ask why Adler had yet to become a member. With a look of concern, Seifert told them, "Unfortunately you've come too late, gentlemen. Herr Adler recently joined the Christian Democratic Union." No sooner were they gone than Seifert picked up the phone and made a few calls.

"I've taken care of everything," he explained to a bemused Adler. "All you have to do is come here and sign, and you'll have been a member of the CDU since the beginning of the year."

Adler spent a year attending Leipzig's city council meetings. He had no intention of sitting around and doing nothing, so he advocated for a women's rights group, and—far more scandalous—decried the city's air pollution. Eventually his fellow party members suggested that it would probably be better for him to withdraw from active participation in politics. Still, something good came out of his brief foray: the Socialist Unity Party left him alone from then on.

Now, Adler had to tell his mentor that his request to emigrate would soon be granted. "I'll be going," he said softly.

Siegfried Seifert had always been only as loyal to the regime as was absolutely necessary, but he could hardly hide his disappointment. After a moment of silence he said, "But I wanted to make you my successor."

Adler was flattered, but he didn't think he'd be the right person for the Leipzig Zoo. And besides, he'd made up his mind. He wanted to get out.

Still, he refused to abide by the Stasi's demand to keep a low profile—he wasn't about to be intimidated. Together with his wife and some four thousand other demonstrators, he spent October 7 on Leipzig's Karl Marx Platz at the corner of Grimmaische Strasse, facing water cannons used for riot control. Throughout the country, people were taking to the streets. There were more than two hundred arrests in Leipzig alone, but Jörg Adler was not among them.

Then came the evening of October 9. It was a Monday, which meant that there would be protests in Leipzig, as usual. Nobody knew what would happen. There were reports that orders had been given to shoot, and that hospitals had stepped up their requests for blood donations. Everyone remembered the images from Beijing where only that summer the Chinese military had brutally suppressed protests on Tiananmen Square. In the GDR rumors of a "Chinese solution" were making the rounds.

Even so, seventy thousand people showed up that evening in Leipzig. They moved through the streets with candles in their hands, singing the socialist anthem, "The Internationale." Government officials weren't prepared for such crowds, and could only look on. Shouts, not shots, filled the air as the marchers made their way through the city streets. Jörg Adler and countless others sensed that on this evening a movement had started that could no longer be stopped. Still, no one anticipated what would happen one month later in Berlin, when, on November 9, Socialist Unity Party spokesman Günter Schabowski announced a relaxing of travel laws at a press conference in Berlin. When asked by a journalist when the new legislation would take effect, he distractedly said immediately. That night, East Germans stormed the Wall. They streamed past astonished border guards and through the doors to West Berlin. When traditional entrances wouldn't let them out quickly enough, the crowd hacked new ones. After twenty-eight years, the Wall was finally falling. After that, Adler knew it was just a matter of time until his application to emigrate was approved. There was no reason for the state to drag things out any longer. By this point, the Adlers could simply travel to Berlin and climb over the remnants of the Wall.

Over the coming days East Germans streamed en masse into West Berlin and the Federal Republic of Germany. Eight hundred thousand people who'd been penned in for so long used their newfound freedom to have a look at the animals at the Berlin Zoo, which offered them free admission for two weeks. Most knew the zoo only from their parents' and grandparents' stories. From the main entrance on Hardenbergplatz, the lines stretched out for several blocks, all the way to Budapester Strasse. People stood in amazement in front of the enclosures, although here and there a child chimed in with comments like, "But our elephant house is much bigger."

Nine miles to the east, at the Tierpark, only a skeleton crew had showed up for work. Everyone wanted to see for themselves whether the Wall was truly down.

◆

In all the confusion, Dathe worried what would become of his Tierpark. For the closing paragraph of his 1989 annual report—which listed all the special distinctions members of staff had been awarded as well as which animals had given birth, how many visitors had come, and how much bratwurst and broiled chicken they had consumed—he wrote:

> Societal changes in our country necessitate not only an adjustment in thinking, but also an enhanced personal commitment from the entire Tierpark collective in order to achieve a successful activation of the new aspects of our endeavors. This should also function as a pledge on behalf of the Tierpark collective for 1990 and the years ahead.

Dathe understood the danger of having two zoos in one city. When the Tierpark first opened, the "zoo of the future" seemed to be putting the cramped, old zoo in the West out of business. The Wall made for clear boundaries—and a reliable stream of visitors for decades. But now Heinrich Dathe and Heinz-Georg Klös were again rivals in a city that maybe wasn't big enough for the both of them. Dathe had actually wanted to retire at some as yet unspecified time, but with this turn of events he felt it was his duty to remain. Who else besides him would do what was needed?

Lothar Dittrich, his longtime acquaintance from their time together in Leipzig, advised him to step down. "You've accomplished everything," he said to Dathe, who was more than twenty years his senior. "Now would be the right time to leave the future of the Tierpark to others."

Dathe saw the situation differently. "No, no, you're wrong," he replied. "I'm the only one here who has seen how a zoo is run under nonsocialist conditions."

Dittrich was astonished and a bit amused, and shook his head as he explained, "This is a completely different capitalism from the one you got to know in the 1930s."

But Dathe wasn't listening.

Inge Sievers-Schröder, the widow of former aquarium director Werner Schröder, also warned him, "Klös will throw you out, just as he did my husband." Dathe didn't believe her either and made light of her concerns. "Nothing will happen to me," he insisted.

Several days after the fall of the Wall he met up with his rival to talk about the future of the two zoos. The West Berlin city government was responsible for financing the zoo, but the Tierpark was still under the control of the cultural affairs department of the East Berlin municipal authorities.

"Believe me, dear colleague," said Klös, who wanted to persuade Dathe to place both facilities under the control of the Department of Finance. "That has always worked well for the zoo. It would definitely be the best thing for everyone, including you."

"That may be your experience," Dathe replied. "But a zoo is a cultural institution. And I see no reason to change that."

◆

Still, many changes did occur—and not only in Berlin. Members of the German Federation of Zoo Directors pondered how to deal with colleagues from the foundering GDR. In 1968 they had left the association under pressure from their government. Now they could be readmitted, but some had misgivings about the East German directors, especially about Dathe. There were those who figured that a man in his position—the director of the most important zoo in the GDR—could only have made it as far as he had by being extremely loyal to the regime.

Heinz-Georg Klös suggested that all newcomers be evaluated on a case-by-case basis to see whether they'd cozied up to the Socialist Unity Party. Lothar Dittrich, who had known Dathe longer than most, and Wolfgang Gewalt, who didn't think much of any of Klös's suggestions, were against this idea. "We don't want to sit in judgment on a man with as complicated a life as Dathe," Dittrich said. He recommended readmitting all of the East German directors.

And that's the way it was handled. In 1991, the zoo directors from the former GDR were invited back, and Wolfgang Puschmann, from Magdeburg, was elected to the executive board. Only Dieter Schwarz, from Rostock, who was exposed as an Informal Collaborator, was barred from the association.

◆

Meanwhile, at Tierpark Friedrichsfelde, the animal keepers found that the Free German Trade Union Federation no longer represented their interests effectively, so in January 1990, elephant keeper Patric Müller and several colleagues set up a spokesmen's council, one of the first in the GDR. The old East German trade unionists offered no resistance. Presumably they weren't eager to grapple with the problems facing animal keepers, or maybe they had a sense that a new era was dawning, and it might be better if representatives of the old system stepped aside.

The animal keepers weren't aiming for a revolution; they just wanted greater worker participation in decision making. They asked their colleagues in the various sections what they'd like to see improved day to day, and compiled wish lists from what they learned. They also sought more of a say in determining the overall composition of the animal collection. In the past, keepers often hadn't learned that animals had been sold until they were gone. That had to change.

Dathe was known for his fits of rage, which were generally directed at his research associates. His ire usually pertained to everyday operations or construction work that failed to move ahead at the pace he thought they should. But Müller had also seen another side to the director. Dathe listened to what he had to say and seemed to take staff concerns seriously. Müller finally felt that he could contribute his ideas.

But this state of affairs didn't continue for long. It took just half a year for West German trade unions to impose themselves on the East.

The Eagle Lands in the Aviary

In Leipzig, Jörg Adler's expatriation had finally been approved. Shortly before Christmas of 1989 he and his wife, his daughter, and his two sons traveled southwest to a reception camp in Giessen and from there north to a field office in Schöppingen, where they were given train tickets to a destination of their choice. They took a bus to the train station in nearby Münster, and because it would be a while before their train left, went on a short walk to the historic city center.

All Jörg Adler had known about Münster came from a couple of black-and-white photos of the newly opened zoo taken in the 1970s. They'd made quite an impression on him back then, but that was no comparison to what he now saw when he reached the Prinzipalmarkt on the final day of the Christmas market. The medieval gabled houses were aglitter with festive lights. Everyone was hurrying past to make one last purchase. The Adlers were standing right in the middle of a strange, seemingly idyllic world that was so different from gray Leipzig, where even at Christmastime the stench from the lignite and cars with old two-stroke engines was overpowering.

From Münster they continued their travels to Kempten in Bavaria to celebrate Christmas with friends. Then it was on to spend New Year's at the Wilhelma Zoo in Stuttgart, where they stayed in a staff apartment within the ape house, sharing a wall with the gorillas. All the while, Adler was searching for a new job. Luckily he knew a few zookeepers in the West. And if there was one person who could help him, it was Wolfgang Gewalt in Duisburg.

Since the late 1980s, the Duisburg Zoo had been a veritable reception camp for zookeepers from the entire Eastern Bloc. Gewalt was happy to help everyone who had turned his or her back on communism. The former director of the Erfurt Zoo, Fritz Dietrich Altmann, who had fled to Austria by way of Hungary, had stayed in the Duisburg ape house, and two Eastern European animal keepers were given lodgings on the grounds. Gewalt—who had ulterior motives of his own—made a staff apartment available for the Adler family in the aviary, and lost no time in communicating this fact to the local press. A few days later, Adler read the headlines—which played on his surname (which meant "eagle"): "Adler family from the East finds sanctuary in the aviary."

Over the coming days, Gewalt took Adler along to public appointments. At a Christian Democratic Union function he even introduced him to West German chancellor Helmut Kohl, who was impressed by Adler's story and immediately sent for one of his aides to help him out, although not much came of that.

In the long run there was no place for Adler in Duisburg either, so his odyssey went on. In late January he and his family went to Berlin. He had met Heinz-Georg Klös back in Leipzig, and Adler would have liked to move to the capital and work in the zoo. But Klös had no opening for him, although he did have an idea of who might. He called up several colleagues and finally got the information he sought from Lothar Dittrich in Hanover: the all-weather zoo in Münster was looking for another section head.

This was the city in which Adler's journey had begun a good

month earlier. Even more serendipitous, this was the very zoo whose massive concrete buildings he had so admired all those years before, when they'd seemed so much more progressive than the ramshackle ape house in Leipzig. This new position seemed meant to be.

The Gray Giant Comes Tumbling Down

In less than a year the GDR would be history, but no one thought that 1990 would also be Dathe's final year in his Tierpark. The animal keepers were preoccupied with more quotidian concerns.

On April 7, early in the morning, Dathe was called into the pachyderm house. When he arrived, several zookeepers were standing in front of the Asian elephants' area, trying to calm down the agitated females, who were pulling at the chains on their feet. When Dathe approached, he saw Dombo, the matriarch, lying on her back in the moat.

"She must have torn herself away from the chain at night and fallen down," one of the keepers said. What his colleagues had feared as far back as the construction phase had come to pass. Unable to turn herself right-side-up in the moat's tight space, Dombo had suffocated under the weight of her own legs.

Two days later, readers of *Neues Deutschland* could see for themselves, on the bottom left corner of page three, how the lifeless body of the elephant was attached to ropes and pulled out of the moat of the pachyderm pavilion. Two despondent zookeepers stood next to her, trying to heave the huge cadaver in the proper direction.

It was another blow for Dathe. His son Falk had never seen him so disconsolate. The elephant's death came at a time when the director feared for the continued existence of the Tierpark and for the future of its more than four hundred employees—not to mention his own life's work. The demise of the gray giant seemed like an omen of things to come.

In spite of his fears for the future, Dathe appeared confident in public. He was quoted in *Neues Deutschland* on September 8, saying, "I agree with Prof. Dr. Heinz-Georg Klös, my colleague in West Berlin, that a city like this one needs two cultural institutions of this kind, particularly as they have different characters." When asked whether he'd thought about retiring, he answered simply, "I have. But here there's still so much I have to do." The next month he again emphasized, this time to the *Berliner Zeitung*, that the city's two zoos were "of differing structure and differing character."

◆

Still, the two halves of Berlin would have to coalesce. Decades of division had required everything to be duplicated, including the city's government. Since the local elections the previous May, the two municipalities had been governing jointly, with politicians commuting back and forth between two city halls, the Rathaus in Schöneberg in the West and the Rotes Rathaus on Alexanderplatz in the East. With cutbacks looming, the public now began to discuss whether Berlin really needed, and could finance, two zoos.

Heinrich Dathe considered it his duty to keep the Tierpark open. In the nearly four decades he had lived in Friedrichsfelde, he had grown up, grown old, and grown together with his zoo. His villa on the Tierpark grounds was chockful of things he had accumulated over the years—from scientific articles and books to unfinished manuscripts, all piled high on his desk. "I live to work" had always been his motto.

On November 7, 1990, the Tierpark held a celebration to mark

Heinrich Dathe's eightieth birthday. A horse-drawn carriage brought him to the austere, flat-roofed administration building. Sitting beside him was his new wife (named Elisabeth like his first), whom he had met a year earlier at an ornithology meeting in Neubrandenburg. The Tierpark staff, accompanied by a band, serenaded the newlyweds upon their arrival. Some of them took animals out of their cages to join in the birthday celebration. One zookeeper brought along a young Catalan donkey for Dathe to pet in front of the cameras. Dathe's face looked gaunt; the past few months had taken a toll on him. Hardly anyone outside the family knew that he was suffering from stomach cancer.

He was asked to grant interviews by the dozens. Everyone wanted to know what was in store for the Tierpark, and what was in store for him.

"I have enjoyed my work, and I still do," Dathe said to the cameraman in a faint voice. "During this rather difficult time in particular I find it essential for me to keep on going for a few more days in order to guide my institution into calm waters."

Numerous well-wishers crowded around him, his West Berlin adversary among them. Klös couldn't pass up the opportunity to give a speech on behalf of his "valued colleague":

Anyone who knows me knows that I am an ambitious man who always wants the best for his Zoo, 24 hours a day, 365 days a year. And when I profess to you, my dear colleague, on this special day, that much in Tierpark Friedrichsfelde so delights me that I could picture it between the Kurfürstendamm and the Landwehrkanal [the borders of his own zoo], please regard it as an expression of the highest respect.

It sounded like a threat. Anyone who knew Klös knew that he liked to be in charge of everything, especially here in Berlin.

The city government resolved that the Tierpajrk would continue to exist. But one month to the day after the festivities, Dathe received a letter written by Richard Dahlheim, the deputy to Irana Rusta, East Berlin's city councilor for culture, who had been placed in charge of Friedrichsfelde—at least for now. Dathe had already received many letters about upcoming changes, but never one like this. At first he could hardly believe what he was reading:

> . . . as you are aware, the unification treaty makes it mandatory for all persons employed in the public service sectors of the former GDR who have reached retirement age . . . to be placed in retirement automatically at this time. In your case we have adopted an interim solution because of your indisputably great accomplishments for the Tierpark and in consideration of your upcoming 80th birthday. . . .
>
> In view of the swift implementation of the Tierpark's changeover to a legal sponsorship it seems essential for us to appoint a younger person to tackle the problems arising from this change in order to spare you any additional burdens. Therefore, on Monday, December 10, 1990, you will turn over your official functions to your deputy, Herr Grummt, who has been appointed temporary director of the Tierpark. You will have until Friday, December 14 to surrender your office.
>
> Unfortunately we also have to instruct you to vacate your official lodgings by the end of the month, which, we hope, will not be a problem for you. . . .
>
> We thank you sincerely for your decades of work, which

were marked by competence and dedication, and wish you all the best for your future.

Dathe had seven days to clear out his office, which held not only mountains of books and papers, but also heaps of gifts he'd just received for his eightieth birthday. The city council was in a hurry, for as of December 15, West Berlin's Department of Finance would be overseeing the Tierpark as well as the zoo. Klös had prevailed.

Dathe had three weeks to leave the home where he had lived for more than three decades. He'd been aware that he would soon have to bow out of his directorship, but he still found it difficult to cope with so abrupt a departure.

The shift in oversight from East to West and cultural affairs to finance sowed confusion throughout the Tierpark. In early December, a letter arrived from the cultural affairs administration, stating that the 439 employees would be "placed on waiting lists and only absolutely necessary areas would continue to be staffed for the time being." No information as to which of them would stay on, face retraining, be asked to retire, or get laid off was shared. The staff of the Department of Finance were themselves befuddled at first, as they claimed to have heard only one week before the handover that they were now in charge of the Tierpark, a representative explained at a gathering of the outraged staff. People were afraid that the zoo might be closed down altogether, as had already happened with other establishments in the GDR.

In mid-December, several thousand people met up in Friedrichs-felde for a mass march. Some 7,500 patrons signed their names to support the preservation of the Tierpark and to express their solidarity with Dathe, while others fired off letters to various newspapers to vent their indignation at his dismissal. One reader of the *Berliner*

Zeitung asked sardonically whether Dathe might have been "teaching the elephants about Marxism and Leninism" and had to go for that reason.

Even though politicians from all parties gave their assurances that the closing of the Tierpark was "never up for debate," the battle lines had been drawn. Many at the Tierpark were angry at the West Germans (dismissively dubbed "Wessis"), at Klös, and at the zoo. But they were also afraid of being let go, and so hardly anyone on staff dared to make a peep. The time for grassroots democracy was over. Patric Müller felt even more silenced than before the fall of the Wall.

Even Dathe seemed to have given up hope. "The Tierpark will likely continue to exist, but maybe as a plain old deer park, which would not be a source of competition for a zoo," he told *Neues Deutschland* on December 29. "We were always a research center, while the West Berlin zoo was more a spectacle," he continued, pessimistically. "And the research center is what has to go."

The retiring director was able to postpone moving out of his home by half a year, but in the end, it hardly mattered. On January 6, 1991, Heinrich Dathe died at the age of eighty, right in his Tierpark. People in both East and West said that the stress of knowing he'd soon be thrown out of his home had done him in.

The day was Heinz-Georg Klös's sixty-fifth birthday.

Farewell to Dathe

On the morning of January 17, a large crowd gathered at the Baumschulenweg funeral home. "Berlin bids farewell to a native-born Saxon, arguably the most famous one in Berlin" since turn-of-the-century illustrator Heinrich Zille, the GDR TV youth broadcast *Elf99* reported the next day. Several thousand people had come, so many that the funeral home was quickly filled to capacity.

Lothar Dittrich had arrived from Hanover only a short time before the service began. Unable to get a seat he, like hundreds of others, had to listen to the eulogy from outside over the loudspeakers. Heinz-Georg Klös was observed pushing his way into the funeral home to lay a wreath at Dathe's coffin.

Rumors had been swirling for some time that Klös had played a part in Dathe's dismissal. The day before the funeral, the *Berliner Zeitung* reinforced this speculation by scooping an article due to run in the *Neue Berliner Illustrierte*:

> As the *Neue Berliner Illustrierte* will be reporting in tomorrow's edition, an *NBI* reporter witnessed a telephone call between [deputy counselor for cultural affairs] Dahlheim and the head of the West Berlin Zoo, Heinz-Georg Klös (who had praised Dathe to the skies in November at Dathe's 80th birthday celebration). Dahlheim's remarks included this: "Now I am the gravedigger. And yet it was actually an act of mercy to finally send him off to retirement." Referring to Klös, he added, "Well, we share the burden of his corpse." In speaking to the journalist, Dahlheim evidently claimed that Dathe was "totally senile" and "far from a martyr," and was regarded as the "Ceaușescu of the zoo world." Dahlheim regretted only that Dathe had "died at an absolutely inopportune time."

Two months later, Dahlheim's rebuttal was published in the *Berliner Zeitung*; he disputed the quotations attributed to him, such as the claim that Dathe was a totalitarian on par with an infamous Romanian dictator. But the feeling that the Tierpark director had been cast aside with Klös's help, "like some annoying bug" in the words of one letter to the editor of *Neue Zeit*, remained.

Many institutions were shuttered in the course of German reunification, but Heinrich Dathe's treatment seemed to infuriate people the most. Maybe the outcry was so strident because his dismissal meant that a part of their own history—their own identity—was being erased. In an obituary for his former boss and friend, Lothar Dittrich wrote, "Perhaps one cannot accept in Berlin that an exceptionally gifted man could achieve something behind the Wall that attracted attention around the world."

Dathe's death showed that poor losers may be unpleasant, but poor winners are the greater evil. "The way things are going now," a reader wrote to *Neue Zeit* in January 1991, "we will never really come together."

That impression would endure for quite some time. And as far as Berlin's two zoos are concerned, it remains true to this day.

OLD MEN, NEW ERA

The cost of being a master of one's trade is also being its victim.

—Friedrich Nietzsche, *The Gay Science*

In the fall of 1993, less than three years after Dathe's death, the staff of the Berlin Zoological Garden contacted the city's mayor, Eberhard Diepgen, with the following message: "Cooperation between the Zoo and the Tierpark has reached rock bottom."

Everything had been going along so well. After half a year of uncertainty, the Tierpark had been converted into a state-owned company in March 1991. Of the animal park's 439 employees at the time of reunification, only 285 still had jobs, but fears of a complete phase-out had faded. A peaceful coexistence between the zoos seemed to be developing, and animals were even being traded: great apes moved from the Tierpark to the Zoo, while red deer, boars, and owls were sent to Friedrichsfelde. In September 1993 *Neue Zeit* reported that the Zoo would acquire the Tierpark company holdings from the state. "The city will pay only for operating losses, revenue shortfalls incurred by reduced admission fees, and investment subsidies," the paper wrote.

By that time, East Berliners were starting to notice that something more was afoot. There had been an announcement that two thousand reptiles from the Tierpark's snake farm and cafeteria aquariums would be relocated to the Zoo; the old installations were in need of renovation, but the Tierpark had no money to pay for improvements. Tensions ran high, and fears of a phase-out returned. The head of the snake farm appeared weeping on television, pleading for the preservation of his life's work. There was a groundswell of outrage; letters of protest reached Berlin from as far away as the San Diego Zoo. Tierpark employees collected thirty thousand signatures in support of the snake farm, which had been around since 1956. It had a unique diversity of species. In the days of the GDR, Tierpark visitors could watch venom being taken from snakes for use in developing serums.

Many enthusiasts' fury was directed at Heinz-Georg Klös, who had been presiding over the Tierpark's supervisory board since 1991. When he went to see Friedrichsfelde with members of Parliament, angry visitors were there to take him to task over the snakes. "Dathe is to blame for this," he blurted out. That made them even angrier. "If you're short on money, shut down the Zoo," they shouted.

After weeks of back-and-forth, a decision was made in early November: the snake farm would remain in Friedrichsfelde. Shortly afterward the Tierpark's transfer went through, and it became a subsidiary of Zoo, Inc.

Klös had been wary enough to insist on a contractual stipulation that the zoo could be returned to the state if the Tierpark didn't get back on track financially. For him, Friedrichsfelde was "a bottomless pit," and someone from the West needed to plug it up. After Klös reached out to several qualified individuals, all of whom turned him down, he settled on Bernhard Blaszkiewitz, a thirty-seven-year-old who was over six feet tall and almost as wide. Blaszkiewitz had begun his career as a zookeeper in 1974, before leaving to earn a doctorate in biology, after which he returned to Berlin as a research associate. "The fat guy will get it done," Klös said.

Blaszkiewitz's first challenge was to improve on a less appealing part of Dathe's legacy. Operating in an economy in which building materials were often in short supply, Dathe had needed to improvise, leading to a mismatched patchwork of fences and latticework. Some parts of the hoofed animal enclosure had been pieced together from railway ties. Dathe had also never taken full advantage of the park's expansive grounds. Not until 1997 was the zoo completely fenced.

Blaszkiewitz's critics thought he was taking this fencing business a bit too far. His functional enclosures with their green, chest-high fences looked monotonous; his wooden stables resembled the garden sheds sold by the thousands at any home improvement store.

In 2007, after more than a decade at the Tierpark, Blaszkiewitz took over management of the Berlin Zoo as well. While the two institutions now shared a director, they remained competitors—although perhaps less in the minds of the staff than of the visitors; nowhere else in Berlin was the Wall still as present as in people's identification with either the Zoo or the Tierpark. A 2014 survey revealed that even a quarter of a century after reunification, former West Berliners go mainly to "their" zoo, former East Berliners to theirs.

Other zoos are getting competitive too. Anyone changing trains at Berlin's central station can't help but notice big billboards luring visitors to zoos in Hanover and Leipzig, which have each been recently modernized at a cost of more than 100 million euros. These two institutions, which came close to closing in the early 1990s, are now vying to steal visitors away from Berlin's two zoos. Thanks to direct trains, both are only about an hour and a half outside the city.

Since the fall of the Berlin Wall, there's been little publicity for the Tierpark, and its lack of playgrounds and its long pathways have kept many families with children away. On weekends, even families who live close to the Tierpark prefer to travel to the town of Eberswalde, twenty-five miles away, where a former *Heimattiergarten* has been transformed into a small, family-friendly zoo. Some residents of Berlin, especially newcomers, don't know that the Tierpark even exists, or confuse it with the public park that bears a similar name (Tiergarten) and borders on the Zoo.

Unlike the Tierpark, which relies on public funding, the Berlin Zoo draws profits—and three million visitors—every year. Andreas Knieriem, who replaced Bernhard Blaszkiewitz as director in 2014, intends to modernize both zoos over the next fifteen years. Even he, however, had to wonder whether Berlin really needed two zoos.

But while the Zoo may be home to more species than any other, its limited space makes it feel like something of a holdover from the old West Berlin. There isn't much room for expansion, and on public holidays its paths and buildings feel congested. "If Berlin had only *one* zoo," Knieriem concluded shortly after taking his new post, "we would now have to build a second one."

◆

With the fall of the Wall and the end of the Cold War, state gifts of animals became a rarity. In 1991, Chancellor Helmut Kohl brought the Berlin Aquarium Komodo dragons from Indonesia, and in 2007 President Horst Köhler gave the Zoo an aye-aye, a rare nocturnal species of lemur from Madagascar. But the days of panda diplomacy are gone. Today, any animals that China places with foreign zoos are loans for which the People's Republic gets an annual fee of about one million euros.

Within zoos, the emphasis has shifted from political systems to ecosystems. Zoos have set themselves the task of presenting animals as representatives of their species in the wild, housed in something close to their natural habitat. It's no longer enough to display pandas in a simple glass pavilion. Today everyone knows what a panda looks like; people come to zoos to learn about their endangered habitat.

The zoos of our time are no longer self-contained fiefdoms, with autocrats at their heads; most work collaboratively with peer institutions. And a majority of animals are no longer sold. Animal trapping has been all but eliminated, and animal traders merely handle the logistics of transporting species shared between zoos. Modern zoos breed their own endangered species, and even try to release them—if possible—back into suitable reserves, whether in Mongolia (for Przewalski's horses) or the Alps (bearded vultures). Nevertheless, zoos do remain competitors when it comes to finding new funding and devising attractive ways of displaying animals. But the competition is economic now, not political. Everything revolves around catering to visitors' tastes.

Neither Man Nor Bear

Heinrich Dathe was convinced that zoos were "primarily for people," and on this issue he and Heinz-Georg Klös likely saw eye to eye. Today's zoogoers learn about the destruction of the environment and how to better protect nature—but at the end of the day, they should also feel good. And they do. According to the German Federation of Zoo Directors, more than 65 million people visited Germany's zoos, animal parks, and game reserves in 2014, making them some of the country's most popular recreational facilities. Even so, they've never before been subjected to so much criticism by animal rights activists—criticism that Dathe and Klös hardly ever encountered. The only zoo critics at their time were the occasional irate visitors who complained about admission prices or about not being allowed to feed the animals.

The sad case of a polar bear named Knut illuminates many of the issues zoos grapple with today. For more than thirty years, there were no polar bears born in the Berlin Zoo. At last, Knut was born in December 2006. But his life got off to a troubled start when his mother abandoned him shortly after his birth, and zookeeper Thomas Dörflein was assigned to care for him around the clock for several months.

From 1986 to 2006, seven polar bears had been born in the Tierpark Berlin—but none of them attracted nearly as much attention as Knut, the first animal to become an Internet celebrity. Just as Berliners had once come to Friedrichsfelde by the thousands to catch a glimpse of Chi Chi the panda, polar bear enthusiasts and journalists from across the world now crowded around the bear enclosure at the Berlin Zoo. Knut brought in a stampede of visitors that lasted for months, and increased the zoo's revenue for that year to five million euros. The zoo secured the rights to Knut's name, and tried to use all the hoopla surrounding the bear to do some good: Knut was named ambassador for wild polar bears and their endangered Arctic habitat. Sigmar Gabriel, Germany's minister for the environment, showed up in person for an official petting, wearing a brownish yellow parka. The idea was to get people thinking about melting polar caps.

As time went by, Knut grew into an awkward adolescent. His white fur was now the same color as Gabriel's jacket. The cult of

Knut continued nonetheless, especially after his keeper, Dörflein, died of a sudden heart attack. Some visitors claimed they could see the grief in Knut's eyes.

When the polar bear was moved to a larger installation, the females there bared their teeth to him. Outraged fangirls loudly demanded protection for Knut, whom they called a "victim of mobbing." Then, in March 2011, Knut dropped dead in front of zoo visitors. Scientists spent four years investigating the cause. "The pressure was enormous," said Alex Greenwood of the Leibniz Institute for Zoo and Wildlife Research at the concluding press conference.

The most tragic part of Knut's brief life was the way it ended. The polar bear, whom many idolized like a pop star, died of a brain disease that had previously been observed only in humans.

Passing into Memory

On the face of it, Heinz-Georg Klös came out ahead in his rivalry with Heinrich Dathe. Well into the new millennium he remained the éminence grise on the supervisory board that governed both the city's zoos. "Father had no other life," Heiner Klös, his son, has said. "He had only the Zoo." The statement sounds at once like forgiveness and a reproach.

Klös was unable to get his son to succeed him as director, even though the board had promised years earlier to offer the position to Heiner when his father was ready to step down. Nothing came of the dynasty he had hoped for. Privy councilor Ludwig Heck, and then his son Lutz, had led the Berlin Zoo for more than six decades. But that was in the nineteenth and twentieth centuries—times had changed.

Klös's influence ebbed—as did his strength in his final years. He kept a low profile. When an old acquaintance, a professor of veterinary medicine at Berlin's Humboldt University, visited him in the spring of 2014, Klös bore little resemblance to the man who had once been able to pull rabbits out of hats and talk anyone into donating money to his zoo. Klös, who even in middle age still had something boyish about him, now looked old. He had trouble recognizing his guest, but tried to gloss over his inability to figure out whom he was talking to.

They chatted about rhinoceroses, his favorite animal. He had retained a keen interest in zoology, and they talked for quite a while until Klös eventually said, "I'm getting tired."

Half a year later, on July 28, 2014, Heinz-Georg Klös died at the age of eighty-eight.

Klös, who had spent his entire career vying for the recognition that seemed to have simply fallen into Dathe's lap, outlived his old rival by more than thirteen years. When his time came to go, the public paid little heed to his death; it received barely more attention than his arrival at the zoo had fifty-seven years earlier. There were a few brief statements by the zoo staff and the mayor, a couple of bureaucratically worded obituaries—and that was that.

Heinz-Georg Klös had headed the Berlin Zoo for over three decades, but his status never rose above that of one more director in a long line. Klös had brought the Berlin Zoo back to prominence after World War II, reclaiming its title as the world's most biodiverse, but he himself never became as great as his zoo.

Heinrich Dathe would always be more than just an episode in the story of Friedrichsfelde. He was its first director—he *built* the Tierpark over nearly four decades. But while his sad end led some to glorify him as a martyr of the sinking GDR, and while the manner in which he was pushed out was thoughtless and shameful, the truth is that things got to that point because Dathe stayed on too long.

Klös—the consummate manager—may have prevailed in the power politics of the war between the zoos, but the way Berliners remember it, Dathe—the educator—was the victor. A local secondary school and a square have been named after him; only a foundation that Klös himself created bears his name. Today, Dathe is regarded as the godfather of modern German zoos. Klös is, simply, a zoo director from sometime in the Cold War.

But not so long ago, and for a great many years, the two men were equals—major figures who made their zoos famous beyond the borders of the two Berlins. They were Cold Warriors in an era of confrontation, a time when Berlin's two zoos were political arenas, and everyone in the divided city had a stake in the zookeepers' war.

WHAT BECAME OF THEM

Jörg Adler was sitting in his study on one of his first days at Münster's all-weather zoo when he suddenly realized that everything had gone quiet. He looked at the clock: it was a quarter after five in the afternoon. Where was everyone? He must have missed an important meeting—and he was still so new at his job! Feeling uneasy, he ran through the other offices to see what was going on, but he couldn't find anyone. Unlike in Leipzig, where the workday dragged on into the evening, everyone had already gone home. In the early years, Adler missed the chummy familiarity of the East, but he did appreciate the fact that all the doorknobs worked and the roofs weren't leaky. In 1994 Adler was named director of the Münster Zoo. He remained in this position until his retirement in 2015.

◆

Bao Bao was sent to the London Zoo on honeymoon in 1991, but he didn't get along with his bride and was returned to Berlin, now overweight, two years later. In 1995 he got a new partner, Yan Yan, but no offspring resulted from this liaison. After Yan Yan's death in 2007, Bao Bao remained alone. When he died in 2012 at the age of thirty-four, he was the oldest panda in any zoo in the world. In 2017 the Berlin Zoo was lent a young pair of pandas from the People's Republic of China. The female's name is Meng Meng ("Little Dream"), the male Jiao Qing ("Little Darling").

◆

Chi Chi once again caught the attention of the international press after moving to London in 1958. It was hoped that the female panda would bear cubs once sexually mature, but there was only one other member of her species in Europe—a male named An An, who was living in the Moscow Zoo. The wish for rare panda offspring proved stronger than any political misgivings, so the two zoos agreed to send Chi Chi to Moscow in March 1966. She stayed there for seven months, and gave An An quite a few scratches, but that was the extent of their contact. In October Chi Chi returned to London, where she eventually died at the age of sixteen.

◆

Falk Dathe rejected an offer to become director of the Dresden Zoo and chose to remain at the Tierpark as head of the reptile section. He went on to serve as the Tierpark's zoological director until his retirement in 2016.

◆

Lothar Dittrich requested early retirement from the Hanover Zoo in 1993. He felt that he had no way of helping the zoo out of its crisis: the enclosures were old and in want of repair, but there was no money for improvements and no visitors. So he heeded the advice his father had once given him: "When you can't make any more good moves, it's time for you to move on." He wanted to spare himself Dathe's fate. Dittrich promised his wife that they would do whatever she liked, as she'd spent so long taking care of things for him. Together they wrote a book, *Animals as Symbols in Painting from the 14th to the 17th Century.*

◆

Wolfgang Gewalt also retired in 1993. Eleven years later the last white whale left the Duisburg Zoo for San Diego. Gewalt died on April 26, 2007, at the age of seventy-eight, at his retirement home in the Black Forest; the official cause of death was an accident. In 2010, the bust that had been displayed in his honor at the Duisburg Zoo was stolen. The bust of his predecessor, Hans-Georg Thienemann, remained in place. Two years later, a cleaning woman stumbled across the missing bust in the broom closet of a men's residential facility in the neighboring town of Mülheim an der Ruhr. The question of whether it was stolen in a belated protest against Gewalt remains a mystery. It's certainly true that while zoologists are held in high regard among experts, they face frequent hostility from the public.

◆

Katharina Heinroth came close to experiencing the fall of the Berlin Wall. The former director of the Berlin Zoo died on October 20, 1989. In accordance with her will, she was buried on zoo grounds, next to her husband, Oskar.

◆

Heiner Klös had been approved by the board to succeed his father as director of the Berlin Zoo, but this approval was later overturned when doubts rose about his lack of experience. Klös remained in Berlin anyway, not wanting to subject his children to a move. He is currently responsible for the zoo's predators.

◆

Kosko, the Tierpark's oldest female elephant, had her tail bitten by Angkor, an adolescent male, in 1994. The wound became infected and required surgery. Kosko couldn't be revived from the anesthesia and died at the age of thirty-eight.

◆

Mao, the China alligator who arrived at the Tierpark in 1957, is the only animal from Dathe's era that still lives in the Friedrichsfelde crocodile house.

◆

Bernd Matern began working at the Frankfurt Zoo as a trainee in the mid-1960s, after he was released from prison and allowed to settle in the West. He later became an animal keeper and a veterinarian. In 1991 Heinz-Georg Klös offered him the directorship of the Berlin Zoo, but Matern turned him down. He still knew too many of the zookeepers from his days in Friedrichsfelde.

◆

Patric Müller stayed with the Tierpark's elephants until 1992, when, after wrangling with the new director, Bernhard Blaszkiewitz, he was transferred to the hoofed animal section and forbidden from entering the pachyderm house. Müller eventually left for Carl Hagenbeck's zoo in Hamburg, where he worked as an elephant keeper for another two years. Today he trains apprentices in the art of zookeeping at the Peter Lenné School in Berlin.

◆

Tuffi was sent to Cirque Alexis Gruss in France when Zirkus Althoff ceased operations in 1968. The female elephant lived with the circus until her death in 1989 at the age of forty-three.

◆

Ralf Wielandt was in charge of the Berlin Zoo's rhinoceros section from 1966 to 2005, during which time sixteen calves were born. His colleagues claimed he had a sixth sense when it came to female rhinoceroses, and knew when they were in heat even before the males. Wielandt always laughed off that idea. In 2005, Wielandt, the longest serving keeper at the Berlin Zoo, retired after forty-eight years on the job. These days, he shows up in his old section just often enough for his colleagues to say, "It's nice to have you with us again," and not, "What are you doing here?"

ACKNOWLEDGMENTS

I would first like to express my thanks to Falk Dathe and Heiner Klös, both of whom agreed to tell me about their fathers, Heinrich Dathe and Heinz-Georg Klös, in such great detail. I am also grateful to Andreas Knieriem, the director of the Berlin Zoo and Tierpark, for generously supporting this book project right from the start.

There is never just one truth, especially in the case of the explosive relationship between the two Berlin zoos, which has remained emotionally charged to this day. All the way through, it was my aim to depict both their relationship and that of the two main characters in the most multifaceted mosaic I could create. Numerous people helped me in this process by sharing their diverse recollections, perceptions, and suggestions. I would like to thank:

Jörg Adler, Lars Brandt, Reinhard Coppenrath, Lothar Dittrich, Walter Encke, Theodor Hiepe, Helmut Höge, Jürgen Jahr, Manfred Kofferschläger, Jürgen Lange, Bernd Matern, Resi Mohnhaupt, Gerd Morgen, Patric Müller, Werner Philipp, Mieke Roscher, Carsten Schöne, Ulrich Schürer, Inge Sievers-Schröder, Martin Stummer, Heinz Tellbach, Frans van den Brink, Ralf Wielandt, and Reiner Zieger.

I would also like to thank Martina Borchert and Klaus Rudloff for making photographic material from the archives of the Berlin Zoo and Tierpark available to me, Katrin Passens of the Berlin Wall Memorial for providing helpful insights about the Stasi, and Clemens Maier-Wolthausen for information on the role of the Berlin Zoological Garden in National Socialism. I thank Bruno Treu for pointers about everyday life and animal keeping in the GDR as well as for proofreading and revision suggestions. Special thanks go to Christiane Reiss, Bruno Hensel, and Dirk Petzold for facilitating contacts and initiating interviews.

I have Grit Thönnissen and Claus Vetter to thank for the fact that I did not have to languish in hotel rooms at the end of long days of research in Berlin libraries and archives; they took me in, and also helped me obtain archival materials.

I would like to thank my editors at Hanser Verlag, Nicola Bodman-Hensler and Christian Koth, for their trust in and support of my work. I thank my agent, Thomas Hölzl, for his foresight and critical judgment about the book proposal and texts, which greatly improved them. I would also like to give my thanks to Annette Kögel, whose collegiality and generosity made it possible for me to report about zoos in *Der Tagesspiegel*, and especially to Jens Mühling, who ultimately gave me the idea for writing a book on this subject.

I never would have dreamed that my book would eventually be translated into English. In an additional stroke of luck, it was Shelley Frisch who took on the translation. The great love of linguistic detail she brought to this book is evident throughout, most delightfully in her droll and poignant rendering of a farewell poem to a hippo, which captures to perfection that special brash charm of Berlin without resorting to the use of dialect.

I would also like to thank Megan Hogan at Simon & Schuster for a wonderful working relationship. Her contagious enthusiasm might well enable the polar bear on the cover to take flight . . .

ACKNOWLEDGMENTS

I have been drawn to zoos and animal parks since the age of fourteen. My visits were not only frequent, but also long enough to include every single enclosure. I cannot express my full appreciation for the way my family not only put up with this, but also joined right in with me.

Last but not least, I would like to thank Juliane Kuhns for her support and advice, her keen intuition, and her critiques, and above all for not being sick and tired of zoos even now.

SOURCES

In addition to personal descriptions provided by interviewees, this book draws on the sources listed below. The dialogues used in the text are in part direct or indirect quotations from these sources as well as conversions into direct speech of recollections or descriptions of people I interviewed. In order to preserve the narrative form and flow of the book, I opted against using footnotes and refrained from quoting excessively in the text.

Works Consulted

Anhalt, Utz. *Tiere und Menschen als Exoten. Die Exotisierung des "Anderen" in der Gründungs- und Entwicklungsphase der Zoos.* Saarbrücken: VDM Publishing, 2008.

Artinger, Kai. "Lutz Heck: Der 'Vater der Rominter Ure.'" In: *Der Bär von Berlin—Jahrbuch des Vereins für die Geschichte Berlins,* 1994, pp. 125–39.

Bell, Catherine E., ed. *Encyclopedia of the World's Zoos.* Chicago: Fitzroy Dearborn, 2001.

Blaszkiewitz, Bernhard. *Elefanten in Berlin.* Berlin: Lehmanns, 2007.

Blaszkiewitz, Bernhard, ed. *Picassofisch und Kompassqualle: 100 Jahre Zoo-Aquarium Berlin.* Berlin: Lehmanns, 2013.

SOURCES

Blaszkiewitz, Bernhard. *Tierpark Berlin 1955–2013. Eine Chronik in Bildern*. Berlin: n.p., 2013.

Böhme, Kathrin, Ekkehard Höxtermann, and Wolfgang Viebahn, eds. *Heinrich Dathe—Zoologe und Tiergärtner aus Leidenschaft*. Rangsdorf: Basilisken-Presse im Verlag Natur & Text, 2015.

Bresselau von Bressensdorf, Agnes. "Frieden durch Kommunikation—Das System Genscher und die Entspannungspolitik im Zweiten Kalten Krieg 1979–1982/83." In: *Studien zur Zeitgeschichte* 88 (2015), p. 70.

Dathe, Falk, Holger Heinrich Dathe, and Almut Fuchs, eds. *Heinrich Dathe—Lebenserinnerungen eines leidenschaftlichen Tiergärtners*. Munich: Koehler & Amelang, 2001.

Dathe, Heinrich, ed. *Wegweiser durch den Tierpark*. Berlin: Tierpark Berlin, series of editions published from 1968 to 1989.

Dathe, Heinrich. *Im Tierpark belauscht*. Lutherstadt Wittenberg: A. Ziemsen Verlag, 1971.

Dathe, Heinrich. *Erlebnisse mit Zootieren*. Lutherstadt Wittenberg: A. Ziemsen Verlag, 1974.

Dathe, Heinrich, ed. *Tierpark Berlin. Jahresbericht*. n.p., 1989.

Dolder, Willi, and Ursula Dolder. *Wunderland Zoo*. Stuttgart: Deutscher Bücherbund, 1978.

Frank, Mario. *Walter Ulbricht. Eine deutsche Biografie*. Berlin: Siedler Verlag, 2001.

Goldner, Colin: *Nazi-Zoos*. "Die deutschen Tiergärten zwischen 1933 und 1945." In: *Tierstudien* 7 (2015), pp. 54–66.

Gräfe, Manfred. "Katharina Heinroth." In: *Berlin—Stadt der Frauen. Couragiert & feminin—20 außergewöhnliche Biografien* (exhibition catalogue, Ephraim-Palais, Berlin 2016). Stiftung Stadtmuseum Berlin, Paul Spies, and Monika Weinland, eds. Berlin: Verlag M, 2016, pp. 170–78.

Grzimek, Bernhard. *Mein Leben. Erinnerungen des Tierforschers*. Munich: Piper, 2009.

Haikal, Mustafa, and Jörg Junhold. *Auf der Spur des Löwen: 125 Jahre Zoo Leipzig*. Leipzig: Pro Leipzig, 2003.

Halbrock, Christian. "Die Westarbeit der HVA im Norden—das Königreich Schweden im Visier ostdeutscher Spitzel und Agenten." In: *Horch und Guck—Zeitschrift der Gedenkstätte Museum in der "Runden Ecke" Leipzig* 55 (2006), pp. 22–36.

Heck, Lutz. *Tiere—mein Abenteuer. Erlebnisse in Wildnis und Zoo.* Vienna: Ullstein, 1952.

Heinroth, Katharina. *Mit Faltern begann's. Mein Leben mit Tieren in Breslau, München und Berlin.* Munich: Kindler Verlag, 1979.

Herter, Konrad. *Begegnungen mit Menschen und Tieren. Erinnerungen eines Zoologen 1891–1978.* Berlin: Verlag Duncker & Humblot, 1979.

Höge, Helmut. *Elefanten. Reihe Kleiner Brehm,* vol. 7. Helmut Höge, ed. Ostheim vor der Rhön: Peter Engstler, 2013.

Hürtgen, Renate. "'Die Erfahrung laß ick mir nicht nehmen!' Demokratieversuche der Belegschaften in den DDR-Betrieben zwischen Oktober 1989 und Januar 1990." In: . . . *das war doch nicht unsere Alternative. DDR-Oppositionelle zehn Jahre nach der Wende.* Bernd Gehrke and Wolfgang Rüddenklau, eds. Münster: Westfälisches Dampfboot, 1999, pp. 200–221.

Kempe, Frederick. *Berlin 1961. Kennedy, Chruschtschow und der gefährlichste Ort der Welt.* Munich: Siedler, 2011.

Klös, Heinz-Georg. *Von der Menagerie zum Tierparadies. 125 Jahre Zoo Berlin.* Berlin: Haude & Spener Verlag, 1969.

Klös, Heinz-Georg. *Berlin und sein Zoo.* Vol. 50 of *Berlinische Reminiszenzen.* Berlin: Haude & Spener Verlag, 1978.

Klös, Heinz-Georg, and U. Klös. *Der Berliner Zoo im Spiegel seiner Bauten 1841–1989.* Berlin: Zoologischer Garten, 1990.

Klös, Heinz-Georg, Hans Frädrich, and Ursula Klös. *Die Arche Noah an der Spree. 150 Jahre Zoologischer Garten Berlin. Eine tiergärtnerische Kulturgeschichte von 1844 bis 1994.* Berlin: FAB Verlag, 1994.

Klös, Heinz-Georg. *Freundschaft mit Tieren. Der Altdirektor des Zoologischen Gartens Berlin erzählt.* Berlin: Edition in Quintessenz Verlag, 1997.

Klothmann, Nastasja. *Gefühlswelten im Zoo. Eine Emotionsgeschichte 1900–1945.* Bielefeld: Transcript Verlag, 2015.

Kofferschläger, Manfred. *Unbedingt mausgrau. Frühe Episoden aus dem Tierpark Berlin.* Kückenshagen: Scheunen-Verlag, 2007.

Körner, Torsten. *Die Familie Willy Brandt.* Frankfurt am Main: S. Fischer Verlag, 2013.

Lai, Fanny, and Bjorn Olesen. *A Visual Celebration of Giant Pandas.* Singapore: Didier Millet, 2013.

Lemke, Karl. *Tiergärten. Zoos, Aquarien, Wildgehege.* Berlin, Leipzig: VEB Tourist Verlag, 1987.

Lubrich, Oliver, ed. *Reisen ins Reich 1933 bis 1945. Ausländische Autoren berichten aus Deutschland.* Munich: Eichborn, 2009.

Mladek, Jürgen. *Professor Dathe und seine Tiere.* Berlin: Das neue Berlin, 2010.

Philipp, Werner, and Friedrich Seidenstücker. *Das Berliner Zoo-Album.* Berlin: Nicolai, 1984.

Pies-Schulz-Hofen, Robert. *Die Tierpflegerausbildung.* Stuttgart: Enke, 2004.

Raethel, Heinz-Sigurd. "Erfahrung mit der Cervidenhaltung im Zoologischen Garten Berlin in der Zeit von 1945–1997." In: *Bongo* 29 (1999), pp. 89–105.

Rieken, Bernd. *"Nordsee ist Mordsee"—Sturmfluten und ihre Bedeutung für die Mentalitätsgeschichte der Friesen.* Münster: Waxmann Verlag, 2005.

Roscher, Mieke, and Anna-Katharina Wöbse. "Zoos im Wiederaufbau und Kalten Krieg, Berlin 1955–1961." In: *Tierstudien* 7 (2015), pp. 67–77.

Sailer-Jackson, Otto. *Löwen—meine besten Freunde. Die Lebensdarstellung eines Tierfängers und Tierlehrers.* Leipzig: Paul List, 1962.

Schmidt, Monika. "Die 'Arisierung' des Berliner Zoologischen Gartens." In: *Jahrbuch für Antisemitismusforschung* 12 (2003), pp. 211–29.

Schneider, Karl Max. *Erlebnisse im Zoo*. Leipzig: Urania Verlag, 1962.

Schröder, Werner. *Zum Abschied ein Krokodil. Heiter-Besinnliches über Mensch und Tier*. Berlin: Westkreuz Verlag, 1999.

Sewig, Claudia. *Der Mann, der die Tiere liebte: Bernhard Grzimek*. Bergisch Gladbach: Gustav Lübbe Verlag, 2009.

Smeets, Marte. *Arche Noah—Zwischendeck. Geschichten und Skizzen einer Tierzeichnerin*. Hattingen (Ruhr): Hundt-Verlag, n.d., ca. 1960.

Spitzer, Gabriele, ed. *Heinrich Dathe: ein Leben für die Tierwelt* (exhibition catalogue, Staatsbibliothek zu Berlin—Preussischer Kulturbesitz, Berlin 1995/96). Berlin: Reichert, 1995.

Staadt, Jochen. "Deutsch-Deutsche Beziehungen von 1949 bis 1989." In: *Die Bundesrepublik. Eine Bilanz nach 60 Jahren*. Hans-Peter Schwarz, ed. Cologne: Böhlau, 2008, p. 162.

Stummer, Martin. *Das Vermächtnis des Inselkönigs. Dokumentation eines ungewöhnlichen Lebens*. Norderstedt: Books on Demand, 2015.

Synakiewicz, Werner. *Berliner Zoo—Die schönsten Geschichten*. Berlin: Berlin Edition im Be.Bra Verlag, 2004.

Wöbse, Anna-Katharina, and Mieke Roscher. "Zootiere während des Zweiten Weltkriegs, London und Berlin 1939–1945." In: *Werkstatt-Geschichte* 56 (2011), pp. 46–62.

Wölbern, Jan Philipp. "Die Entstehung des 'Häftlingsfreikaufs' aus der DDR 1962–64." In: *Deutschland Archiv* 41, no. 5 (2008), pp. 856–67.

Additional Newspaper and Journal Articles

R.B. "Ein neuer Zungenschlag—Nach dem Besuch Robert Kennedys." In: *Die Zeit* (1962), no. 9.

Baier, Tina. "Woran Eisbär Knut starb." In: *Süddeutsche Zeitung*, August 27, 2015; http://www.sueddeutsche.de/wissen/tiermedizin -woran-eisbaer-knut-starb-12623515 (consulted on September 30, 2016).

"Bärendienst." In: *Stern* (1980), no. 39.

Baumann, Peter. "Wilde Tiere unter Dach und Fach." In: *Der Tagesspiegel*, November 22, 1970.

Berlau, Oliver. "Abwicklung im Reich der Tiere." In: *Die Zeit* (1991), no. 5; http://www.zeit.de/1991/05/abwicklung-im-reicht-der-tiere /kom plettansicht (consulted on August 25, 2016).

"Berliner Tierpark öffnet seine Tore." In: *BZ am Abend*, July 2, 1955.

"Biber-Umsiedlung." In: *Der Tagesspiegel*, December 20, 1964; quoted in: *Der Morgen*, December 17, 1964.

Blaszkiewitz, Bernhard. "Heinz-Georg Klös in memoriam." In: *Der Zoologische Garten* (2014), vol. 83.

Boller, Andreas. "Vor 60 Jahren setzte Tuffi zum Wuppersprung an." In: *Westdeutsche Zeitung*, July 17, 2010; http://www.wz.de /lokales/ wuppertal/vor-60-jahren-setzte-tuffi-zum-wupper-sprung -an-1172475 (consulted on August 17, 2016).

Borgeest, Bernhard. "Sind Delphine die besseren Menschen?" In: *Zeit-Magazin* (1996), no. 10.

Brandt, Bodo. " 'Knautschke' – Neue Erkenntnisse zur Herkunft des berühmten Berliner Flusspferdes." In: Bulette. Mitteilungen aus der Tiergartenbiologie. Band 5 (2017). S. 8-25.

Burger, Reiner. "Als Elefantenkuh Tuffi aus der Schwebebahn sprang." In: *Frankfurter Allgemeine Zeitung*, July 21, 2015; http://www.faz .net/ aktuell/gesellschaft/tiere/wuppertal-1950-sprang-ein-elefant -aus-der- schwebebahn-13714026.html (consulted on August 27, 2016).

Carpenter, Julie. "Panda-monium." In: *Daily Express*, August 19, 2009; http://www.express.co.uk/expressyourself/121247/Panda-monium (consulted on August 27, 2016).

Chinoy, Michael. "Pandamonium OR Everything You Always Wanted to Know About Pandas." In: *New China* (1975), no. 1, pp. 15–17.

Dathe, Heinrich. "Viel Lärm um Chi-Chi." In: *BZ am Abend*, July 30, 1958.

Dehmer, Dagmar. "Artenschutz: Die DDR war schneller." In: *Der Tagesspiegel*, June 19, 2001; http://www.tagesspiegel.de/politik/artenschutz-die-ddr-war-schneller/235302.html (consulted on October 5, 2016).

Deutsch, Michael. "Interesse an großen Tieren galt nicht denen der Partei." In: *Mitteldeutsche Zeitung*, March 12, 2010; http://www.mz-web.de/7833142 (consulted on August 17, 2016).

Ehlert, Stephan. "Alt-Zoodirektor Heinz-Georg Klös wird 75." In: *Berliner Zeitung*, January 6, 2001; http://www.berliner-zeitung.de/16212720 (consulted on August 17, 2016).

R.F. "Willy Brandt hinter Gittern." In: *Neue Zeit*, March 2, 1962.

General, Jochen. "Eine solche Stadt braucht zwei Zoos." In: *Neues Deutschland*, September 8, 1990.

Gerhardt, Rainer. "Berliner Gesichter: Heinz-Georg Klös. Zoodirektor i. R." In: *Neue Zeit*, August 31, 1991.

Granin, Daniil. "Schauen und sehen." In: *Neues Deutschland*, October 12, 1969.

Grzimek, Bernhard. "Um diesen einen Beluga sorgen sich Hunderttausende." In: *Der Spiegel* (1966), no. 23.

Hardick, Stefanie. "Jagd auf Moby Dick." In: *Der Freitag*, April 17, 2013; https://www.freitag.de/autoren/franz-viohl/jagd-auf-moby-dick (consulted on September 30, 2016).

Henning, Gustav Adolf. "Leipziger Tigerhochzeit." In: *Hamburger Abendblatt*, December 30, 1989.

"Hinter Gittern." In: *Neues Deutschland*, March 2, 1962.

"Hitzewelle—'Wie Plagen aus alter Zeit'." In: *Der Spiegel* (1976), no. 28.

Höfer, Werner. "Der Mann, der den Wal jagte." In: *Die Zeit* (1966), no. 23.

Höge, Helmut. "Rettet die Ossifanten!" In: *Die Zeit* (1993), no. 44.

Hucklenbroich, Christina. "Und jeden Nachmittag ins Paradies—Tiergärten im Wandel der Zeit." In: *Frankfurter Allgemeine Zeitung*, April 27, 2015; http://www.faz.net/aktuell/feuilleton/tiergaerten -und-zoos-im-wan del-der-zeit-13554789.html?printPagedArticle =true#pageIndex_2 (consulted on September 30, 2016).

"Jagd auf weissen Wal im Rhein geht weiter." In: *Neues Deutschland*, May 23, 1966.

H.K. "Tier mit Tick—Im Rhein schwimmt ein weißer Wal." In: *Die Zeit* (1966), no. 22.

Karau, Gisela. "Nur Wochen später der blaue Brief." In: *Neues Deutschland*, December 29, 1990.

Kern, Ingolf. "Zoo und Tierpark streiten um Reptilien." In: *Neue Zeit*, September 18, 1993.

Kern, Ingolf. "Dauerkartenbesitzer lassen auf den alten Dathe nichts kommen." In: *Neue Zeit*, September 22, 1993.

Klee, Ralf. "Heile Welt im Hippodrom." In: Spiegel Online, February 27, 2009, https://www.spiegel.de/einestages/alltag-im-zweiten -weltkrieg-a-948178.html (consulted on May 14, 2019)

Kroll, Hartmut. Letter to the editor: "Leben nur mit Ungerechtigkeit?" In: *Neue Zeit*, January 21, 1991.

Lietzmann, Sabina. "Guanaco zu verschenken." In: *Die Zeit* (1956), no. 16.

Loy, Thomas. "Der Witwentröster." In: *Der Tagesspiegel*, March 27, 2011; http://www.tagesspiegel.de/berlin/raubtier-chef-der-witwen -troester-im-zoo/3992644.html (consulted on October 5, 2016).

"Marvin Jones, 77; Was a Pioneer Record-Keeper of Zoo Animal's Longevity." In: *Los Angeles Times*, May 2, 2006; http://articles .latimes.com/ 2006/may/02/local/me-passings2.2 (consulted on August 27, 2016).

Menzel, Björn. "Die 70 000 SanftMutigen von Leipzig." In: *Die Zeit*, October 9, 2014; http://www.zeit.de/wissen/geschichte/2014–10

/mauerfall-leipzig-montagsdemonstration-9-oktober-1989
(consulted on August 18, 2016).

Mielke, André. "Der Superlativ von Herzlos." In: *Berliner Zeitung*,
January 16, 1991.

Mohnhaupt, Jan. "Ein Fossil sagt Tschüss." In: *Der Tagesspiegel*, March
26, 2014; http://www.tagesspiegel.de/berlin/zoochef-bernhard
-blaszkiewitz-ein-fossil-sagt-tschuess/9667076.html (consulted on
October 5, 2016).

Mohnhaupt, Jan. "Die Konkurrenz der Tiere." In: *Der Tagesspiegel*, June
20, 2015; http://www.tagesspiegel.de/berlin/60-jahre-tierpark-das
-prestigeprojekt-in-ost-berlin/11943338.html (consulted on October
5, 2016).

Mohnhaupt, Jan. "Der Wal im Rhein." In: *Der Tagesspiegel*, May 15,
2016; http://www.tagesspiegel.de/weltspiegel/sonntag/moby
-dick-in-duisburg-der-wal-im-rhein/13594010.html (consulted on
October 5, 2016).

"Neuer Zoodirektor machte Vertrag." In: *Der Tagesspiegel*, June 24,
1956.

"Neuer Zoodirektor stellte sich vor." In: *Der Tagesspiegel*, January 3, 1957.

"Noch eine Chance für den Tierpark?" In: *Berliner Zeitung*, December
15, 1990.

Orgeldinger, Mathias. "Notausgang zur Natur." In: *Der Tagesspiegel*,
January 14, 2008; http://www.tagesspiegel.de/wissen/zoologische
-gaerten-not ausgang-zur-natur/1140252.html (consulted on
October 5, 2016).

"Die Pandas sind da: Ihre 1. Nacht im Zoo." In: *B.Z.*, November 6,
1980.

Philipp, Werner. "Der Zoo erwägt den Wiederaufbau des historischen
Elefantenportals." In: *Der Tagesspiegel*, June 2, 1974.

Philipp, Werner. "Die Drachen wohnen im 2. Stock—Berliner
Aquarium im Strom der Zeit." In: *Der Tagesspiegel*, September 21,
1980.

Renneisen, Hans-Jürgen. "Haus für Dickhäuter ist schon Besucher-magnet." In: *Berliner Zeitung*, September 30, 1989.

Renneisen, Hans-Jürgen. "Park mit tierischen Perspektiven." In: *Berliner Zeitung*, October 3, 1990.

Renneisen, Hans-Jürgen. "Einfach gefeuert: Dathe, der 'Chef'." In: *Berliner Zeitung*, December 15, 1990.

Renneisen, Hans-Jürgen. "Forderung: Tierpark bleibt." In: *Berliner Zeitung*, December 18, 1990.

Richter, Marina. "Graue Riesin starb unter Narkose." In: *Berliner Zeitung*, July 20, 1994.

Riechelmann, Cord. "Vom Blockwart zum Tiergärtner." In: *Jungle World* (2009), no. 32; http://jungle-world.com /artikel/2009/32/36915.html (consulted on October 5, 2016).

Scherer, Marie-Luise. "Mein Affe braucht Wärme." In: *Die Zeit* (1968), no. 19.

Scherer, Marie-Luise. "Es zieht im Europa-Center." In: *Die Zeit* (1968), no. 48.

Schmidl, Karin. "Von Harpyien und anderen Viechern." In: *Berliner Zeitung*, June 3, 2000, http://www.berliner-zeitung.de/16623158 (consulted on August 30, 2016).

Schmidt, Ulrike. "Reinhardt Coppenrath gibt Zoopräsidentschaft ab." In: *Neue Osnabrücker Zeitung*, August 14, 2013; http://www.noz.de/ lokales/osnabrueck/artikel/9341/reinhard-coppenrath-gibt-zoopra -sidentschaft-ab (consulted on September 9, 2016).

Seher, Dietmar. "Wie der Himmel über der Ruhr wieder blau wurde." In: *Westfalenpost*, April 25, 2011; http://www.derwesten.de/wp /region/ rhein_ruhr/wie-der-Himmel-ueber-der-ruhr-wieder-blau -wurde- id4577658.html (consulted on November 30, 2016).

"Sehnsucht und Liebe." In: *Der Spiegel* (1984), no. 7.

Steffahn, Harald. "Machen Tiere uns menschlicher?" In: *Die Zeit* (1978), no. 43.

"Strichvogel Willy lendenlahm." In: *Berliner Zeitung*, May 12, 1962.

"Ein Stück Zoogeschichte verschwindet unbemerkt." In: *Wochenanzeiger Duisburg*, January 6, 2015; http://www.lokalkompass .de/ duisburg/kultur/ein-stueck-zoogeschichte-verschwindet -unbemerkt- d505818.html (consulted on August 27, 2016).

"Tran und Tränen." In: *Der Spiegel* (1966), no. 23.

Tuohy, William. "Talks by Kohl and Bradley Highlight Opening of Berlin's Birthday Festivities." In: *Los Angeles Times*, May 1, 1987; http://articles. latimes.com/1987–05–01/news/mn-1854_1_east -berlin (consulted on August 15, 2016).

"Ungeschickt oder böswillig?" In: *Neue Zeit*, December 14, 1990.

"Urmacher unerwünscht." In: *Der Spiegel* (1954), no. 26.

von Kuenheim, Haug. "Ihr Auftritt, Frau Walross!" In: *Die Zeit* (2007), no. 18; http://www.zeit.de/2007/18/A-Hagenbeck (consulted on October 5, 2016).

von Viereck, Stefanie. "Trauer um Tian Tian—Himmelchens Ende." In: *Die Zeit* (1984), no. 8.

Wahl, Torsten. "Ein Porträt des Zoologen Curt Heinrich Dathe: Der Tierpark war sein Werk—und sein Leben." In: *Berliner Zeitung*, September 7, 2010; http://www.berliner-zeitung.de/15072476 (consulted on August 27, 2016).

Werz, Günter. "Die Pandabären sind unterwegs." In: *Hamburger Abendblatt*, November 3, 1980.

"Zu blauen Himmeln." In: *Der Spiegel* (1961), no. 33.

Additional Sources

"Bundesregierung: Herbst 1989: Umweltverschmutzung kein Tabu mehr." https://www.bundesregierung.de/Content/DE/ StatischeSeiten/Breg/ Deutsche_Einheit/Artikel/bilder/2009–11 –01-umweltverschmutzung. html (consulted on August 20, 2016).

Bundeszentrale für politische Bildung & Robert-Havemann-Gesellschaft e. V., ed. "Oppositionszentrum Leipzig." www

.jugendopposition.de/themen/145316/oppositionszentrum-leipzig (consulted on August 16, 2016).

Bundeszentrale für politische Bildung & Robert-Havemann-Gesellschaft e. V., ed. "Mahnwache in der Gethsemanekirche." www .jugendopposition.de/index.php?id=645 (consulted on August 29, 2016).

Haubner, Petra. "Die Elefantenkuh Tuffi springt aus der Wuppertaler Schwebebahn." In: *SWR2 Zeitwort*, July 21, 2011; http:// swrmediathek. de/player.htm?show=8cb3ceco-b8f4–11e0-b31b -0026b975f2e6 (consulted on August 27, 2016).

Köpcke, Monika. "Mit Bolzenschneidern gegen ein System." In: *Deutschlandradio Kultur*, June 27, 2014; http://www.deutschland radio- kultur.de/1989-mit-bolzenschneidern-gegen-ein-system.932 .de.html?dram:article_id=290238 (consulted on August 16, 2016).

Landesarchiv Berlin, ed. "Berlin-Chronik, June 8, 1954." Online-Version; http://www.berlin-chronik.de (consulted on September 9, 2016).

Litfin, Jürgen. "Gedenkstätte Günter Litfin—Geschichte"; http://www .gedenkstaetteguenterlitfin.de/gedenkstaette/geschichte (consulted on August 27, 2016).

Mieder, Rosemarie, and G. Schwarz. "Die geteilte Arche—Berlin und seine zoologischen Gärten." In: *Deutschlandfunk*, January 15, 2016; program script: http://www.deutschlandfunk.de /die-geteilte-arche-berlin-und-seine-zoologischen-gaerten.1170 .de.html?dram:article_id=337679 (consulted on August 17, 2016).

"Mitteldeutscher Rundfunk: Das Chemiedreieck der DDR." In: *Damalsim Osten—Hintergrund*; http://www.mdr.de/damals/archiv /artikel 85418.html (consulted on August 20, 2016).

Schwartz, Horst. "Das Nashorn. Nachruf auf Heinz-Georg-Klös." August 4, 2014; https://schwartzaufweiss.wordpress.com/2014/08/04 /tagebuch-das-nashorn/ (consulted on August 26, 2016).

Steiner, Walter. "Nationale Front und Nationales Aufbauwerk." In:

Damals im Osten—Steiners ABC; http://www.mdr.de/damals
/archiv/artikel 7710.html (consulted on September 1, 2016).

Verband der Zoologischen Gärten e. V. "Das Tiergartenwesen der
DDR, 18. August 2010"; http://www.zoodirektoren.de/index
.php?option= com_k2&view=itemlist&task=category&id=69:das
-tiergartenwesen- der-ddr (consulted on August 26, 2016).

Wasserschutzpolizei Nordrhein-Westfalen. "Das Wal-Jahr 1966." Web
memento, November 17, 2009; https://web.archive.org
/web/ 20091117210310/http://www.polizei-nrw.de/wasserschutz
/WSP- Geschichten/article/Das_Wal-Jahr_1966.html (consulted
on August 27, 2016).

Westdeutscher Rundfunk. "Stichtag 21. Juli 2005—Tuffi springt aus
der Schwebebahn"; http://www1.wdr.de/stichtag/stichtag948.html
(consulted on August 27, 2016).

World Wide Fund for Nature. "WWF in the 60's." http://wwf.panda
.org/ who_we_are/history/sixties/ (consulted on August 26, 2016).

Zoo Hoyerswerda. "Vom Tiergehege zum anerkannten Zoo." http://
www.kulturzoo-hy.de/index.php?language=&m=2&n=3#content
(consulted on August 27, 2016).

Archives and Libraries

Behörde des Bundesbeauftragten für die Unterlagen des Staatssicher-
heitsdienstes der ehemaligen DDR.

Dathe-Nachlass, Staatsbibliothek zu Berlin Landesarchiv BerlinArchiv,
Zoologischer Garten BerlinArchiv, Tierpark Berlin, www.zootier
liste.de.

Film and Television

"Abschied von Prof. Dr. Dr. Dathe." In: *Elf 99—Jugendsendung des
Deutschen Fernsehfunks*, January 18, 1991; http://www.mdr.de

/damals/ archiv/avobjekt614_zc-d3058531_zs-a8c40657.html
(consulted on August 23, 2016).

*Geheimnisvolle Orte: Der Zoologische Garten Berlin—Geschichte einer
Großstadtoase.* Dir.: Dorothea Schildt, Birgit Wolske. RBB (2006).
DVD. 45 min.

Ost-Legenden: Curt Heinrich Dathe. Dir.: Jens Rübsam, Dagmar
Wittmers. MDR (2009). Internet. 43 min.

Der weisse Wal. Moby Dicks Abenteuer im Rhein. Dir.: Stephan Koester,
Carl-Ludwig Rettinger. Lichtblick Film (2001). DVD. 90 min.

INDEX

INDEX

Göring, Hermann, 5, 42–43, 176
  animal breeding projects of, 8
  pet lion cub of, 7–8
Götting, Gerald, 145
Graffunder, Heinz, 15, 43–44, 46,
  47–49, 1927
Granin, Daniil, 153–54
Great Britain, postwar German
  occupation zone of, 18, 22, 62
Greece, 25
Greenwood, Alex, 221
Grete (hippo), 22–23
Grotewohl, Otto, 35
Grummt, Wolfgang, 87, 116, 210
Grzimek, Bernhard, 71, 90, 131,
  141, 145
  as Frankfurt Zoo director, 60,
  62, 98, 134, 166
guanacos, 52

Hagenbeck, Carl, 42, 46, 228
Hagenbeck animal trading
  company, 90
Hagenbeck circus, 62
Halle, 87, 130, 197
Halle Zoo, 35, 48, 52, 59, 98, 99,
  149
Hamburg, 42, 67, 100, 111
Hamburg American Line, 100
Hamburger Abendblatt, 180
Hamburg Zoo, 42, 228
Hanover, 10, 106, 163, 206
Hanover Zoo, 4, 125, 148, 163,
  217–18, 226
Happy (panda), 84, 85
Hase, Karl-Günther von, 135
Havel River, 118
Heck, Heinz, 8
Heck, Ludwig, 9, 60, 221
Heck, Lutz, 5, 13–14, 15, 16, 29
  as director of Berlin Zoological

Garden, 7–10, 28, 42–43,
  175–76, 182, 183, 221
Heimattiergärten (domestic animal
  gardens), 149, 150, 218
Heinemann, Gustav, 4, 174
Heinroth, Katharina, 11–14, 16–25,
  53, 95, 163
  background and education of,
  11–12, 29
  character and personality of, 12,
  14, 17, 21–22, 26–27, 28, 42
  critics of, 26–27, 29, 30
  death of, 227
  as director of Berlin Zoological
  Garden, 19–30, 41–43, 57–61,
  70, 72–74, 173, 227
  rape of, 16
Heinroth, Oskar, 11, 12, 13–14,
  16–17, 19, 59, 227
Hellabrunn Zoo, 8
Henselmann, Hermann, 43
Herre, Wolf, 166–67
Heuss, Theodor, 174
hippopotamuses, 5, 11, 12, 17,
  22–24, 30, 57, 58, 73, 74, 84,
  156, 185–86, 192
Hitler, Adolf, 8
Ho Chi Minh, 92
horses, 15, 16, 24, 62, 144, 219
Hua Guofeng, 178
Hudson Bay, 136
Humboldt University, 125, 167, 222
Hungary, 196, 206
"Hyena Heinrich," 152
hyenas, 68, 99, 100, 190

ibises, 151
India, 24, 52
  Kaziranga National Park in, 90
  nature reserves in, 89
Indian chain viper, 112

ABOUT THE AUTHOR

J.W. MOHNHAUPT has written for many of Germany's leading newspapers and magazines, and covered both the Zoo and the Tierpark for Berlin's *Der Tagesspiegel* for several years. *The Zookeepers' War* is his first book to be translated into English. Mohnhaupt prefers to stay close to famous zoos—just like U.S. Army officer Marvin Jones in the 1960s—and so recently moved to Munich, in southern Germany.

SHELLEY FRISCH's translations from German, which include biographies of Friedrich Nietzsche, Albert Einstein, Leonardo da Vinci, Marlene Dietrich, Leni Riefenstahl, and Franz Kafka, have been awarded numerous translation prizes. She lives in Princeton, New Jersey.